PRAISE FOR *MARKETING THAT WORKS*

"A comprehensive look at ways to increase enterprise results through efficient marketing."
—*Bill Campbell, Chairman, Intuit*

"The principles and insights outlined in this highly engaging book have been invaluable to me in leading the marketing efforts at Victoria's Secret Stores as well as on several P&G brands."
—*Jill Beraud, Executive Vice President, Marketing/Limited Brands and Victoria's Secret*

"Practical guidance for creating sustainable value from marketing for companies of all sizes."
—*Mark Leslie, former CEO and Chairman, Veritas*

"Finally a marketing guide that is supported by research and validated by real business examples."
—*Catherine Muriel, Chief Marketing Officer, E-Loan*

"Marketing and sales excellence were essential to building Autodesk. This book really tells you how to do it."
—*Carol Bartz, Executive Chairman and former CEO, Autodesk*

"Effective marketing is critical to the success of any business. This book is full of proven methods and tools to help companies of all sizes successfully compete in today's saturated market."
—*John W. Thompson, CEO, Symantec*

"It's refreshing to read a marketing book that is full of sensible concepts backed up by factual examples."
—*Ben Horowitz*

D1213263

MARKETING
THAT
WORKS

MARKETING
THAT
WORKS

How Entrepreneurial Marketing Can Add Sustainable Value to Any Sized Company

Leonard M. Lodish • Howard L. Morgan •
Shellye Archambeau

Vice President, Publisher: Tim Moore
Editor: Yoram (Jerry) Wind
Acquisitions Editor: Martha Cooley
Editorial Assistant: Pamela Boland
Associate Editor-in-Chief and Director of Marketing: Amy Neidlinger
Publicist: Amy Fandrei
Marketing Coordinator: Megan Colvin
Cover Designer: Chuti Prasertsith
Managing Editor: Gina Kanouse
Project Editor: Michael Thurston
Copy Editor: Water Crest Publishing
Proofreader: Debra Williams
Indexer: Erika Millen
Compositor: Fastpages
Manufacturing Buyer: Dan Uhrig

© 2007 by Pearson Education, Inc.
Publishing as Prentice Hall
Upper Saddle River, New Jersey 07458

Prentice Hall offers excellent discounts on this book when ordered in quantity for
bulk purchases or special sales. For more information, please contact U.S. Corporate and
Government Sales, 1-800-382-3419, corpsales@pearsontechgroup.com. For sales outside the U.S.,
please contact International Sales at international@pearsoned.com.

Company and product names mentioned herein are the trademarks or registered trademarks of
their respective owners.

Printed in the United States of America

First Printing March, 2007

ISBN 0-13-702133-x

Pearson Education LTD.
Pearson Education Australia PTY, Limited.
Pearson Education Singapore, Pte. Ltd.
Pearson Education North Asia, Ltd.
Pearson Education Canada, Ltd.
Pearson Educatión de Mexico, S.A. de C.V.
Pearson Education—Japan
Pearson Education Malaysia, Pte. Ltd.

Library of Congress Cataloging-in-Publication Data is on file.
This product is printed digitally on demand. This book is the paperback version of
an original hardcover book.

The authors dedicate this book to our best venture partners,
our spouses who have supported us in so many ways
for over 100 years of happily married life—
Susan Lodish for 41 years, Eleanor Morgan for 39 years,
and Scotty Scott for 22 years. We love you.

ACCESSING MARKETINGALLOCATION.COM

Throughout this book, and especially in Chapter 11, we use a free tool which we have created to help optimize the tracking and management of marketing dollars. Following are instructions for accessing the site:

- On your first visit to the site, click on "First time user? Register here."

- Your username will be your email address and you will choose your own password.

- Please type in BOOK for the registration key.

- After you have logged in you will be able to enter your own data into the system and it will be stored for you and available each time you return to the Web site.

- On future visits to the site you will only need to enter your email address (for the username) and your password.

CONTENTS

About the Authors

Leonard M. Lodish, Ph.D., is Samuel R. Harrell Professor of Marketing and Vice Dean, Wharton West. He is co-founder and Chair of Wharton's Global Consulting Practicum, and innovator of Wharton's MBA Entrepreneurial Marketing course. His research specialties include marketing decision support systems, marketing experimentation, and entrepreneurial marketing. He has consulted with clients ranging from Procter & Gamble and Anheuser Busch to Tropicana and Conagra.

Howard L. Morgan is Vice Chairman of idealab!, the pioneering Internet incubator; and President and founder of the First Round Capital, a consulting and venture capital investment firm. He has served as Professor of Decision Sciences at The Wharton School and Professor of Computer and Information Sciences at The Moore School of the University of Pennsylvania, and as Visiting Professor at the California Institute of Technology and Harvard Business School.

Shellye Archambeau is CEO of MetricStream, Inc., a recognized leader in compliance and governance. She previously served as CMO and EVP of Sales for Loudcloud, Inc., responsible for all global sales and marketing activities. There, she led Loudcloud's transformation into an enterprise-focused company while growing sales by 50 percent year over year. As President of Blockbuster, Inc.'s e-commerce division, she was recognized by *Internet World* as one of the nation's Top 25 click and mortar executives.

Acknowledgments

This book is an outgrowth of the Entrepreneurial Marketing Course that Len Lodish teaches in The Wharton School M.B.A. program. Aside from the invaluable help and wise counsel of Howard Morgan and Shellye Archambeau, there are many people who have helped the course and this book. Amy Kallianpur administered the questionnaire and tabulated the results, as well as developed some of the content on franchising. Jill Beraud, the Chief Marketing Officer of Limited Brands, and Len's student, was very kind to be interviewed about the marketing strategies that made Victoria's Secret so successful. Yosi Heber provided some very interesting conceptual structure for our discussion of Web search advertising. Lisa Cain designed and built the Web-based deployment software for the book.

The Wharton M.B.A. students who participated in the class for the past 10 years have been inspirational to us all. The entrepreneurs who have either spoken to the class or helped the book by sharing their real-world experience have been invaluable to this effort. A partial list of those entrepreneurs includes: Mark Stiffler of Synygy, Inc.; Craig Tractenberg, the franchise law guru at Nixon Peabody; Gary Erlbaum of David's Bridal and other ventures; Eric Spitz of Trakus, Inc. and the Know Fat Lifestyle Grill; Mel Kornbluh of Tandem's East; Bob Tumulo of Rita's Water Ice; Steve Katz of SEI Corp and many ventures; Jim Everett of Country Junction; Bill Gross of Idealab; Alan Markowitz of many ventures; Ralph Guild of Interep; Ken Hakuda of Allherb.com; Dwight Riskey of Frito Lay; Barry Feinberg of many ventures; Chuck Holroyd and Mike Perry of IndyMac Bank; Barry Lipsky and Mort David of Franklin Electronic Publishing; Bob Brisco of Internet Brands; Andrew Beebe of Energy Innovations; Jim Simons of Renaissance Technologies; Gerry Shreiber of J&J Snack Foods; Marc Lore of

1-800-Diapers; Brett Hurt of Coremetrics and other ventures; Angelique Irvin of ClearAlign; Don Mclagan and the management of Compete, Inc.; Max Lodish of Aerial-Media Services; Jake Lodish of Papa Jakes Subs; Steve Woda of Buy Safe; and Josh Kopelman of half.com and First Round Capital. Tovah Feldshuh, the actress, demonstrated to Len how valuable excellent sales execution and dedication are to a successful venture.

The Wharton Global Consulting Practicum has also been a source of rich entrepreneurial and strategy experiences of foreign companies entering the United States. Over the years, this book has benefited from the insights of Therese Flaherty, Guri Meltzer, Shlomo Kalish, Ron Waldman, and David Ben Ami of that program, as well as all of the M.B.A. students and faculty in Israel, Chile, Mexico, India, China, Peru, and Colombia who have added their insights.

Many colleagues at Wharton and other academic institutions, and other Marketing Scientists, have helped with concepts, methodologies, and paradigms. In particular, John Little, Pete Fader, Magid Abraham, Gerry Eskin, Abba Kreiger, Jerry Wind, David Reibstein, Russ Palmer, Terry Overton, Erin Anderson, CB Bhattacharya, David Aaker, Robert Nason, and Irwin Gross have been very helpful over the years. The participants in the Wharton-Insead "Leading the Effective Sales Force" program, which is co-directed by Erin Anderson, have also contributed many valuable ideas and insights over the years as well as being a beta site for the deployment software. Thirty years of experience working with Information Resources, Inc. has helped Len Lodish with significant learning about how consumers react to advertising and other marketing mix elements. Working with the entrepreneurs of the more than 100 companies of idealab! and First Round Capital has given Howard Morgan many exciting experiences with all types of marketing, both consumer and industrial.

We want to also thank Charlene Niles and the staff of Inc. Magazine and Ian Mac Millan, Greg Higgins, Mark Dane Fraga, and the staff of the Wharton Entrepreneurial Center and Wharton Small Business Center for making our survey possible and helping with its administration.

In addition, Shellye Archambeau would like to acknowledge the value of the experience gained working with the teams at IBM under Abby Kohnstamm; NorthPoint under Liz Fetter; Loudcloud under Ben Horowitz; and the entire MetricStream team. Her mentors and advisors over the years have helped shape her approach to marketing and sales. Special thanks go to Bill Campbell, Tim McChristian, Vinod Khosla, Mark Leslie, Robin Sternbergh, and Ken Thornton.

INTRODUCTION

THE BOOK'S MISSION

Truly successful businesses over the long term have achieved greater-than-market levels of profit return to their investors because they have been able to somehow insulate themselves from competitive pressures. If a company cannot insulate itself from competitors, it becomes doomed to market-level rates of return as competitive forces continually attack its profit margins and revenue sources. In this book, we show how entrepreneurial marketing can help firms both large and small to differentiate themselves and insulate themselves from some competitive pressures. The entrepreneurial marketing techniques, concepts, methods, and paradigms we provide will help your venture make more money—extraordinary money—on a sustainable basis. Not only will you be able to position and target your product/service offering to leverage your firm's distinctive competencies and potential sustainable competitive advantages, but the way you do marketing will make you more efficient than your competition as well.

Marketing, more than technology, is most often the reason for the success or failure of new ventures or new initiatives of mature corporations. Yet there are few detailed guides, and fewer serious studies, on what does and does not work when dealing with these situations. This book is designed to help modern-day marketers make the best use of their time, money, and effort in growing their businesses in a way that gives them some competitively sustainable differential advantage. The book is itself the product of cost-effective, entrepreneurial marketing thinking. There is a target market that has a need for help that we hope to provide. We have seen no books that combine conceptually sound marketing concepts and paradigms with practical guidance on how to apply them in real situations in order to leverage the resources used for marketing and attain sustainable competitive advantage.

This book has a very pragmatic objective. We are not trying to deliver a complete compendium on marketing or on entrepreneurship or intrapreneurship (entrepreneurship within a larger corporation). We cover only marketing concepts, methods, tactics, and strategies that "work"—that is, can add value to real ventures as we move into a more connected "global village" era. We have been guided in our thinking, not only by our academic research and practical experience with dozens of companies, but also by a survey of the Inc. 500 companies conducted jointly by the authors and *Inc. Magazine*. These results provide new insights into what types of marketing programs and channels are most effective in diverse business settings.

You, our target reader, are someone who needs to get results quickly, and has limited financial resources and people resources—you are someone who often does not have any staff to help with speculative research or analysis. Although some bigger, older companies may have the luxury of waiting for longer-term impact of their marketing and sales strategies, the company we write for has to worry about the short term. Like it or not, for many managers today, and for all startup firms, without a short-term cash flow, the longer term is impossible. Even if you work for a large, "deep pockets" organization, acting as though resources are limited often produces the best results. No matter what size your entity, your responsibility is to get the biggest return from your resources you can. One of the ways this book can help you to be better than your competition is that your competition will still be thinking in outmoded, less-productive ways about marketing. You will be much more able to get increased productivity from your marketing budget and will be able to develop offerings that are part of sustainable competitive advantage.

THE AUTHORS' AND THE BOOK'S HERITAGE

Marketing That Works is possibly the best of both the academic and practical approaches to marketing issues—it comes from the intersection of both approaches. This book got started as a by-product of the entrepreneurial marketing course that Len Lodish developed at The Wharton School of the University of Pennsylvania. In the class, MBA students worked in groups to develop marketing plans for entrepreneurial ventures they were possibly starting. Along with the instructors' comments on how marketing could be used to help entrepreneurial ventures, the students were exposed to successful entrepreneurs who spoke and answered questions. In the nine years since the course was begun, over 30 different entrepreneurs have come to share their experiences. A favored presenter in each semester was Howard Morgan, who has over 25 years experience with over 30 high-tech ventures as a consultant, director, sometimes executive, and financial resource. Shellye Archambeau was one of the first entrepreneurs to speak with the entrepreneurial marketing class when it was given at Wharton's San Francisco campus. Shellye was really elegant in showing how basic entrepreneurial marketing concepts, methods, and paradigms are useful at both large and small firms—from IBM to MetricStream, where she is currently the CEO. Len Lodish has over 30 years of applying marketing and strategic thinking to entrepreneurial ventures. One of Len's early entrepreneurial ventures has become Information Resources, Inc (IRI). As a corporate director and consultant to IRI, Len has worked with many of the major packaged goods firms to improve their marketing productivity—including Procter & Gamble, Pepsico, and Campbell's.

This book's intellectual parent is the first book that came out of Wharton's entrepreneurial marketing class: *Entrepreneurial Marketing: Lessons from Wharton's Pioneering MBA Course*, by Len Lodish, Howard Morgan, and Amy Kallianpur. This book updates many of the concepts, methods, and paradigms from that book and expands them for application by any size firm that wants to make more money by acting like a successful entrepreneurial marketer.

THE IMPORTANCE OF MARKETING

Marketing, depending on how broadly you define it, is becoming the most important way many firms differentiate themselves. As you will see, marketing's biggest job is impacting how your product offerings are perceived by your target market(s). What's the difference between Jet Blue, Southwest Airlines, or US Airways? While they all fly customers from one location to another, the perception of what it is like to use their services is very different. Other examples are Ikea, Levitz, and Ethan Allen. They all sell furniture; Ikea's positioning is affordable furniture solutions, Levitz offers a broad selection to fit multiple lifestyles, and Ethan Allen positions itself as high quality and upscale. Mis-targeted marketing would spend dollars attracting low-end buyers to Ethan Allen, when they are unlikely to buy. Proper targeting would get the college student and first-time buyers to Ikea, which has been extremely successful.

Marketing is of critical importance to the success of most entrepreneurial ventures. In a recent survey, fourteen venture capitalists that backed more than 200 ventures rated the importance of business functions to the success of the enterprise. The marketing function was rated 6.7 on a scale of 7.0, higher than any other business functions, in terms of importance to success of entrepreneurial ventures. In-depth interviews with the same venture capitalists concluded that venture failure rates can be reduced as much as 60% using pre-venture marketing analysis. Too many ventures are focused on the technical superiority or inventiveness of their product, but "build it and they will come" often fails, since the customers need to be educated with new products. Early attempts at pocket organizers, such as Franklin's Rex, did not succeed because enough of the market never found out the product existed.

As part of the preparation of a 1997 Inc. 500 list of the fastest-growing private companies in the U.S., the CEOs of those companies were asked to outline their greatest weaknesses and strengths. Their responses are shown in Table I-1. Note that sales and marketing strategies are perceived as their biggest strengths compared to other strategic assets.

Table I-1   1997 Inc. 500: Greatest strength and weakness

Numbers of CEOs Who Cite the Following as a:	Strength	Weakness
Sales and Marketing Strategies	145	19
Managing People	112	89
Financial Strategies	53	75
Information Technology	28	19
Product Innovation	12	2
Other	59	35

Entrepreneurial marketing is the tool that every manager needs to help his or her product or service be perceived as more valuable than the competition by target segments. Marketing strategies and tactics help guide the development of products and services that the market wants, help target the firm's offering to the right customers, get the product or service to the customer, and help ensure that the customers perceive the incremental value of the offering better than the competition and will pay for the added value.

Entrepreneurial marketing is also geared to make the resources supporting marketing go as far as possible, squeezing every penny used for marketing to make it as profitable as possible. We will show how to balance incremental lifetime revenue with incremental lifetime costs to be more efficient with marketing activities such as sales forces, advertising, promotion, and public relations. We will also show how in marketing, **adaptive experimentation** can be a very efficient way to estimate the incremental revenue and incremental costs of many marketing activities. Many executives feel that they have to decide "once and for all" how best to get to market. However, the reaction of the marketplace is often very difficult to forecast in advance. Many times it is preferable to try two or three different ways to get to the market, measure the incremental impact of each method, and then roll out the one that works the best.

ONE MARKETING PLAN ISN'T ENOUGH

Marketing is important, but not just in its traditional role of aiding in developing, producing, and selling products or services that customers want. We will demonstrate in the first chapter that **positioning** and **segmentation** are the real core of what makes ventures financially successful or not successful and provide the basis for sustainable competitive advantage.

Positioning is how the product or service is to be perceived by a target market compared to the competition. It answers the question: "Why will someone in the target market(s) buy my product or service instead of the competition?" An equivalent question is: "What should be the perceived value of my offering compared to the competition?" Positioning is intimately related to core distinctive competencies that the firm has or can develop.

Segmentation answers the question: "Which is (are) my target market(s)?"

The marketing plan, including appropriate pricing, distribution channels, public relations, advertising, promotion, and sales efforts, flows directly from the positioning and targeting decision.

This one marketing plan is not enough, however. Although the basic plan is focused on getting acceptance and purchase of the product or service by someone who is paying money to the company, other positioning and marketing challenges are just as important. These focus on other stakeholders who may be at least as important as the end customer:

- **Investors** and potential investors in the venture
- **Market intermediaries** between the company and the end customer
- **Employees** and potential employees
- **Strategic partners**
- **Users**—Non-paying parties who may influence customers (e.g., viewers of advertising-supported programs)

Each of these stakeholders is concerned about the end customer product positioning and segmentation, but they are also concerned about other issues that are at least as important to them—the **equity** and **image** of the venture. The successful cost-effective marketer has a big job. He or she needs to manage **how his or her venture is perceived on all three issues— its product offering, corporate image, and equity—by all of the different constituencies**. The positioning challenge is even more daunting because all the stakeholders have different values that they typically seek in the venture's product offering, image, and equity. Table I-2 summarizes this multidimensional positioning and multiple plans. Each chapter of this book will shade the boxes at the intersection of the appropriate stakeholders and which of the plans for Products/Services, Equity, or Image will be covered.

Table I-2 Multiple marketing plans required

	Products/Services	Equity/Shares	Image
Customers			
Users			
Investors			
Supply Chain/Channel Partners			
Employees			

As Bo Peabody points out in his book *Lucky or Smart*, an entrepreneur is always selling his or her stock. In the early stages of almost every venture, there is no revenue coming in, and expenses are covered by loans or equity. Marketing to investors requires a different plan than marketing to customers, because to them, the product is those shares they're buying. How will they become more valuable? And hiring needs a marketing plan since getting the best and brightest to work with your venture, a task on which companies such as Microsoft and Google have focused, requires them to believe in your mission, people, and image, as well as the value of stock options. Even in the product area, the customers (those who actually pay for the goods and services) are often not the same as the users (those who consume the goods or services). In most media companies—whether a new cable channel, an Internet site, or print publication—other businesses are the customers (advertisers), while these customers can only be drawn in by having lots of users. The plan for marketing to the customers needs to be quite distinct from the one designed to draw users.

THE IMPACT OF THE INTERNET ON MARKETING PLANS

The rise of the Internet has been one of the most explosive growth phenomena of our times. In the past decade, stock trading on the Internet has grown from zero to more than twenty million accounts. The success of specialized retailers—such as **Amazon.com** in selling books, records, and now everything, **eBay** in creating a global auction market, and **Google** and **Yahoo!** in targeted ad sales—has shown that direct one-to-one marketing to consumers, on a 24 hours/7 days per week basis, can lead to success. Thus, the Web is both an opportunity for new businesses, and a way to market old ones in a much more quantifiable, targeted way.

Getting visibility and name recognition as one of more than 30 million domain names now requires a major marketing effort or creative, leveraged approaches. The Web is important for its ability to connect an organization not only to its customers, but also to its suppliers, investors, and any other stakeholders who have an interest in its operations. Each such connection is an opportunity for marketing and promotion, and for the building of a brand. Any entrepreneur or marketer who ignores the Web does so at his or her own peril. This book will try to help describe how to leverage the Internet across the various constituencies.

CHALLENGES OF THE NEXT DECADE

There are a number of key challenges to any organization that will operate over the next decade. Globalization, corporate consolidation, ecological issues, increasing sensitivity to privacy and data ownership issues, and new governmental regulation must all be considered when designing marketing efforts.

Marketing across national boundaries creates challenges that once could only be profitably managed by large companies. Because the Internet immediately puts one's products and service information at the fingertips of the world, it is important to be ready for the global customer from day one. In addition, one must be prepared for competition from very far away, for on the Internet, no one cares if you're next door or halfway across the world, as long as the goods or services can be delivered in a timely, reliable manner. A publishing executive in Australia said he routinely orders his books from Amazon.com because they arrive in Australia within 48 hours, often months before the Australian bookstores get the same books.

Continuing merger and acquisition growth, and the increased number of strategic alliances, are altering the competitive structure of many industries. This creates opportunities for some ventures, and problems for others. Many new Internet ventures have been bought, often for large amounts of money, in order to reach their customer bases. Hotmail, started as a free email service, was purchased by Microsoft for more than $200 million so that they could have access to the 8 million members. But their aggressive expansion has led to over 80 million Hotmail accounts. Similarly, Yahoo! bought Overture, and eBay bought half.com to access technologies and large user bases. Acquisitions are also a method for gaining or improving domain expertise, customer references, and credibility in target markets. EMC is known as a data storage company. But did you also know they are in the top 10 largest software companies? To move into information management solutions, they have acquired Documentum, Legato Systems, and Astrum Software, just to name a few.

Other key issues for entrepreneurial marketers in the next decade include the changing demographics, values, and expectations of the population. In the developing world, the boomer generation will begin retiring in the early 2000s. At the same time, the lesser-developed populations are beginning to acquire technology and consumerism. China, India, and other

parts of the world offer growth opportunities, but require closer cooperation with government, and better understanding of different cultures than
most U.S. ventures have shown. The fact that these emerging growth
countries are actively getting their citizens connected to the Internet
allows foreign companies to inexpensively reach markets that would have
been prohibitively costly with old media. Entrepreneurial marketers can
take the lead in taking advantage of these new opportunities.

The key to any marketing that impacts sustainable competitive advantage
is an understanding of "What am I selling to whom?" Chapter 1,
"Marketing-Driven Strategy to Make Extraordinary Money," begins to
address this question.

1

Marketing-Driven Strategy to Make Extraordinary Money

	Products/Services	Equity/Shares	Image
Customers			
Users			
Investors			
Supply Chain/ Channel Partners			
Employees			

POSITIONING TO ENHANCE THE VALUE PROPOSITION

"What am I selling to whom, and why will they buy?" Determining the answers to this seemingly simple question will have more impact on the success of your venture than anything else. The answers will drive the essence of your unique value proposition to your customers.

What is a unique value proposition, and why is it important?

First, a *value proposition* is the promise of intrinsic worth that your product, service, or offering can provide to customers. It is the statement of benefits a customer can expect when buying from you. Simply stated, it's what they get for their money. A *unique value proposition* is one that is distinguished from the value propositions offered by competitors.

Value is usually created along three dimensions:

- Performance value (superior functionality)
- Price value (low cost)
- Relational value (such as personalized treatment)

Value is also relatively perceived. For instance, one company will place more weight on low cost, while another will place it on reliability. For example, Cisco will charge over ten times the price as former competitor and now subsidiary Linksys for wireless routers that have the same operating characteristics, but higher perceived (and actual) reliability. For IT buyers to whom reliability and system uptime are crucial, the Cisco value is there. The home wireless networker is much more concerned about the price paid and will sacrifice some extreme reliability for a significant price reduction. Therefore, it is critical to know whom you are selling to in order to position your venture to provide a unique value proposition.

Segmentation and positioning represent the foundation of the venture. It is on this foundation that the unique value proposition is built and upon which the customer-oriented marketing plan is based. All of the venture's important decisions and tactics are critically dependent on these basic elements. However, determining segmentation and positioning is not easy. If other marketing decisions are made before the segmentation and positioning is defined, there is a danger that resources such as money and time will be poorly used and that expected results will not be realized. The customer-oriented marketing plan must be based on the target market(s), the positioning of the venture, and the unique value proposition offered.

Segmentation answers the first half of the question: **"What am I selling to whom. . .?"** It is through segmentation that the market is divided into categories of like-minded buyers. Once the categories are determined, the target market can be determined.

Positioning answers the second half of the question: **". . .and why will they buy?"** Positioning is determining how the product or service should be perceived by the target market as compared to the competition. Two related concepts of management strategy must be considered to most productively answer the positioning question. These are the venture's distinctive competence and its sustainable competitive advantage.

DISTINCTIVE COMPETENCE AND SUSTAINABLE COMPETITIVE ADVANTAGE

Sustainable competitive advantage is the Holy Grail that most ventures continually pursue. If a way can be found to continually be ahead of competition, then the venture will probably return higher-than-normal returns to its owners. Being ahead of competition means that the venture can more easily sell more, and/or charge higher prices, and/or have lower costs than "normal" firms. Let's look at competitive advantage from an entrepreneurial marketer's point of view. As you will see, the entrepreneurial marketer's point of view is the customer's point of view. Your competitive advantage is why the customer or potential customer will more likely buy from you than from your competition. If you have succeeded in developing a competitive advantage that is sustainable from competitive encroachment, you are creating sustainable value.

Distinctive competence is how some people refer to the advantage that is the source of the sustainable competitive advantage. If the advantage is sustainable, then your venture has something that is difficult for your competition to emulate and must be somewhat distinctive to your venture. What are sources of distinctive competence for entrepreneurs that might be sources of sustainable competitive advantage? Creative entrepreneurs seem to be finding new distinctive ways to get customers to prefer them to the competition. Here are some of them:

- Many companies use technology to obtain competitive advantage. Patents and trade secrets are weapons to keep competition from imitation. For software companies, source code for their products is a key competitive advantage. Priceline.com has a patent on their method for having consumers try to name their own price for goods and services. This is a great source of sustainable competitive advantage.

- Other companies may rely on excellent design, perceived high quality, or continual innovation as distinctive competencies. Dell Computers, for example, was able to offer the unique value proposition that it would custom build a computer, exactly as and when a customer orders it, and deliver it at a very competitive price. Dell is able to execute on this because its investment in supply chain and order management systems created a "just in time" system eliminating the cost of overhead, inventory, and mistakes in calculating demand. However, as other competitors, such as Lenovo and Hewlett Packard, have found alternative low-cost manufacturing and distribution systems, Dell's competitive advantage is being eroded.

- Other businesses use excellent customer service by loyal employees who have adopted corporate service values. Southwest Airlines is an excellent example of a venture that differentiates itself from competitors with both excellent customer service and technology for scheduling and turning flights around. Many customers fly Southwest, not only because it is economical, but also because it is fun. Other airlines have tried to imitate Southwest and have been unsuccessful.

- Reputations and other differences in customer perception of products, services, and companies can be extremely valuable sources of sustainable advantage. If consumers perceive you as being a preferable source, they will more likely choose your products or service. Industry-leading quality of service has always been a Lexus hallmark. Think about how Lexus focuses on providing a great customer experience. They collect lots of information from each customer and use it the next time the same customer interacts with the company to make his or her experience even better, from service scheduling, to loaner cars, to doing a good job explaining the work that was done on the vehicle, to completing a quality vehicle inspection process. This is a major reason why Lexus became the top luxury import in 1991 and the number-one luxury car overall in 2000, a title it has kept for seven years running.

All of these are ways that entrepreneurs search for sustainable competitive advantage. They relate to how customers choose one product or service versus another. Key positioning and segmentation decisions are intertwined with why customers will choose you versus your competition. These decisions, which feed your unique value proposition, are best made to leverage the distinctive competence of the venture.

GETTING STARTED: SEGMENTATION AND TARGETING

In reality, the positioning and segmentation decisions are typically developed together. However, for ease of communication, we will take them one at a time, but consider the interrelationships as we go. Conceptually, segmentation is a process in which a firm's market is partitioned into sub-markets with the objective of having the response to the firm's marketing activities and product/service offerings vary a lot across segments, but have little variability within each segment. For the entrepreneur, the segments may, in many cases, only amount to two: the group we are targeting with our offering and marketing activity and "everyone else." The targeted segment(s) will obviously be related to the product/service offering and the competitive strategy of the entrepreneur.

There are some very important questions that need answers as part of the selection of target market segment(s), as follows:

1. The most important question is: *Does the target segment want the perceived value that my positioning is trying to deliver more than other segments?* Sometimes targeting may involve segments that differ on response to other elements of the marketing mix. However, many successful ventures differentiate target segments on the value they place on the differential benefits they perceive the firm to deliver. If a firm can target those people who value their offering the highest compared to competition, it has many benefits, including better pricing and higher margins, more satisfied customers, and usually a better barrier to potential and actual competition.

2. Almost as important to profitable segmentation is: *How can the segment be reached? And how quickly?* Are there available distribution or media options or can a self-selection strategy be used? Are the options for reaching the segment cost effective? Can enough of the segment be reached quickly enough so that you can be a leader before competitors (particularly on the Internet) can target the same segment?

3. *How big is the segment?* If the segment is not big enough in terms of potential revenue and gross margin to justify the cost of setting up a program to satisfy it, it will not be profitable.

4. Other questions to also keep in mind include: What are likely impacts of changes in relevant environmental conditions (e.g., economic conditions, lifestyle, legal regulations, etc.) on the potential response of the target segment? What are current and likely competitive activities directed at the target segment?[1]

VIRTUAL COMMUNITIES: THE ULTIMATE SEGMENT?

The Internet has fostered thousands of virtual communities. These are made up of groups of people who are drawn together online by common interests. Just as enthusiasts for certain activities such as hobbies, sports, recreation, and so on have gotten together in metropolitan areas for years, the Internet lets enthusiasts from all over the world "get together" virtually. The same phenomenon holds for business users of certain software or specialized equipment. Users or potential users like to get together to help each other with mutual solutions to common problems, helpful hints, new ideas, or evaluations of new products, which might help the community members. It is much easier to post notices on a blog or an online virtual bulletin board than to physically go to an enthusiast's meeting. A virtual community member can interact with his counterparts any time of the day or night and reach people with very similar needs and experiences.

These virtual communities can be an entrepreneur's penultimate segment. In terms of the preceding segmentation selection questions, the answers to the first two questions are almost part of the definition of an online virtual community. If your product or service offering is tailored (or as importantly, *is perceived to be tailored*) to the members of a virtual community, then it will be positioned as very valuable to that segment compared to any other group. The size of the segment is easily determined as the size of the virtual community.

The incentives for entrepreneurial companies to get involved with virtual communities are great, but it is not a one-way street. All elements of the marketing program need to be cleverly adapted to the new segmentation environment. The challenges of marketing in virtual communities are summarized nicely by McKinsey consultants John Hagel III and Arthur G. Armstrong:

> Virtual communities are likely to look very threatening to your average company. How many firms want to make it easier for their customers to talk to one another about their products and services? But vendors will soon have little choice but to participate. As more and more of their customers join virtual communities, they will find themselves in "reverse markets"—markets in which customers seek out vendors and play them off against one another, rather than the other way around. Far-sighted companies will recognize that virtual communities actually represent a tremendous opportunity to expand their geographical reach at minimal cost.

AN ENTREPRENEURIAL SEGMENTATION EXAMPLE—TANDEM'S EAST

A clever entrepreneur can use target segmentation as a prime reason for beginning a venture. An example is Mel Kornbluh, who began a company called *Tandem's East* in his garage in the late 1980s. Mel is a specialist in selling and servicing tandem bicycles—bicycles built for two (or three or four). Mel realized that there was a segment of bicycling couples that would appreciate the unique benefits of tandeming. It is the only exercise that two people can do together, communicate while they exercise, appreciate nature together, and do all this even though they may have very different physical abilities.

When he began his venture, intuitively Mel had very good answers to the previous questions. There were actually two target segments that Mel could target. The first was existing tandem enthusiast couples—those who already had a tandem and would need an upgrade or replacement. The other target segment was relatively affluent bicycling couples who had trouble riding together because of differences in physical abilities. The couples needed to be affluent because tandems are relatively expensive when compared with two regular bicycles. They are not mass-produced and do not take advantage of mass scale economies.

At the time Mel started, there was no one on the East Coast who had staked out a position as a specialist in tandems. As tandem inventory is expensive and selection is very important to potential buyers, he could establish barriers to potential competitors by being first to accumulate a substantial inventory. He was also able to establish some exclusive arrangements with some suppliers by being first in the area and offering them a new outlet.

It was relatively easy for Mel to reach both of his segments. Existing tandem enthusiasts were members of the Tandem Club of America that has a newsletter they publish bi-monthly. It is relatively inexpensive to advertise in the newsletter that reaches his first segment precisely. Not only does it reach the segment, but because the readers are already enthusiasts, they pay attention to every page of the newsletter. Over time, Internet user groups dedicated to tandeming were also formed. They are also natural vehicles for effectively reaching the segment.

His second segment was also relatively easy to reach cost effectively. Affluent bicycling couples read cycling magazines—the major one being *Bicycling Magazine*. Again, because they are enthusiasts, the target segment pays a lot of attention to even small ads. This segment also attends bicycling rallies and organized rides.

Both segments were much larger than Mel needed to make the business viable. With very small response rates in either segment, he could afford to pay his overhead and to begin to accumulate a suitable inventory. In fact, his advertising costs are significantly under 10% of revenues, indicating that reaching the segments is extremely cost effective.

Thus, Tandem's East was begun and flourished by creatively seeing target segments that valued what Mel was selling. The segments were substantial and very easily reached cost effectively, and competitive barriers could be erected.

AN ENTREPRENEURIAL SEGMENTATION AUDIT

Figure 1-1 shows a segmentation audit that the entrepreneurial marketer can use as a checklist to make sure that s/he has not forgotten an element of segmentation to consider. For an entrepreneur, many of the issues in the audit can cost effectively be answered only qualitatively. However, not considering these issues can cause big problems.

The goal of the rest of this book is, in fact, to flush out the seventh group of issues. How does segmentation relate to all the other elements of the marketing mix for an entrepreneurial venture? Just as fundamental as the targeting decisions, however, are the interrelated positioning decisions to which we turn next.

	Completely Describes Us (A)	Somewhat Describes Us (B)	Does Not Describe Us At All (C)	Don't Know (D)
1. Our business strategies recognize the need to prioritize target segments.	_ _ _	_ _ _	_ _ _	_ _ _
2. Our marketing plans include specific plans for each of the selected segments.	_ _ _	_ _ _	_ _ _	_ _ _
3. We have specific product and service offerings for each target segment.	_ _ _	_ _ _	_ _ _	_ _ _
4. We have detailed information about segments, including:				
• Current size of the segment	_ _ _	_ _ _	_ _ _	_ _ _
• Potential size of the segment	_ _ _	_ _ _	_ _ _	_ _ _
• Key business needs of the segments	_ _ _	_ _ _	_ _ _	_ _ _
• Information systems needs of the segment	_ _ _	_ _ _	_ _ _	_ _ _
• Their prioritized needs/benefits sought	_ _ _	_ _ _	_ _ _	_ _ _
• Their prioritized preference for product and service features	_ _ _	_ _ _	_ _ _	_ _ _
• Demographic characteristics of the segments	_ _ _	_ _ _	_ _ _	_ _ _
• Product ownership and usage	_ _ _	_ _ _	_ _ _	_ _ _
• Competitor's strength in each segment	_ _ _	_ _ _	_ _ _	_ _ _
• Perceived positioning of each competior by the members of the segment	_ _ _	_ _ _	_ _ _	_ _ _
5. We have a process for updating the information on our segments on an ongoing basis.	_ _ _	_ _ _	_ _ _	_ _ _
6. Our segments are developed across countries, but recognize unique country requirements and subsegments.	_ _ _	_ _ _	_ _ _	_ _ _
7. Information about the target market segments is incorporated effectively into the following categories:				
• Positioning	_ _ _	_ _ _	_ _ _	_ _ _
• Product and service offering	_ _ _	_ _ _	_ _ _	_ _ _
• Pricing	_ _ _	_ _ _	_ _ _	_ _ _
• Promotion	_ _ _	_ _ _	_ _ _	_ _ _
• Public relations	_ _ _	_ _ _	_ _ _	_ _ _
• Advertising	_ _ _	_ _ _	_ _ _	_ _ _
• Distribution	_ _ _	_ _ _	_ _ _	_ _ _
• Sales force	_ _ _	_ _ _	_ _ _	_ _ _
8. We have an effective process for implementing segmentation research.	_ _ _	_ _ _	_ _ _	_ _ _
9. We have an effective process for implementing segmentation strategies.	_ _ _	_ _ _	_ _ _	_ _ _
10. We have P&L reports and accountability by segment.	_ _ _	_ _ _	_ _ _	_ _ _

Figure 1-1 A segmentation audit*

* Adapted from correspondence of Yoram J. Wind, 1997.

POSITIONING

Positioning answers the question: "Why should a member of the target segment buy my product or service rather than my *competitor's*?" A related positioning question is: "What are the unique *differentiating* characteristics of my product or service as *perceived* by members of the target segment(s)?" The italicized words in these positioning questions are crucial for effective implementation. First, the word "perceived" must be analyzed. It is obvious that people make decisions based only on what they perceive. Many entrepreneurial firms are happy when they have developed products or services that are *actually* better than the competition on characteristics that they know should be important to people in their target market(s). What they forget is that the job is not done until the targeted people actually *perceive* the differences between their product and the competition. In fact, in the Internet space, many companies try to gain the perception that they're better long before they can deliver on that in reality.

One of the hindrances to effective positioning is that most humans cannot perceive more than two or three differentiating attributes at a time. It is important that the targeted positioning be easy to remember. If there are too many differentiating attributes, the potential consumer can get confused. The marketer's job is to isolate the most important differentiating attributes of her offering and use those in all the elements of the marketing mix. In many cases, it is very cost effective to do concept testing or other research with potential consumers to isolate the best combination of attributes (see the "Concept Testing" section in Chapter 2, "Generating, Screening, and Developing Ideas"). In other cases, the entrepreneur can instinctively isolate a good combination of attributes.

Entrepreneurs who have been successful may overstate how easy it was to get a good combination of attributes for their positioning. Companies such as Starbucks (just great-tasting, excellent-quality coffee) or Apple Computer (fun and easy to use) were successful at least partly because of very effective positioning. What has not been documented has been how many entrepreneurial ventures failed (or were not as successful as they could have been) because their positioning and associated target segments weren't very effective. The venture capitalists' estimate (cited in the introduction)—that as many as 60% of failures can be prevented by better pre-launch marketing analysis—underscores the importance of getting your positioning right and testing with real consumers to confirm that it is right.

A big mistake many ventures make is to position based on *features* of their product offering compared to their competitors. It's amazing how many entrepreneurs we have encountered who have great ideas that are based on technical features that are somehow better than their competitors. The fundamental paradigm that "customers don't buy features, they buy *benefits*" has been lost on many entrepreneurs. Even more precisely, customers buy based on *perceived benefits*. Not only does the entrepreneur need to develop the best set of benefits versus the competition; he or she must also somehow get the customers to perceive these benefits.

In his book, *What Were They Thinking? Lessons I've Learned From Over 80,000 New Product Innovations and Idiocies*, Robert McMath also says that communicating features instead of perceived benefits is "one of the most common mistakes marketers make."[2] He describes a training film in which British comedian John Clease illustrates how a surgeon might explain a new surgical procedure to a patient lying in a hospital bed:

> "Have I got an operation for you. Only three incisions and an Anderson Slash, a Ridgeway stubble-side fillip, and a standard dormer slip! Only five minutes with a scalpel; only thirty stitches! We can take out up to five pounds of your insides, have you back in your hospital bed in 75 minutes flat, and we can do ten of them in a day."[3]

The surgeon is concerned only with technical features that he as producer (entrepreneur) is excited over. The customer has very different concerns. All that the customer probably wants to know is whether he'll get better, perhaps what his risks of complication are, and whether he'll be in pain.

TYING TOGETHER THE VALUE PROPOSITION: DISTINCTIVE COMPETENCE, SUSTAINABLE COMPETITIVE ADVANTAGE, AND POSITIONING

Now that we have explored segmentation and positioning, and established their relationship to the strategic concepts of distinctive competence and sustainable competitive advantage, we can return to the unique value proposition. The unique value proposition is the public face that is put on the target market and positioning decisions that were based on the venture's distinctive competence and sustainable competitive advantage. We can now determine the answer to "What am I selling to whom and why will they buy" based on the decisions discussed previously. Be careful, however—these decisions are not easily changed. It typically takes more effort to change a value proposition than to attempt to establish a new one in a vacuum. To change a value proposition is more than changing a slogan. It means undoing a market perception that has been established based on how a venture executes and replacing it with another.

For entrepreneurial companies, deciding on the value proposition—the intertwined positioning, distinctive competence, and sustained competitive advantage decisions—is the most important strategic decision made before beginning a new business or revitalizing an older business. Take the time to do it right. If the market doesn't value "what they perceive to be the distinctive competence of your firm versus the competition" (another way of defining "positioning"), then the positioning will not be successful. If the positioning is not successful, the value proposition will fail to attract customers. Furthermore, because it is difficult to change perceptions, the perceived distinctive competence should be sustainable over time. Thus, it is crucial to get the positioning reasonably close to right *before going public the first time*. In Chapters 2 and 3, you will explore cost-effective ways of getting market reaction to positioning options before going public.

ORVIS CO.—EXCELLENT ENTREPRENEURIAL POSITIONING

The Orvis Company has done an excellent job over the years of capitalizing on a unique positioning in a very competitive industry. They sell "country" clothing, gifts, and sporting gear in competition with much bigger brands like L.L. Bean and Eddie Bauer. Like their competitors, Orvis sells both retail and mail order. How is Orvis differentiated? They want to be perceived as the place to go for all areas of fly-fishing expertise. Their particular expertise is making a very difficult sport "very accessible to a new generation of anglers."[4] Since 1968, when their sales were less than $1 million, Orvis has been running fly-fishing schools located near their retail outlets. Their annual sales are now over $350 million. The fly-fishing products contribute only a small fraction of the company's sales, but the fly-fishing heritage adds a cachet to all of Orvis's products. According to Tom Rosenbauer, beginner fly fishermen who attend their schools become very loyal customers and are crucial to continuing expansion of the more profitable clothing and gift lines. He says, "Without our fly-fishing heritage, we'd be just another rag vendor."[5]

The Orvis positioning pervades their entire operation. Their catalog and their retail shops all reinforce their fly-fishing heritage. They also can use very targeted segmentation to find new recruits for their fly-fishing courses. There are a number of targeted media and public relations vehicles that reach consumers interested in fishing. Their margins are higher than the typical "rag vendor" because of their unique positioning. The positioning is also defensible because of the consistent perception that all of their operations have reinforced since 1968. A competitor will have a very difficult time and large expense to reproduce the Orvis schools and retail outlets. It also will be difficult for a competitor to be a "me too" in an industry where heritage is so important. The positioning and segmentation decisions Orvis made in 1968 probably added close to $1 billion of incremental value to their venture since that time. That value is our estimate of the difference of Orvis's actual profit since 1968 compared to what the venture's profitability might have been had they just been "another rag vendor." Victoria's Secret is another company that has really leveraged excellent positioning, as discussed next.

VICTORIA'S SECRET AND THE LIMITED—EXCELLENT INTEGRATION OF POSITIONING, SEGMENTATION, AND DISTINCTIVE COMPETENCIES[6]

The original Victoria's Secret store and catalog was in Palo Alto, California. In 1982, when the Limited Brands founder, Les Wexner, first saw this store, it was very sleazy stuff. However, after seeing the store, Les got the idea to reinvent underwear as lingerie and make underwear emotional—have underwear make you feel good. Les was influenced by how he thought European women viewed underwear much differently than American women. A brilliant idea early on was to use supermodels as part of the PR and advertising for Victoria's Secret (VS).

Limited bought the first VS store for $1 million in 1982. By 1995, they had a catalog, 300 retail stores, and an $800 million business. The catalog was the greatest revenue contributor. In 1995, VS products were perceived by women and men as suited mainly for *Saturday night and special occasions*. In 1995, VS marketers identified an opportunity for a much-expanded positioning for VS—addressing "everyday" needs while maintaining the "special" image. They began the transformation of VS by segmenting by usage occasion. Their first products in the repositioned lines were everyday cotton, but positioned and designed as "sexy." There was a lot of uncertainty in the Limited management about whether it was possible to have women perceive cotton as lingerie. The risk was that cotton underwear might be perceived as comparable to Haines as opposed to as sexy lingerie. This was a big communication challenge.

All the elements of the marketing mix needed to be changed to support the new positioning. VS had never advertised before and had only used their catalog as an advertising vehicle. The catalog was very low in reach and very high in frequency—not suited for getting new people into the brand on a large scale or for changing the perception of the product. Thus, large-scale TV advertising and PR were appropriate, using their successful supermodel icons as part of the repositioning. The supermodels were the embodiment of the emotion of the new VS positioning. The VS supermodel fashion shows on the Web were extremely effective at reinforcing their positioning. So many people came to their Web site that they overwhelmed the Internet servers.

In 1995, before the repositioning, VS bras were priced two for $15, and VS was a merchant-driven business. It needed to be made into a fashion business. By 2006, the average price for a VS item had more than doubled, and their revenue had risen by a factor of over 4 due to the repositioning. One key to the success of the repositioning was that the VS bras were not only sexy, but they were extremely comfortable. The consumer didn't have to compromise between feeling sexy and feeling comfortable. The loyalty levels for VS doubled with the new bras. Increasing loyalty makes the long-term value of a customer larger, thus justifying larger expenses for obtaining new customers—a nice virtuous circle for VS.

The VS stores were an integral element of the repositioning. The in-store experience is designed to be much different from other stores—it is designed to make customers feel special, intimate, and personal. There is much more pampering.

VS has evolved sub-brands over time—segmented by lifestyle:

- Provocative—"Very Sexy"
- Romantic—"Angels"
- Glamorous

- Girly—"Such a Flirt?"
- Clean and simple—"Body by Victoria"
- Younger-flirty-modern—"Pink"

VS has succeeded in doing what Starbucks has also done—changing how people view a commodity—by changing VS into a relatively inexpensive way for women to feel good about themselves. In subsequent chapters, we will go into more depth as to how VS and the Limited were able to use entrepreneurial marketing strategy and tactics to accomplish making VS the crown jewel of Limited Brands.

POSITIONING, NAMES, AND SLOGANS

Many entrepreneurs miss positioning opportunities when they name their products, services, and companies. As we will discuss in-depth later, entrepreneurs have very limited marketing funds to educate their target markets about the positioning of their products and services. If the names chosen do not themselves connote the appropriate positioning, then the entrepreneur has to spend more funds to educate the market in two ways instead of one. They have to not only get potential customers to recognize and remember their product name, but they also have to educate them about the attributes and benefits of the product that goes with the name. The Please Touch Museum in Philadelphia is a perfect example. Its name tells parents and their children exactly what they can expect. Many new technology and Internet-based ventures have also been very intelligent and creative in their names to connote the appropriate positioning. Companies such as CDNow (CDs on the Internet), ONSale (online Internet auctions), Netscape Communications (Internet browsers), and NetFlix (movie rentals on the Internet) made it easy for potential customers to remember what they do and at least part of their positioning. However, CDNow's flawed positioning and business model caused the firm's demise, even when the name was excellent. On the other hand, all you know just from its name about Amazon.com is that it is an Internet company. The fact that it sells books is not evident from its name, and the education needs to be done with other marketing activity.

Some fortunate companies have gone even further by making their names not only support their positioning, but also simultaneously let their potential customers know how to get in touch with them. Examples would be 1-800-FLOWERS, 1-800-DIAPERS, and 1-800-MATTRESS or Reel.com.

Other companies gain leverage by having their product name and company name be the same. Do you know which Fortune 1000 company was named Relational Software? Relational Software's product was named Oracle. To improve market awareness, the company changed their name to Oracle, the name of their popular product. Oracle has become one of the top database software companies in the world. However, the gain in awareness has been a hindrance in diversifying. Oracle is known for database but, despite large investments and marketing activities, Oracle has been relatively unsuccessful in selling their own application software. Oracle is not perceived as a strong applications software company. Oracle = database.

If the name of the company or product is not enough to position it in the customer's mind, then the next need is for a slogan or byline that succinctly (and hopefully memorably) hammers home the positioning. If the positioning has been done well, then a slogan or byline can in many cases fairly completely communicate the appropriate attributes. One good example is FedEx: "When it absolutely, positively has to get there overnight." The positioning inherent in this byline is a good example of concentrating on only the few, most important attributes to stress in order to position the company. Visa has been using "It's everywhere you want to be" for many years to differentiate itself as a ubiquitous charge card, accepted around the world. On the other hand, Michelin uses "Because so much is riding on your tires" to try to differentiate itself as better on the safety attribute for tire buyers.

Just as brevity and simplicity are valuable in positioning, they are also as valuable in slogans and bylines. The slogan that goes with a company or product name should be one that can be retained for quite a long time, as long as the positioning will be in force. Robert Keidel proposed other ground rules for effective slogans:[7] Avoid clichés, such as "genuine" Chevrolet, Miller, and so on; be consistent; use numbers, but have them backed up; be brief; take a stand; and make it distinctively your own. All of these rules are consistent with our effective positioning paradigm and make good sense.

Hindustan Lever represents an interesting example that illustrates many of the points discussed in this chapter.

HINDUSTAN LEVER: POSITIONING AND TARGETING TO THE BOTTOM OF THE GLOBAL PYRAMID

The positioning and targeting decision should be made like any effective management decision. Develop criteria, generate many decision options (including creative, "out of the box" options), and then evaluate the options on those criteria. The implicit criteria for evaluating positioning and targeting decisions are typically related to the long-term and short-term impact on the entity's shareholder value. However, there are also many constraints that may limit the options, such as ethical issues, environmental issues, legal issues, corporate values and culture, and so on. The Hindustan Lever example also illustrates how the positioning and targeting decision is deeply intertwined with decisions on how to promote, distribute, and sell the products. C.K. Prahalad in his very valuable book, *The Fortune at the Bottom of the Pyramid*, documents the need for the new positioning and how Hindustan Lever responded to the need with a very innovative product positioning, targeting, and marketing mix strategy.

Hindustan Lever Limited, HLL, is the largest detergent manufacturer in India, with $2.4 billion in sales in 2001, 40% from soaps and detergents.[8] One constraint that exists on their positioning options is their corporate mission:

> Our purpose at Hindustan Lever is to meet the everyday needs of people everywhere—to anticipate the aspirations of our consumers and customers and to respond creatively and competitively with branded products and services, which raise the quality of life.
>
> Our deep roots in local cultures and markets around the world are our unparalleled inheritance and the foundation for our future growth. We will bring our wealth of knowledge and international expertise to the service of local customers.

In their history from 1990–2000, HLL has targeted the mass market in India. They have developed some distinct competencies that should provide sustainable competitive advantage versus their competition. Products are manufactured in about 100 locations around India and distributed via depots to almost 7,500 distribution centers. HLL reaches all villages with at least 2,000 people. It has a number of innovative programs to involve the rural women in selling and servicing their products.[9] It is very difficult for their competition to reach the rural population because of the costs of building the infrastructure and developing products that are appropriate for the rural market.

One of their competencies that they continue to leverage is their ability to introduce and profitably market products that the poorer parts of the society are willing to pay for. Instead of looking at costs first, they look at what the people are willing to pay. This willingness to pay is determined by the perceived value of the product by the potential customers. According to HLL Chairman Manvinder Singh Banga:

> Lifebuoy is priced to be affordable to the masses. . . Very often in business you find that people do cost-plus pricing. They figure out what their cost is and then they add a margin and figure that's their selling price. What we have learned is that when you deal with mass markets, you can't work like that. You have to start by saying I'm going to offer this benefit, let's say it's germ kill. Let's say it's Lifebuoy. You have to work out what people are going to pay. That's my price. Now what's my target margin? And that gives you your target cost—or a challenge cost. Then you have to deliver a business model that delivers that challenge cost.[10]

Why did HLL decide to use the "germ kill" positioning? They saw a way to fulfill an important unfulfilled need of many consumers. However, they had a number of interacting issues and stakeholders to deal with in order to make the positioning and associated targeting work.

THE UNMET NEED

Globally, in terms of infectious diseases, only acute respiratory infections and AIDS kill more people than diarrhea, which kills 2.2 million people annually. In India, 19.2% of the children suffer from diarrhea, and India accounts for 30% of all the diarrhea deaths in the world.[11] The solution for this problem is very simple and well known. Washing hands with soap reduced the incidence of diarrhea by 42 to 48% in a number of well-documented research studies.[12] In 2000, the solution was not being used by the masses in India. Only 14% of the mass rural population was using soap and water after defecating and before and after every meal. 62% used water plus ash or mud, and 14% used water alone.[13]

There have been a number of attempts to solve this problem globally, but without a lot of success. In India and other developing countries, the problem was seen as too large and costly for a big public health initiative. Additionally, the solution needed to be coordinated among three different government departments—Public Health, Water, and Environment—a daunting task. Because other diseases such as AIDS got most popular attention, there wasn't a champion for diarrhea. Lastly, behavioral change in the diarrhea area is difficult to design and implement. In 2000, HLL was a participant in a public-private partnership for encouraging hand washing. It was a consortium of communities, government, academia, and the private sector and was targeting a pilot in the Indian state of Kerala. However, controversy around the consortium's mission from various community groups hampered its implementation in 2002.

HLL had a long history of marketing 107-year-old Lifebuoy, with a bright red color and a crisp carbolic smell, as "healthy clean." Since the 1960s, they marketed the product using a sports idiom to illustrate healthy clean. Their target market was the Indian male, 18–45 years old, with a median income of approximately $47 per month, a semiliterate farmer or construction worker living in a town of 100,000 or less.[14] However, by the late 1980s, competition had also copied the positioning so that health became perceived as the base level of cleaning, and Lifebuoy was not as differentiated. By 2000, in the developed, higher income areas of India (and the world, for that matter), the soap market was saturated and very competitive. Proctor & Gamble and Colgate were world-class competitors for the relatively affluent consumer all over the globe.

Because of this phenomenon, Unilever as a whole was expecting developing markets to account for approximately 50% of their sales over the next ten years.[15]

If HLL did not have the sales and distribution channels available to deliver the newly positioned Lifebuoy profitably at the price the market dictated, it would not be a good or even feasible strategy. The sales and distribution channel is a unique public/private mix of micro-credit lending and rural entrepreneurship that began in 1999. Hindustan Lever noticed that dozens of agencies were lending micro-credit funds to poor women all over India. Hindustan Lever approached the Andra Pradesh state government in 2000 and asked for clients of a state-run micro-lending program. The government agreed to a small pilot program that quickly grew. The initiative, now called Project Shakti (strength), has expanded to 12 states, and CARE India, which oversees one of the subcontinent's biggest micro-credit programs, has joined with HLL.[16]

The *Wall Street Journal* illustrates the power of this channel by describing the activities and attitudes of one independent micro-credit entrepreneur associated with HLL—Mrs. Nandyala:

When one of Mrs. Nandyala's neighbors, who used a knock-off soap called Likebuoy that comes in the same red packaging as Unilever's Lifebuoy brand, balked at paying an extra rupee (about two U.S. cents) for the real thing, Mrs. Nandyala gave her a free bar to try. A skin rash caused by the fake soap cleared up after a few days, and the neighbor converted to Lifebuoy.

When another neighbor asked why she should pay more for Unilever's Wheel detergent than a locally made bar of laundry soap, Mrs. Nandyala asked her to bring a bucket and water and some dirty clothes. "I washed the clothes right in front of her to show her how it worked," she says.

Project Shakti women aren't Hindustan Lever employees. But the company helps train them and provides local marketing support. In Chervaunnaram, a Hindustan Lever employee, who visits every few months, demonstrates before a gathering of 100 people how soap cleans hands better than water alone. Dressed in a hospital-style smock, she rubs two volunteers' hands with white powder, then asks one to wash it off with water alone and the other to use soap. She shines a purple ultraviolet light on their hands, highlighting the specks of white that remained on the woman who skipped the soap. As the crowd chatters, the Hindustan Lever worker pulls Mrs. Nandyala to the front of the hall, and tells the crowd she has got plenty of soap to sell.

Mrs. Nandyala wasn't always comfortable with her new, public role. She first applied for a micro loan from a government-run agency to buy fertilizer and new tools for her family's small lentil farm four years ago. In 2003, the agency introduced her to a Hindustan Lever sales director from a nearby town. She took out another $200 loan to buy sachets of soap, toothpaste, and shampoo—but was too shy to peddle them door to door. So a regional Hindustan Lever sales director accompanied Mrs. Nandyala and demonstrated how to pitch the products.

Mrs. Nandyala has repaid her start-up micro loan and hasn't needed to take another one. Today, she sells regularly to about 50 homes, and even serves as a mini-wholesaler, stocking tiny shops in outlying villages a short bus ride from her own. She sells about $230 of goods each month, earning about $15 in profit. The rest is used to restock products.[17]

In 2005, 13,000 entrepreneurs like Mrs. Nandyala were selling Unilever's products in 50,000 villages in India's 12 states. HLL is targeting expanding this project to 40,000 rural women by 2006. HLL expects that Project Shakti could account for as much as 25% of HLL's rural sales in 2008–2010.[18]

An important reason for the success of this very integrated marketing strategy for rural India is the consistencies of goals between the private entity (HLL), the government entities, and the NGOs (e.g., CARE). Because the Lifebuoy product is positioned and targeted for the socially desirable improved health goal, the other entities are happy to cooperate with HLL. This targeting and positioning is strategically very valuable for HLL. As C.K. Prahalad states:

> Differentiating soap products on the platform of health takes advantage of an opening in the competitive landscape for soap. Providing affordable health soap to the poor achieves product differentiation for a mass-market soap and taps into an opportunity for growth through increased usage. In India, soap is perceived as a beauty product, rather than a preventative health measure. Also, many consumers believe a visual clean is a safe clean, and either don't use soap to wash their hands, use soap infrequently, or use cheaper substitution products that they believe deliver the same benefits. HLL, through its innovative communication campaigns, has been able to link the use of soap to a promise of health as a means of creating behavioral change, and thus has increased sales of its low-cost, mass-market soap. Health is a valuable commodity for the poor and to HLL. By associating Lifebuoy's increased usage with health, HLL can build new habits involving its brand and build loyalty from a group of customers new to the category. A health benefit also creates a higher perceived value for money, increasing a customer's willingness to pay. By raising consumers' level of understanding about illness prevention, HLL is participating in a program that will have a meaningful impact on the Indian population's well-being and fulfill its corporate purpose to "raise the quality of life."[19]

It is clear that this integrated positioning, targeting, and marketing sales and distribution strategy delivered sustainable competitive advantage for HLL. However, there is one area in which we feel that HLL could have improved the productivity of the whole process—with their newly developed communication channels.

HLL worked with Ogilvy and Mather to develop teams that would visit the villages—targeting the 10,000 villages in nine states where HLL stood to gain the most market share, as well as educate the most needy communities. They spent a lot of effort in designing low cost ways of communicating with their rural target. HLL grew to 127 two-person teams in 2003 and estimates that the program is reaching 30–40% of the rural population in targeted states.[20] Each team went through a four-stage communications plan. Stage 1 is a school and village presentation using an interactive flip chart. At the end of the day, they assign school teachers to work with the students to develop skits and presentations for their next visit in two to three months. Stage 2 is a Lifebuoy village health day, which includes the skits and a health camp in which the village doctor measures height and weight to give "healthy child" awards to those who fall within healthy norms. Stage 3 is a diarrhea management workshop geared toward pregnant women and young mothers who might not be reached by the first two stages. Stage 4 is the formation of the Lifebuoy health club that includes activities on hygiene and keeping the village clean. The two-person team will return four–six more times to run health club activities.

As we will discuss in more detail in Chapter 6, "Entrepreneurial Advertising That Works," there is a big opportunity for improving productivity of advertising and, in this case, other communications methods, by applying adaptive experimentation. In the HLL case, they assumed that the Ogilvy and Mather-generated communication plan was the best that could be generated, and they rolled it out. However, given that each village or state could be an experimental unit, and given that some other way of efficiently communicating with the targeted rural villagers could have been more effective, there was an opportunity cost of not developing and trying and measuring the impact of other communications methods in different villages as they rolled out the program. We will go into more detail on how this might have been done in Chapter 6.

SUMMARY

Each venture must answer the "what am I selling to whom, and why will they buy?" question before it can create a successful marketing strategy and plan. Segmentation selects the subgroup of all consumers to whom we think we can sell our products. Positioning tries to inform members of the segment of the benefits of using our product or service, vis-à-vis any competitors. The unique value proposition is the public communication of the promise of intrinsic value that customers will receive from your products and services that they won't receive from others. All of these are based on the venture's distinctive competence and sustainable competitive advantage. With this foundation, an effective marketing plan can be built.

So far we've focused on the foundation for the customer-oriented marketing plan, which is the first priority. However, the marketing challenge today expands beyond customers. All of the venture's other stakeholders— such as users, investors, supply chain/channel partners, and employees— care about the customer, but they are also concerned with equity and image of the venture. Each stakeholder needs a relevant value proposition on why to stay engaged with the firm. So the same concepts of segmentation and positioning apply to them.

ENDNOTES

1. Some of these segmentation questions come from personal discussions and correspondence with Professor Yoram Wind of The Wharton School, University of Pennsylvania.

2. McMath, Robert and Forbes, Tom, "Look Before You Leap," *Entrepreneur*, April 1998, pp. 135–139.

3. Ibid, p. 135.

4. Greco, Susan, "Reeling them in," *Inc. Magazine*, Jan. 1998, p. 52.

5. Ibid.

6. This section comes from two interviews done by Leonard Lodish with Jill Beraud, the Chief Marketing Officer of Victoria's Secret from 1995–2005 and the Chief Marketing Officer of Limited Brands from 2005–, on July 8, 2004 and April 6, 2005.

7. R.W. Keidel, *Wall Street Journal*, June 16, 1997, p. B1.

8. C.K. Prahalad, *The Fortune at the Bottom of the Pyramid*, Prentice Hall, 2005, p. 211.

9. Ibid, p. 213.

10. Ibid, p. 222.

11. Ibid, p. 207.

12. Ibid, p. 209.

13. Ibid, p. 209.

14. Ibid, p. 220.

15. Ibid, p. 214.

16. Cris Prystal, "With Loans, Poor South Asian Women Turn Entrepreneurial," *The Wall Street Journal*, May 25, 2005, p. B1.

17. Ibid.

18. Ibid.

19. Prahalad, *op.cit.*, pp. 229–230.

20. Ibid, p. 226.

2

Generating, Screening, and Developing Ideas

	Products/Services	Equity/Shares	Image
Customers			
Users			
Investors			
Supply Chain/ Channel Partners			
Employees			

Most entrepreneurs or Strategic Business Unit (SBU) managers have at least one product or service concept in mind when they begin planning new initiatives. In this chapter, we describe some helpful methodologies and concepts, as well as codified entrepreneurial experiences, which can help generate and screen new product and service concepts. We then describe cost-efficient methods for getting marketplace and channel participants both to help improve the design and to gauge the potential sales outlook for the idea. The old stock market adage of "cut your losses and let your profits run" applies equally well to the development of new ideas. Strong filtering is essential if long-term success is to be achieved. We first review some very interesting research that helps the entrepreneurial marketer choose a better battlefield to enter, if he or she has the option of choosing different kinds of products or services to consider.

FINDING MORE RECEPTIVE BATTLEFIELDS

Are there better markets for entrepreneurial survival? Are there characteristics of products/markets that make them more likely to be receptive to successful entrepreneurial activity? Are there differences in these characteristics when the new initiative is from a part of a big corporation versus an entrepreneurial venture? Three European researchers, Hay, Verdin, and Williamson, analyzed 30,000 new U.S. businesses to find characteristics that were more likely to be associated with entrepreneurial ventures that would survive for ten years or more.[1] The researchers developed measures of three groups of characteristics: the first was customer buying patterns, the second was competitor's marketing and channel strategies, and the third was production requirements.

Customer buying patterns were described by the following characteristics: The first was *purchase frequency*, which was measured by the proportion of product line that was generally purchased less than once per year compared with products that were purchased more frequently. The second was *purchase significance*, which was measured by the percentage of the product line that represented a major purchase for the ultimate buyer. The third measure of consumer buying patterns was the *degree of customer/distributor fragmentation*. This was measured by the percentage of product lines for which there were over 1,000 customer accounts at the manufacturer level.

Competitors' marketing and channel strategies were described by three variables: The first variable was *pull marketing*, which was measured by the expenditures on media advertising as a percentage of total sales revenue. The second variable was *push marketing*, which was defined as the cost of marketing excluding media spending as a percentage of sales revenue for the product lines in each group. Finally, *channel dependence* was described as the percentage of products that pass through an intermediary before reaching the user.

Production requirements were described by four variables: The first was *labor vs. capital intensity*, which was measured by calculating the ratio of total employees to the total book value of plant and equipment in the industry producing each group of products. The second variable was *employee skill requirements*. It was defined as the number of "high skills" jobs as a percentage of total employees involved in producing the product group. The third variable was *service requirements*. It was calculated as the percentage of products requiring a moderate to high degree of sales or technical service as classified by the suppliers who were surveyed. The last variable in this group was *made-to-order supply*. It was defined as the percentage of product lines that were made to order based on customer specifications.

Hay, Verdin, and Williamson analyzed almost 30,000 independent start-ups for a five-year period ending in the mid-1980s. They performed a statistical analysis of the relationship of survival rates of independent start-ups and the preceding product/market characteristics. Their main results are summarized in Figure 2-1,[2] which shows hostile and fertile product/market segments for independent start-ups.

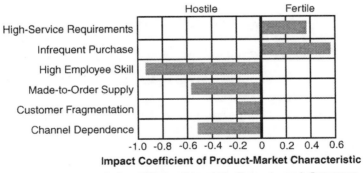

Source: Hay, Verdin, and Williamson, "Successful New Ventures: Lessons for Entrepreneurs and Investors," *Long Range Planning* 26 (5), 1993, 31-41

Figure 2-1   The impact of product and market characteristics on the survival of independent start-ups

The data showed that entrepreneurial start-ups had significantly better chances of survival in two product/market segment types: those that had high service requirements and those that had low purchase frequency. The high service requirements results imply that the greater attention to customer needs and flexibility an entrepreneurial start-up can offer can give it an advantage over less-attentive established vendors for that product/market segment.

The results that product/market segments that made infrequent purchase decisions are also more fertile are consistent with other theories of
business-to-business marketing. Infrequent purchases typically involve
the customer reassessing the attributes of product or service offerings. In
this circumstance, there is a higher likelihood of attending to new information and possibly trying a new alternative product offering.

The figure also shows four product/market characteristics that an entrepreneur should avoid, all other factors being equal. Those segments that
require high employee skill and made-to-order supply are harder for
entrepreneurs to succeed in. These segments may require extensive
employee training and big investments in production assets—both luxu-
ries that are difficult for a new entrepreneur to supply. The other two
entrepreneurially hostile segment characteristics make it very difficult for
the small player to target the segment effectively. Both highly fragmented
customer bases and high-end customer dependence on channels make it
relatively more difficult for the entrepreneurial marketer to reach her target customers. Of course, the Internet makes it easier to reach fragmented customer bases, since geography no longer plays a role, but even on the
Web, if the base is too fragmented, the cost of customer acquisition may
rise to unprofitable levels.

For corporate "intrapraneurs," Hay, Verdin, and Williamson also report
the product market segment types that were hostile and fertile for corporate ventures. The results are summarized in Figure 2-2.[3]

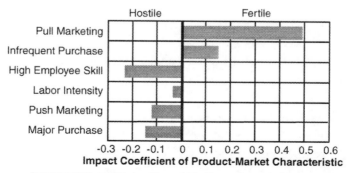

Source: Hay, Verdin, and Williamson, "Successful New Ventures: Lessons for Entrepreneurs
and Investors," *Long Range Planning* 26 (5), 1993, 31-41

Figure 2-2   The impact of product and market characteristics on the survival of corporate ventures

The only segment characteristic common to higher likelihood of survival for both corporate and independent ventures is infrequent purchase. Segments in which a customer is more likely to be receptive to new information are evidently fertile, regardless of the assets that the new venture brings to them. Segments that require high employee skill are also hostile to both independent and corporate entrepreneurs. Evidently, high employee skill is a barrier to entry of established competitors, regardless of whether the new entry is corporate or independent.

The other characteristics differentiate those segments that corporate resources can impact. Pull marketing requires resources for mass marketing and may also leverage the reputation of a corporate parent. Corporate subsidiaries seem to be at a disadvantage when infrastructure to support "push marketing" is required by the segment. Perhaps long periods of experience are necessary to set up effective networks. This experience with the "push marketing" infrastructure can be an effective barrier to entry.

Even though these results can help an entrepreneur or corporate subsidiary to choose a more receptive product/market to enter, keep in mind that all of the positive and negative characteristics are only effective on the average. Certainly, not every entrepreneurial venture that attacks segments with the fertile characteristics will be successful. The results just show that the entrepreneur or corporate subsidiary will be more likely to not fail or to fail in those segments.

EVALUATING SPECIFIC VENTURE IDEAS—CONCEPT TESTING

Before we describe important ways to generate market reaction to your product or service concept, we should stress that there are other evaluations that also need to be performed. Necessary activities include making sure that the production requirements will fit with your operations system; that the logistics for supply will work; that the organization can perform the needed design, production, and operations activities; and that financial resources are available for the launch and ongoing revenue and costs. However, the details of these activities are beyond our scope. We concentrate on the crucial marketing activities that will make or break the success of many new initiatives.

In order to obtain sales, every product or service idea has to be wanted by some market segment more than competitive products or services. Very simply, if customers won't choose your new product or service over the existing product or service, then you won't make any sales. It is amazing to us that so many entrepreneurs and managers do all kinds of analyses of the costs, patent protection, possible competition, and market potential (if everyone who could use one of my widgets bought one, we would have sales of five billion dollars!). What they don't do is get actual reaction from real customers to the product or service concept. The entrepreneur just doesn't know all of the factors that the end customer will consider when she evaluates the new product or service. As we discuss in Chapter 4, "Distribution/Channel Decisions to Solidify Sustainable Competitive Advantage," it is also very important to get channel intermediary reactions to the concept as well. Before we describe methods for getting customer and intermediary's reactions and suggestions for product improvements, we will share with you an example of how valuable these methods can be.

TRAKUS: THE VALUE OF CONCEPT TESTING

Trakus, Inc. was founded by an M.I.T. MBA, Eric Spitz, and two high-tech M.I.T. undergraduates in 1997. The company was originally named Retailing Insights to reflect their initial product concept. They were going to do Videocart right using the latest technology. Videocart was a computerized shopping cart that was developed and introduced in the early 1990s. The cart would know where it was in a store and let the shopper know about specials and other useful information that depended on the cart's location in the store. So if a shopper was in the cereal aisle, the screen on the cart would show the cereal specials for the day. The cart could also show advertisements for cereals when the cart was in the cereal aisle. In order to keep shoppers' attention, the cart had a number of useful consumer functions. These functions included locating items in the store, getting a number for the meat or deli line remotely and being paged when your number is ready, providing recipes and store location for all of the recipe's items, local news, and so on.

The original Videocart venture failed because of poor execution. The carts were not recharged or repaired on a timely basis. Thus, when a consumer went to take one, the odds were that the cart would not function well. Word of mouth among consumers and the early store sites became negative, so no new stores wanted to utilize the carts. From a public market value at one time over $300 million, Videocart Inc. failed and declared bankruptcy in the mid-1990s.

Eric's team was going to do Videocart right using all the new technology. Instead of FM transmitters for location in the store, they had developed an indoor version of the GPS global positioning system to use. They would be able to identify the shopper's frequent shopper card or name and pull information from the Internet. Thus, the shopper could enter their shopping list at home and it would be available electronically at the store. The carts would be of value to store operators because they would get more customers to patronize their store. The retailers would also be able to sell promotion opportunities on the cart to the manufacturers just as they did in their weekly circulars. This was a significant profit opportunity for the retailers. To advertisers, the computerized shopping cart was the perfect opportunity to reach the consumer at the most important point—just as they were making their actual purchasing decision. The new Videocart was going to be much cheaper than the original because of the lower costs of new technology. On paper, the venture looked terrific. Eric obtained $50,000 seed money from an angel investor. The angel investor requested that before the team spend any money on product development, they concept test the idea to both of the customer groups that would need to buy off on the idea. These were the retailers who needed to subsidize putting the carts in the stores in return for promotional funds they would get, and the advertisers who were to pay for advertising on the carts.

The team developed a very compelling description of the new generation Videocart, which included all of the benefits that either the retailer or manufacturer would obtain. They even had a neat simulation of how the system would work and what the cart's screen would look like that they put on their laptops. They then showed this to retailers and manufacturers, and at a given price, asked how likely they would be to buy their role on the carts. After asking the purchase intent question, they also asked a number of questions about what manufacturers and retailers liked and what they disliked about the cart concept. The answers the team received were not very encouraging. For retailers, the cart's previous bad reputation was a big barrier. Retailers were very apprehensive to try another version of a product that had a terrible reputation. This implied that the team would have to establish extensive beta sites (at the venture's expense) to prove over a long term that the carts would work and would provide the benefits the team anticipated. Not only that, but retailers were also very frugal and were very reticent to commit their own funds to investing even partially in the carts. The retailers were used to having manufacturers pay for most new innovations as a way of getting or improving their shelf space and in-store position.

For the manufacturers, they were only willing to pay for advertising on the carts if the carts would demonstrate that they actually had an incremental effect on the manufacturer's sales in the stores. Not only that, but manufacturers also required significant scale to justify their infrastructure to support the new advertising medium. That meant that Eric's team would have to be in a significant fraction of all of the U.S. supermarkets before the manufacturers would begin to commit significant advertising and promotion funds to the medium. It did not take much rough calculating to determine that the cash investment required to reach a break-even (if a break-even were at all possible) would be huge. The probability of convincing venture capital or angel sources to invest that kind of money was very low. Eric's team was discouraged for a couple days by the results. However, they had most of their angel's seed money left and lots of technical skills in the areas of GPS location, communications, and digital signal processing. After the bad concept-testing results sunk in, the team had a brainstorming session where they generated and evaluated a number of product ideas that would leverage their distinctive competence as they viewed it.

The outcome of that brainstorming session took the team in a very different, but much more profitable, direction. Eric, a sports nut, conceptualized a product concept that the rest of the team said could be accomplished technically. They put little rugged transmitters on athletes (in their helmets or on their clothes) and put receiving antennas in a few places in the stadium. They could then determine in real time, digitally, where every athlete on a team is located, record it, and process that data to generate new valuable statistics, and display the information virtually immediately. The information would include speed and acceleration of each player and real-time location of each player. If you know the weight of two players and their acceleration the instant they collide, you can easily calculate a "hit" gauge. This hit gauge would be a valuable addition to the broadcasting of football or hockey. The broadcaster could also analyze any plays by showing the digital picture of the replay and associated speed and acceleration statistics and processing the digital data to illustrate good or poor performance of some players. The digital, real-time data and information would also be perfect for "broadcasting" the games over the Internet.

The team concept tested this idea similarly to the way they had potential customers evaluate the Videocart. They developed a simulation of what the system might look like and presented it to members of potential market segments that might be interested in the system. They also changed their name to Trakus, Inc. to reflect their new orientation. The segmentation and decision process that would be used by each segment was much more complicated for the new Trakus sports product. There were teams, leagues, players associations, coaches (who could use the system for training), advertisers, agents, Internet sports companies, and so on who all could contribute to or influence Trakus' market reception and potential revenue. Before they exposed the concept to all of these market participants, they applied for patents on their ideas to give them some protection after they exposed them to the market.

In contrast to the lukewarm reception they received for Videocart, the Trakus concept "rolled the socks up and down" of almost all the people they interviewed. The biggest concern anyone expressed was whether the team could actually develop the product and have it work reliably. They didn't interview the sports league officials, however. They found out after going through development of the technology that the sports leagues would not let an outside firm make enough money from the technology to make the venture succeed.

Therefore, Trakus found another niche using their technology to track horses for electronic transmission to parimutuel betting parlors around the world. This technology uniquely lets betters "watch" a race digitally in real time and track the horse they have bet on. The existing video technology that Trakus is replacing could only show some of the horses, but not all at the same time.

If the Trakus team had not concept tested their original Videocart idea and had gone ahead to develop and implement that concept, it is not certain that they would have failed. However, given their concept-testing results, the odds of having a huge success were low. On the other hand, the concept-testing results were used the way they should have been used—to screen an idea before a lot of resources were spent on it. The concept testing caused the team to "go back to the drawing board" and generate other product ideas that could best leverage their unique skills and abilities.

The team deserves a lot of credit for interpreting the concept-testing results in a rational manner. Human nature goes against rational interpretation of valuable, but negative, information. When the team had organized itself and made its mission to "do Videocart right," it was very difficult emotionally to receive and rationally process information that said that the market did not want a new Videocart nearly as much as the team thought they did. The U.S. culture seems to reinforce these emotional reactions to negative, but valuable, information. It is not seen as "macho" to decide to give up on an idea, admit you were wrong, and go on to make the best of what you have left. Especially in an entrepreneurial venture that is typically started with the product/service idea as the main motivation for the team to get together, it is very difficult to admit that the initial idea may not be as profitable as the team first thought. As we describe how to do concept testing, you should keep in mind that it is a challenge to use the concept-testing results rationally. We first review the methods that one very successful firm, idealab!, used to generate new concepts and ideas for products and services.

IDEA GENERATION AT IDEALAB!

At idealab!, a generation of new ideas and companies has turned into a multi-hundred million dollar business. Bill Gross, who had created a number of companies since his early school days, realized that his skills at generating ideas (from speakers, to Lotus Hal and Magellan, to the extremely successful Knowledge Adventure's Jump Start learning series) could be codified and used to incubate many successful companies. Since 1996, almost 500 ideas have been tried, leading to dozens of successful companies including CitySearch, Overture Services—the creator of the paid search market, and Internet Brands (CarsDirect.com and other Internet services).

The key methodologies used are trend analysis, brainstorming, filtering, and "sense and respond." Let us examine each one. Groups at idealab! regularly talk about large-scale trends in technology and markets. One such analysis led to work in the alternative energy space. At regular intervals, small (6–10) groups of people, including Bill Gross, have brainstorming sessions focused on an area of interest. During these half-day sessions, the first hour is spent discussing the problem area. People are encouraged to generate ideas, with no criticism permitted. The ideas are then grouped into themes, and each theme is pursued for a few minutes. Finally, and key, someone needs to stand up with the passion to take the ideas forward. That is the key first filter in creating a project.

The next filter is a quick market analysis—with the focus on the potential overall size of market. In creating risky ventures, it is often more valuable to have a few percent of a watermelon-sized market, than 100% of a grape-sized one. Big-enough markets create enough opportunity for several companies, reducing one set of risks any new venture faces.

Finally, a small project is started to do a paper or Internet prototype that can be shown to "real" customers. This use of the Web for concept testing is discussed more fully in the following sections. The results create a feedback loop where reaction to the concept is sensed (measured) and small or large changes are made (response) to hone into what customers will actually buy.

CONCEPT TESTING: WHAT IT IS AND WHERE IT'S BEST USED

Concept testing is a research technique that checks whether the prospective purchaser and/or user of a new product-offering bundle understands the product/service idea, feels that it answers a need, and would be willing to purchase and/or use it. The technique can also help to improve the product-offering bundle by understanding problems and/or improvement opportunities that are perceived by the potential consumers. Its primary purpose is to estimate customer and/or intermediary reactions to a product-offering bundle concept before committing substantial resources to it. Concept testing forces the entrepreneur to expose the idea to the people who will have to receive perceived benefits from it, and to make sure that these people indeed do perceive the benefits. If done well, concept testing and associated procedures can provide a number of important benefits to the entrepreneur:

- First, concept testing can identify likely product failures and limit the amount of resources spent on ideas that the market does not perceive as helpful.
- Second, concept testing can separate the good ideas from the poor ones, and support resource allocation to those ideas that the market does want.

- Third, the concept-testing procedure can supply suggestions for improving the product-offering bundle to make it perceived as more useful to the market participants.

- Fourth, as we will see in Chapter 3, "Entrepreneurial Pricing," concept testing can also be used to generate rough price-sales volume demand curves for new product-offering bundles. Well-designed and executed concept testing can provide estimates of how the demand for a product will change at alternative price levels.

Concept testing is best at estimating consumers' reaction to the product-offering bundle *before* they actually would use it; it is okay for estimating the trial of a new product or service, but obviously not very effective at estimating repeat purchase for goods that are bought more than once. The experience with the physical product or service bundle and whether it delivers on its implied promise will be the most important determinant of whether the customer purchases the product again. Thus, concept testing will be more useful for estimating trial rates for frequently purchased products and potential sales for consumer durable products as well as business-to-business durable products. However, even for durable products and business-to-business products, if the initial customers are not satisfied, then they will tell other potential customers that the product is bad if they are able logistically to do that. Word of mouth can be the biggest help and also the biggest problem for entrepreneurs, depending on whether the initial users are satisfied that the product meets their expectations. You should keep in mind that concept testing can only help estimate revenue *assuming that the product meets the customer expectations* when the customers actually use the product or service.

Given the preceding caveats, concept testing can be a very productive addition to the entrepreneurial marketer's "bag of tricks." It can be done relatively quickly at a relatively low cost. It is also a very flexible technique. A number of ideas can be handled in a single study, as well as the evaluation of different versions of the same basic product-offering bundle. From a cost/benefit viewpoint, concept testing is usually a great value. Not enough managers use concept testing in relation to its value. Hopefully this chapter will help rectify the situation. We next discuss some "nuts and bolts" of actually doing concept testing and then discuss what concept testing doesn't do—that is, some of its limitations.

HOW TO DO CONCEPT TESTING—THE "NUTS AND BOLTS"

In order to use concept testing productively, the following issues are important:

1. What kind of information specifically should be collected from respondents?
2. What should be in the concept statement?
3. What are the best modes of data collection?
4. Who should be exposed to the concept?
5. How should the questions be asked?

We'll take each of the preceding questions in order.

1. What Kind of Information Specifically Should Be Collected from Respondents?

The most valid information you could gather from a respondent is to *actually ask and receive an order* for a purchase of the product based upon the concept statement. We discuss these *dry tests* later in modes of data collection. If you cannot realistically perform dry tests, then the next most valid information is *purchase intention*. Purchase intention is an indication of how likely the respondent would be to buy the product, after he or she was exposed to the concept. The usual scale that is used to scale purchase intention is the following:

I definitely would buy I probably would buy I

might or might not buy I

probably would not buy I and definitely would not buy I.

It is risky to interpret purchase intentions absolutely, especially any answer except "definitely would buy." The exposure of the concept will typically sensitize the respondent to the product concept and may bias them to tell the perceived source of the concept test what they feel the concept tester wants to hear. People want to "be nice." The purchase intent question also implicitly assumes that the respondent has been exposed to the product, has understood the attributes of the product, and is able to find the product available in the channel that the respondent would use to buy the product.

In order to counteract the "be nice" bias, it's best to include somewhere in the concept test a comparison of the new product with some existing product it might replace. Equivalently, some respondents can respond to a concept that describes the existing product in the same form as the new product. The purchase intent scores on the existing product can then be a base from which to compare the intent scores on the new product. For example, if product A is an existing product and product B is the new product, both products would be described by a concept statement (as discussed later in the chapter), and purchase intent would be collected for both products. The fraction who "definitely would buy" can be compared for A and B. If B has 20% more intent to "definitely buy," then it is reasonable to assume that if consumers are aware of product B, understand its attributes, and can find it distributed, then B could reasonably sell 20% more than A. Some researchers will take a small fraction, around 30% of the "probably would buy," into their calculations by adding 30% of the responses to "the second box" (the "probably would buy" box), to the responses for "the top box" (the "definitely would buy" box).

In order to counteract the other awareness and distribution limitations, you should multiply the fraction of the market that the concept test says would buy by at least three estimated reduction factors, all fractions less than one. The first factor, f1, is the fraction of the target population(s) that will be aware of the new product. This will depend on how successful the marketing plan is for the product. The second factor, f2, is whether those who are aware will understand and perceive the attributes and benefits of the product as well as those who were exposed to the concept in the concept test. This reduction factor, f2, also depends on the success of the marketing plan. Finally, the third factor, f3, reflects the odds that members of the target market(s) will be able to easily purchase the product where they would expect to find it. Multiplying the concept test purchase intent fraction by f1 × f2 × f3 will reduce the purchase intent number to one that is much more reasonable and more predictable of in-market performance.

Other questions that might be asked can aid in both improving the actual product and the way it is described to potential consumers. These other questions should be asked *after* the purchase intent question. The purchase intent question is meant to measure the attraction of a concept after the potential customer has been exposed to the concept, not after the potential customer has been asked a lot of questions about the concept, which normally heightens their interest in the concept.

Questions about how well the potential consumer understood the concept and what they liked and didn't like about the product are usually very helpful. The "likes and dislikes" can be very useful in improving either the product or the way the product is communicated. The respondents should be able to "play back" the product's attributes and benefits, as they perceived them after having been exposed to the concept statement. The respondents could also answer questions about how interested they are in the product—extremely interested, somewhat interested, and so on. If lots of respondents are "extremely interested," but relatively few express high purchase intent, then perhaps the price used in the concept test was too high.

Depending on the product and its target market, other questions can be asked such as situations for which the respondent sees the product as useful, or problems the product might solve. If the respondent can tell which products the new product might replace, this is also helpful. Answers to these questions can be valuable for improving the marketing materials for the product's introduction.

Some people put price response questions right into the concept test by asking *the same person* purchase intent questions *at different price levels in the same concept test*—for example, "How likely would you be to purchase the product if it were $140, $130, $120, or $100?" The respondent would give a separate response for each alternative price level. *This procedure is extremely biasing and should be avoided.* The respondent assumes that she is "negotiating" with the concept tester and gives very biased results that are not usually indicative of how the respondent would actually react if she were exposed to the product at different price levels.

The right way to include price response in a concept test is to include *one price* as part of the product's description. *Each respondent* is exposed to only one price as a descriptor of the product. However, *each respondent* can be exposed to *different prices* than other respondents. As we'll see later with some examples, price is a very psychological attribute and can have a big impact on how potential consumers perceive a product or service. This procedure insures that the potential consumer only sees one price, the same way the person will see the product in the real market. This procedure is just one example of the next category of "nuts and bolts" of concept testing.

2. What Should Be in the Concept Statement?

The concept statement should as closely and realistically as possible mimic how the respondent would be exposed to the product and its attributes when the product is actually introduced. Most concept statements look like product brochures or print ads. The concept statement typically also includes where the respondent could expect to buy the product or service, and all the benefits that are part of the positioning plan. As discussed previously, the price of the product is also one of the attributes that should be an integral part of the concept statement. Figure 2-3 shows a concept statement for one product from a new novelty diaper line that has university and sports team logos on them. To be realistic, the concept test should be done in each of the possible target market segments with the specific logo for that segment as part of the concept description. One of the possible market segments was alumni of the University of Pennsylvania. The concept is slightly disguised to protect confidentiality.

Figure 2-3 Logo diaper concept statement (slightly disguised)

Product Concept: Futurewear is a line of designer diapers that feature university and professional sports team logos. One of the diapers has the University of Pennsylvania "Penn Quaker" logo, both on the tape and bottom ("tush") of the diaper. This diaper is made of premium materials and is functionally equivalent to a good disposable diaper. It is a fun, novelty item, which will typically be purchased as a gift (i.e., baby shower, Christmas) rather than as an everyday item by parents. The diapers will be white, packaged in a very nice gift box of 19 that also has the Penn Quaker logo, and be priced at $11.95. The diaper will be available at most stores that have other University of Pennsylvania logo merchandise, as well as Web stores that sell baby merchandise. What a nice, fun, way to help a loyal

Penn alumnus start his or her child showing their support of Penn! The perfect gift for anyone who is a Penn supporter!

3. What Are the Best Modes of Data Collection?

The entrepreneur wants to have the respondent exposed to the concept in a manner as close as possible to how they would be exposed in reality. There are limits and trade-offs of costs versus validity of the concept test results. If you would use a print ad or direct mail piece to introduce your product, it is not very expensive to "dummy up" some sample ads as part of the concept statement and then to expose people to those ads. These kinds of concepts are most validly exposed through personal interviews with the respondent either at her home or at her place of work. Depending on the segmentation targets, it sometimes is cheaper and not less valid to use centralized locations like malls. Telephone interviews can be very cost effective for concepts that are easily understood over the phone and may be advertised on radio when they are introduced. Sometimes a combination of mailing, emailing, or faxing the concept statement can be combined with telephone interviews. These combinations can be very cost effective and for many products and services do not lose much validity compared to in-person interviews.

It is usually cost effective to contract with a local market research firm to actually field the concept test. They have much experience in getting with the right people and can help with the actual test design. However, if the firm tells you to do something that contradicts the major points in this chapter, then you should change suppliers. Depending on your time versus resource constraints, it may be possible to use students at nearby universities who are studying market research. If they use your product as a class project, it may take two or three months to get results. Commercial firms can turn around some concept tests in a few weeks.

For products that will be sold or promoted with the Web as a primary marketing tool, concept testing can very easily be done directly on the Internet. In fact, depending on one's ethics, it is very feasible to "dummy up" online ads and/or product descriptions, and *actually ask for the order online.* When respondents start the order process, you then can explain to them that the product is in development and that you were testing marketplace reaction. You could then send them some kind of a gift as a token of thanks and apology, and put their name on a list of those who will get the first chance to buy the product when it's ready. This "dry test," as direct marketers call it, is the most valid way of getting real consumer demand for a new product or service. The Web is not the only place "dry tests" can and have been used. Direct response marketers have been using dry tests for years. Depending on which media vehicles they use for advertising, they have to consider prematurely letting their competitors know their new product plans. Dry tests with direct mail are much easier to hide than dry tests in radio, TV, or print.

4. Who Should Be Exposed to the Concept?

If your positioning and segmentation planning have been complete, then it is obvious that decision-making members and decision influencers of the target segments should be exposed to the concept. In concept testing, it usually pays to be inclusive with possible target segments. If you are doubtful about a target segment, it makes sense to concept test some members to help decide whether to include the segment in your plans. The cost of concept testing is typically small compared to the foregone profits of missing a possible segment.

For business-to-business products and some complex and/or expensive consumer products, the entrepreneurial marketer must be careful to interview all of the possible influencers of the purchase decision. For example, if the firm is considering introducing a new angiography product to hospitals, she should interview not only the physicians who would use the product, but hospital administrators who would need to approve the purchase, as well as nurses who might influence how the product were to be used. For high-involvement consumer purchases like appliances, computers, telecommunications equipment, and so on, there may be many possible decision influencers that need to be tested. For example, for computers and telecommunications equipment, many consumers will turn to "experts" whose opinions they request before they make purchase decisions. It is very important for the entrepreneurial marketer to seek out and interview these experts.

If the entrepreneurial marketer does not know the decision process in her target markets well enough, before performing the concept testing, it makes sense to do some qualitative questioning of market participants to find out how these type of decisions are typically made. Questions such as "would you consult anyone else before making a purchase decision?" or "who else would have to approve this decision?" can be very enlightening.

CONCEPT TESTING CHANNEL MEMBERS

In Chapter 4 we discuss concept testing for channel members as being as important as for the end purchasers. However, concept testing with channel members *is no substitute* for getting systematic end user reaction to a product. In his book, *The Silicon Valley Way*, Elton Sherwin Jr. describes a disguised, but real, company, The Palo Alto PC Company, which neglected to concept test the end purchaser and solely relied on the results from the distribution channels.[4] This company had been successful designing and building small, good-looking, premium-priced notebook PCs and selling them through a strong network of distributors.

> As Palo Alto PC began designing their fourth generation notebook, they did a cursory survey of their largest distributors. They assumed, and their distributors confirmed, that "customers want it even smaller."
>
> The new Palo Alto PC was a hit with the media. Its innovative keyboard made it both small and cute. Unfortunately, few customers bought it. Sales plummeted. It turns out that executives wanted longer battery life, brighter screens, and thinner PCs—but not smaller keyboards.[5]

Distributors are very good at reacting to the aspects of the product that affect how well they will "push" them—the mark-up, the terms, the logistics, the end-user marketing program, and so on. They also can sometimes tell you what *they think* their customers will want. However, as this example points out, there is typically no substitute for getting end-user reaction to concepts.

5. How Should the Questions Be Asked?

Concept testing for entrepreneurial marketing situations typically involves either *monadic* testing (a person gets exposed to only one concept) or *paired comparison* testing (a person is exposed to a pair of concepts).

Monadic testing should be used when you seek a detailed uncontaminated reaction to a concept. It is typically better to monadic test when direct competitors are hard to identify. Monadic tests also work better when there is little external search for alternatives prior to purchasing.

On the other hand, when there are direct competitors already in the market, it can be useful to also do a *paired comparison* evaluation of the new product vs. others. If there's enough time, the paired comparison can be done after the monadic evaluation. The paired comparison purchase intent can be asked as "which would you prefer to purchase, Product A or Product B?" Here also a scale can be used, just as it was in the monadic purchase intent:

Definitely prefer A | Moderately prefer A | Toss-up |
Moderately prefer B | Definitely prefer B

As we discussed previously, this comparison evaluation helps to ground revenue predictions in what you know about existing products. For example, if your new entrepreneurial product is preferred by 20% more people than existing Product A, you know that its potential is to sell even better than Product A. This is only a *potential*, however. The preceding caveats on any purchase intent measure are also salient here—for example, awareness, understanding the product benefits, and finding the product in distribution.

CONCEPT SCREENING

Getting reactions of potential purchase influencers can be very helpful, not only after one product concept has been determined, but also to help *screen* candidate product ideas before much work or resources have been spent on them. For this screening application, *card sorting and evaluation* is sometimes cost effective. Simply give the respondent several product descriptions, each on a card or a separate sheet. The respondent can sort them into a rank order and can rate each idea on either a semantic (excellent, good, fair, poor, etc.) or numeric scale. The movie *Ten* has made it very easy to use 1-to-10 scales for marketing research.

USING THE WEB FOR CONCEPT TESTING

Many times, the reactions of consumers to concepts are biased by their inability to really understand what would be offered. The Web allows for certain concepts to be tested in a live manner, with direct validation or refutation of the basic concept. When CarsDirect.com was started, there was a lot of skepticism about whether or not people would actually buy

$25–$50,000 items sight unseen on the Web. Rather than do a lot of focus groups, screening, and so on, they elected to do a quick test on the Web.

With less than a week's work, they put up a site that offered "Cars at invoice price." The pricing was already widely available on the net, and a small number of pages were put up, inviting the user to search for the car they desired, and submit an order on the Web. Once their order was received, a phone call was made to verify that they were serious and a deposit was taken, and then the car was delivered.

When the test site was ready, CarsDirect.com bought the top listing for the cars keyword at GoTo.com (now Yahoo! Search Marketing) in order to direct some traffic to the site. Over the course of a single weekend, four cars were ordered. The company bought them at retail prices and subsidized the difference between that price and the invoice pricing that had been advertised. For less than $20,000, they had proven that people would buy very large ticket items on the Web. After that, several million dollars was invested to build the successful Web site that had sold more than $250 million worth of cars by the end of their first year and by 2006 was the largest car dealer in the U.S.

Similarly, with GoTo.com, a search site that charged for higher position in search results, there was great skepticism that either consumers or advertisers would use it. The company put up the site, and verified that advertisers would give them credit cards and pay for their ads. None of the cards were actually charged in the first month, since it was merely a concept-testing experiment. The refined version created a public company worth several billion dollars.

CAVEATS FOR CONCEPT TESTING

Even though concept testing is typically very valuable in terms of cost/benefits for you, it has a number of limitations that constantly need to be kept in mind:

1. As discussed previously, if the product or service does not deliver the benefits promised in the concept, the revenue predictions will never happen. The more costly, risky, and high involvement the product is, the more important is the experience of the innovator and early adopter users. If this experience is worse than the benefits expectation of the concept test and the expectations of these

"lead users" based upon the introductory sales and marketing material, then the product will be severely penalized.

2. Changes in the product between the concept test and the product's introduction will cause possible changes in consumer reactions.

3. Sometimes R&D and production cannot execute the product exactly as promised in the concept test.

4. If the concept has not been tested in a very realistic way, respondents may overstate their preferences in order to "be nice" to the interviewer. It is human nature to tell someone what you think they would like to hear. Thus, respondents may say they like the product, but not buy it when it actually comes on the market.

5. Concept testing can only predict initial purchase. It cannot predict how many people will use the product regularly, or how many will repeat purchase it. For repetitively purchased products, high trial rate alone does not guarantee success.

CONCEPT TESTING SUMMARY

Concept testing really amounts to getting systematic direct reactions of market and channel participants to your product/service concept before you spend the time and resources to develop, produce, and introduce it. Historically, concept testing has been able to predict product trial rates within a 20% range, about 80% of the time for frequently purchased packaged goods. For example, if predicted trial was 50%, the product trial rate would be between 40–60% in 8 out of 10 cases. However, even today, most packaged goods firms do qualitative focused groups rather than systematic concept testing for their new product screening and evaluation. Entrepreneurial firms do not have the luxury of using less than the most cost-effective methods.

The details of exactly how and who should be concept tested are not nearly as important as *just doing it!* The most important thing is to get direct reaction, including some measure of purchase intent from members of your target markets. If you don't do that, you *significantly increase your odds of failure* for your new venture.

If you are fortunate, you sometimes can do it in market testing of new concepts and product ideas.

VICTORIA'S SECRET USES THEIR STORES AS TEST BEDS FOR NEW PRODUCTS AND BRANDS

As we discuss in Chapters 1 and 4, a very important competitive advantage of Victoria's Secret (VS) is that they own their own stores. Not only are there ongoing strategic advantages of this, such as controlling the user experience in the store and the product's display, but another strategic advantage is that not all stores need to have the same product line. It is conceptually very easy to choose some representative stores and use them to get real consumer reaction to potential new lines or new display strategies for old lines. Recently, VS did a consumer segmentation study of current and potential customers. The study showed a need for a younger line for a more casual lifestyle. The new VS brand **Pink** is aimed at filling this need. In each VS store that sells Pink (now all of them), there is a separate "Pink" room and environment. The Pink line was first introduced in only 10 stores chosen to be representative. The product-offering bundle was then modified to reflect the consumer feedback and the sales trends that these test stores exhibited. The line was then rolled out to 30 stores, modified again based on customer feedback, then rolled out to 100 stores, modified again, and then rolled out to all stores. Compared to concept testing with a small sample of consumers, this "real" test marketing is an extremely valid, reliable way of evaluating and launching a new product. Pink has become a $500 million revenue product line in less than two years!

If a company that owns its own end user distribution is not using the sites as possible test beds, the company may be wasting one big asset that can strategically keep them ahead of their competition. VS competition who sells through department stores will have a much riskier proposition trying to evaluate and roll out new product lines. They won't be able to use the very valid, reliable testing methodology that VS used. Given the large investment that is required to develop owned store distribution, it makes sense to leverage this investment in all profitable ways. Testing new products and product lines is almost always a very productive use of the company-owned distribution channels.

As an added bonus, concept testing can be combined with price testing to help maximize the profit contribution of the new product. We explore this in the next chapter.

ENDNOTES

1. Michael Hay, Verdin, Paul, and Williamson, Peter J., "Successful New Ventures: Lessons for Entrepreneurs and Investors," *Long Range Planning*, (1993), Vol. 26, No. 5, pp. 31–41.

2. Ibid., p. 36.

3. Ibid., p. 38.

4. Sherwin, Elton B., Jr., *The Silicon Valley Way*, Prima Publishing, Rocklin, CA., 1998, p. 63.

5. Ibid.

3

Entrepreneurial Pricing— An Often-Misused Way to Garner Extraordinary Profits

	Products/Services	Equity/Shares	Image
Customers			
Users			
Investors			
Supply Chain/ Channel Partners			
Employees			

PRICING

Pricing is typically the most difficult marketing decision for most firms. It is also probably the most important because it ultimately determines how much money a company can make. In today's world, you not only have to price products that have significant manufacturing costs, or services with large human elements in delivery, but also intellectual property that can be replicated for essentially zero cost on the Internet. Unfortunately, some managers think pricing is much too easy. They use very comfortable, precise rules for pricing. These simple rules are usually one of two types: mark-up rules or competitive matching rules. Mark-up rules just take the product or service's costs and mark them up by a margin percentage. This margin percentage may be standard for the industry, or related to what you are used to, or what you need to make your forecasted profit at the forecasted revenue for your venture. The competitive rules usually have the manager planning on pricing just a bit lower than competition, or matching their prices. These "rules" make it very easy to make the pricing decision without having to do much work or careful thinking. However, like many things in life, "no pain, no gain." The problem with these "rules" is that they may leave lots of money on the table.

Why do these common ways of pricing leave lots of money on the table? Very simply, because other prices may be more profitable to the venture. For example, if my widgets cost $1, and I sell them for $2, a "keystone" or doubling mark-up, why shouldn't I as an entrepreneurial marketer be happy? You shouldn't because you haven't asked the proper question. The right question is: *Of all the possible prices I can charge for my widgets, which price will maximize my profitability over my planning horizon?* If when I price my widgets for $2, I will sell 400,000 units per year, is that the best possible price in terms of total profitability from the widgets over the product's life? Selling 400,000 units at $2 per unit brings in revenue of $800,000. From that revenue, product costs of $1 per unit make costs equal to $1 × 400,000 equals $400,000 in product costs. This leaves $400,000 as gross margin or contribution to fixed costs and profit due to the widgets.

As an entrepreneurial marketer, you must ask what would happen to my units sold if I charged other prices than $2? If a reasonable estimate can be made of units that would be sold at other alternative prices (the "elasticity of demand"), then the entrepreneur can easily find the price that does maximize profitability over the planning horizon. We will describe methods for getting estimates of demand at alternative prices later, after we show how valuable they can be if they are integrated into the cost structure of the venture. Let's assume that our widgets would sell the amounts indicated in Table 3-1.

Table 3-1 Contribution and revenue consequences of different prices

Price per Unit	Units Sold	Revenue ($)	Cost @ $1/Unit	Contribution ($)
1.0	600,000	600,000	600,000	0
1.5	500,000	750,000	500,000	250,000
2.0 (original)	400,000	800,000	400,000	400,000
2.5	350,000	875,000	350,000	525,000
3.0 (highest revenue)	300,000	900,000	300,000	600,000
3.5 (highest profit)	250,000	875,000	250,000	625,000
4.0	200,000	800,000	200,000	600,000
5.0	100,000	500,000	100,000	400,000

The maximum revenue price is $3 per widget for revenue of $900,000, only $100,000 greater than the original price of $2. However, the contribution is $600,000, 2.4 times the profitability of the original $2 price! However, there is even a better price—the price of $3.50 per widget has a lower revenue of $875,000, but has a higher contribution of $625,000. This contribution is 2.5 times the contribution that would have occurred had the original price been used. This is an obviously simplified example, but not simplified in isolating how important the analysis of alternative prices is to most ventures. The impact of the initial pricing decision on the venture's ultimate profitability is typically huge. We'll show some real examples later of what this decision has meant to some firms as well as how to estimate the revenue at alternative price levels. However, first, it is now time to give the quick entrepreneurial marketer's guide to *cost accounting!*

The reason for bringing up cost accounting is that the profitability of pricing decisions depends solely on revenue and *variable costs*. Fixed costs are almost irrelevant to the decision on the best price to charge for the product or service. Why is this true? Because if fixed costs, by definition, don't change when the number of units sold changes, then they will be incurred *regardless of the alternative price that would be charged*. All of the "contribution" numbers in Table 3-1 should really be contribution to fixed costs and profit of the venture. The $1 cost assumed in the simple example should be only the variable costs to produce, sell, and deliver an incremental unit. Fixed costs that will be incurred regardless of the price will be subtracted from the contribution to estimate the profitability of the widget product. If any constant number were subtracted from each contribution row, the price that maximizes contribution and profit will not change. Thus, fixed costs do not affect the best price to charge for a product or service. There is only one exception to this rule. If the estimated contribution of the best price is *not enough to cover the fixed costs* associated with the product or service, then the product or service should *not be introduced.*

GETTING PRICE RIGHT EARLY—IT'S HARD TO RAISE PRICES LATER!

It is even more important to get the pricing done well early in the product's life because of human nature. If you lower a price over a product's lifetime, no one will complain (except possibly the customers who just bought it at a higher price). However, if you want to raise a price significantly because you realize the product's perceived value is much higher than you thought, it is very difficult. Human nature does not consider such price rises as "fair." If you can convince potential customers that your costs have gone up, that is usually perceived as a legitimate or fair justification for raising prices. Customers do not typically go through such fairness evaluations when they originally see a price for a new product or service. Human nature and fairness arguments take over only when prices are raised. Thus, it is even more important to have your initial price set at a very good level. In some cases, one can even leave it up to the customer—eBay and Priceline both do, and are big moneymakers, as we shall discuss.

However, for many new products, it is usually the innovators who will take a risk on a new product or service. For taking this initial risk, the first customers want (and deserve) special pricing treatment. Sometimes they even deserve to get the product at no cost to try until they are convinced of its value. It is okay for the entrepreneur to give special pricing to these first innovative customers. However, the prices should be structured as *charter customer discounts* or *introductory discounts* from a *regular price* that is publicized as what will be normal after the introduction. This paradigm gives the entrepreneurial marketer much more room to determine marketplace reaction and adjust his/her actual selling prices by adjusting the introductory discount level and time period.

By having a regular price stated up-front, the entrepreneur is free to charge up to that level without generating market perceptions of unfairness. There are some entrepreneurial marketers that have kept introductory prices for over a year after a product has been introduced.

METHODS FOR DETERMINING REVENUE AT ALTERNATIVE PRICE LEVELS

Reading the preceding, you are probably saying to yourself, "Sure, it would be more profitable to price so as to get the most profit, but how can I get good estimates of the sales I would realize if I charged alternative prices?" There are a number of ways to do this that can be grouped into two categories—in-market and pre-market testing.

IN-MARKET METHODS

The in-market method is usually preferable because it is typically a very valid predictor of what revenue would be at alternative price levels. However, it is not always practical to charge different prices for the same product or service in the marketplace. You cannot charge different prices for what is perceived as the same product bundle if market participants will communicate with each other. If one market participant finds out that another participant bought what they perceived as the same product bundle at a better price, they will feel cheated. Even though rationally, they got enough perceived value from their purchase or they would not have made it, psychologically they feel cheated. If they feel that way, they can begin saying bad things about your product. Bad word of mouth is very damaging to a new product or service that lives based upon customer perceptions. If a potential customer hears bad things about a product from a respected source, it can undermine all the other marketing activities you do.

If the customer perceives the product bundle to be different, then the consumer will not necessarily be upset about hearing that someone else paid a different price. For example, airline seats or concert tickets will be priced differently depending on when the customer decides to buy them or exactly where they are located. We will discuss more about yield management and other methods for charging different prices to different segments for different product bundles of the same physical product later in this chapter.

However, there are circumstances where it is highly unlikely for market participants to become upset. These are products or services that are purchased individually and usually not discussed very much among consumers, or products whose prices may be difficult to compare because they are customized to each potential customer. Many product/market combinations can be tested in-market. For example, if one of your primary marketing vehicles is personal sales and your product price is somewhat dependent on the potential customer's characteristics, it is relatively easy to do evaluation of market reaction to different price levels. The best way to do this is to have each of the salespeople involved in the test use different price levels for every nth potential customer on whom they call. For example, if there were three alternative price policies to test, then every potential customer would be exposed to one of the three different pricing policies, and each customer would have a 1/3 probability of being exposed to each policy. As long as it's pretty difficult for the potential customer to compare the pricing algorithm actually used by your salesperson, it will be difficult to compare prices across different potential customers. Thus, even if two customers do talk who have been exposed to different pricing algorithms, they will not be able to find out that they actually were quoted different pricing options. For example, if the pricing of software is developed based upon a fixed charge for organizational training, another charge for installation, and another set of charges per "seat" or installed computer terminal, then it becomes difficult for two firms of different needs to compare prices.

THE WEB AS THE PERFECT IN-MARKET PRICE-TESTING VEHICLE AND A REASONABLE CONCEPT PRICE-TESTING VEHICLE

Concept testing with different recipients receiving different prices can easily be done on the Web.

USING WEB-BASED CONCEPT TESTING TO GET PRICE RESPONSE FOR COMPUTER PERIPHERALS

A company had developed a new storage medium for portable computers— the Disk on Key (DOK). DOK is a USB device that has flash memory and can be an external storage device. The same physical DOK device can also be programmed to perform functions that make it easier to leverage working on more than one computer. Confidentiality prohibits us from giving more details. The problem of pricing the different versions of the DOK were made to order for concept testing at different price levels. A Web survey was done on samples recruited to be in the various target markets for different potential versions of the DOK. The respondents were shown a picture of the device, a description of the device, and its benefits (depending on how or whether it was programmed), and given a price as part of the description. Each respondent was exposed to one price for each concept. One quarter of the respondents were exposed to a $59 price, one quarter to $95, $195, and $295, respectively. They were then asked a few questions, the main one being how likely they would be to purchase the product.

Figures 3-1 and 3-2 show purchase intent versus price results for two of the concepts. The first concept, the ABCDEF Key, was basically the unprogrammed, storage version of the key. Here, the purchase intent (80% of the top box, plus 20% of the second box) goes down as the price goes up.

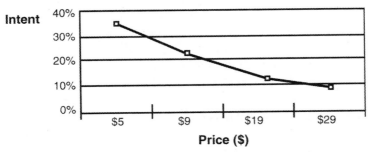

Figure 3-1 Concept testing: price versus purchase intent ABCDEF Key

Another concept was the same physical device (the EFGHI Key), but programmed to perform some functions. Again, the different respondents were exposed to the concept at one of the same four price levels. The concept description portrayed the features and benefits of the programmed device. The purchase intent response was much different for this version of the device. As Figure 3-2 shows, the purchase intent reached a maximum at the prices of $95 and $195 and was much lower at either $59 and $295. The qualitative feedback on the survey and further personal probing of respondents showed that at $59, the value proposition was not credible to some of the respondents: "How could something so valuable be so cheap?" On the other end of the spectrum, the $295 price was not as good as the perceived value for many of the respondents.

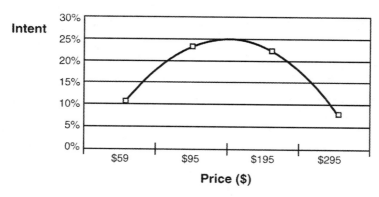

Figure 3-2 Concept testing: price versus purchase intent EFGHI Key

Please keep in mind that this concept testing was done before any DOKs were introduced and when this firm thought competition would not be coming for a reasonable time. The firm used this methodology for two very important and valuable functions. First, they were able to price the versions that they decided to introduce at appropriate levels, given the consumer value perception of the different versions. Second, they were able to prioritize their development resources to bring out the product versions that would be most profitable. This Web-based concept testing cost under $30,000 to perform. The value of the activity was easily in the millions. This is the kind of research that entrepreneurial firms of all size need to do more.

Because purchasing is done individually on the Web, and each person can be exposed to a different, customized Web site, the Web can be an extremely effective and valid in-market price-testing device.

The Internet offers one of the best vehicles for market and price testing ever invented. Immediate feedback, large sample sizes, and live customer reactions make it much more efficient and valid than focus groups or limited city tests. idealab! will often test banner ads and pricing by using 1,000–5,000 banners to drive viewers to specific pages on a site, keeping cookies to track their behavior, and then examining the follow-through once they have reached a site.

With utility.com, a provider of deregulated electric power in a number of states around the U.S., the pricing and messages were honed through a series of tests. The VP of Marketing first stated that he thought we needed to offer 15% off in order to get customers to switch from their existing supplier. Perhaps, he said, we could get away with only 10% off if they chose "green" (environmentally clean) power. There were a number of skeptics that led to the company using a test.

Table 3-2   Experimental offerings tested

Offer at Site	Offer to Get to Site										
	5%	6%	7%	8%	9%	10%	11%	12%	13%	14%	15%
0%	X	X	X	X	X	X	X	X	X	X	X
1%	X	X	X	X	X	X	X	X	X	X	X
2%											
3%	X	X	X	X	X	X	X	X	X	X	X
4%											
5%											

After testing a number of different banners to get the best colors, animation, and messages, we tested offers of 5–15% off, each leading to a page that offered 0–5% additional if you signed up right away. The results were non-intuitive. The offers that drew the most people to the site were 7% off and 11% off. They were significantly higher draws than 15% off or 10% off. Once at the site, the best additional offers were 0%, 1%, and 3% off.

The best combined action came from a 7% offer to get visitors to the site, where they were offered 3% off for immediate signup—a total of 10% off. Green vs. non-green power had only a very small effect, and is now offered as an option on the signup pages. Without the testing, the company would have used the "instinct" of 15%, with both higher cost and lower effectiveness.

The cost for the test was under $5,000, since off-peak banner advertising can be purchased very inexpensively, and it only took several thousand tests to make it work.

The Web is not the only vehicle for profitable in-market price experimentation.

VICTORIA'S SECRET CAN USE ITS MANY STORES FOR IN-MARKET EXPERIMENTATION

Another advantage of the Limited Brands and Victoria's Secret "own store" strategy is that there is an opportunity to do price testing with different stores having different prices for the same item. Originally, VS did their price testing by doing their tests among different stores in the same region. In these tests, different stores in the same region would have different prices for the same items. This method should conceptually be pretty valid because stores in the same region should be comparable on consumer and competitive characteristics that would affect price response. However, VS found that they got into some legal issues in some regions for having different prices in their stores. Also, as we discuss previously, there is a possibility of negative consumer reaction from finding out that your friend paid a different price for an item than you did. There is also a public relations risk if a newspaper or TV news reporter wrote a story on the different prices.

VS then moved to a less valid, but more doable testing method—varying prices across regions and then comparing the sales effects by store across regions. This method has caused no problems and is done a lot because the insights into the revenue price relationship VS obtains are very valuable. Here again, the experimental results may not be as precise as VS would like, but they give them the broad magnitudes of how their products respond to price changes. This is another example of being "vaguely right rather than precisely wrong." VS's price decisions are more profitable using their price tests than they would be if they didn't do them and used some arbitrary, precise formulas for calculating their prices.

PRE-MARKET METHODS—PRICING AND CONCEPT TESTING

Our discussion in Chapter 2, "Generating, Screening, and Developing Ideas," of concept testing before a product or service is introduced mentioned that it could be used as a very effective vehicle for estimating the relative differences in sales that would occur at alternative price levels. The basic idea is very simple. Part of the concept description of the product or service is the price. If you want to concept test four alternative prices, then make every concept description have only one of the four pricing alternatives, with each respondent being exposed at a .25

probability to one of the alternatives. So every fourth concept test will have the same price. The estimates of number of units that would be bought at different price levels can be calculated in the same way as any other concept test. What is very valuable to the entrepreneur is to analyze the resulting revenue implications from the alternative pricing policies.

Because any biases of the concept test would be constant over the four different prices, the relative differences in response of one price versus another will usually be quite valid. For example, if the concept test results indicate that 40% more widgets would be sold at a 20% lower price, that percentage difference will be the same regardless of what the base absolute sales of the widgets would be. Regardless of whether the actual sales of the widgets in market would be 1,000 units or 10,000 units at the base price, the estimate of 40% more units that would be sold at a 20% lower price should hold pretty validly.

A PRICE-CONCEPT TESTING EXAMPLE: ABLE FAUCETS

A small, non-U.S. manufacturer (whom we will call ABLE) of faucets for kitchen sinks had been selling one model of faucet through a major do-it-yourself retailer for two years—and just barely breaking even, when all of the costs associated with the faucet were taken into account.[1] The manufacturer, ABLE, wanted to see if they could convince the retailer to change the retail price from $98 to a higher price, enabling ABLE to raise the wholesale price to the retailer. As part of a larger study, a paired comparison concept test was administered in the retail store to customers who were about to buy a kitchen faucet. The customers were asked to choose which of two alternative faucets they would rather purchase and provided concept descriptions of each. The concept statements included a picture of the faucet and all of the descriptions of the product features and/or benefits that were on the respective faucet boxes. In the large do-it-yourself retailers, the box on the shelf was the major way in which the customer was able to evaluate alternative products prior to making a purchase. The box's perception on the shelf is very important in most mass merchandisers. Each concept statement also had a price associated with it. Each customer that was tested received a concept test with one of four alternative prices for the ABLE faucet—$98, $127, $141, or $160. The other faucet they were given to evaluate was constant throughout the test. It was the major seller at the retailer with a price of $141. An example of part of the concept test survey is shown in Figure 3-3, where the ABLE faucet is B.

1. Looking at the photos and descriptions below, how much do you think each of these faucets sell for?

A. _____

B. _____

- Pull-out spray for hard-to-reach places
- Adjusts from aerated stream to powerful spray
- Can be mounted without deckplate to accommodate accessories
- Easy do-it-yourself installation
- Water-saving aerator
- Washerless, one-piece cartridge
- Lifetime limited warranty

- Pull-out spray
- European design faucet
- Matching deckplane
- Easy installation
- Flexible connector tubes
- Ceramic disc cartridge/washerless design
- 20-year limited warranty
- Solid brass construction

If the price for Faucet A was $141 and $98 for Faucet B, which would you purchase?

Figure 3-3 Portion of ABLE faucets concept test survey

Twenty-five percent of the people received the ABLE faucet concept description priced at $98, a different 25% received the ABLE concept priced at $127, and so on. The competitive faucet was always constant and priced at $141. The results of this part of the concept test are shown in Figure 3-4.

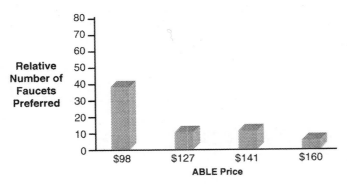

Figure 3-4   ABLE faucets concept test results

From the results, demand seems to go down very significantly at prices over $98. It falls from 40 to 5, a drop of 85%. If this pricing option was the only alternative ABLE could pursue, it would not make sense to raise the faucet's price. However, some entrepreneurial marketers looked carefully at the ABLE box. They observed that the product description on the box was all stated as product *features* as opposed to product *benefits*. For example, flexible connector tubes probably don't mean very much to the typical faucet buyer. However, if the feature was translated into a benefit such as "flexible connector tubes to fit into tight spaces under the sink," it might have more value to a potential purchaser. How many potential purchasers would know the benefit associated with the feature "ceramic disc, washerless cartridge"? How much more valuable is "ceramic disc, washerless cartridge design eliminates leaks and ensures maximum control"?

PRICE RESPONSE DEPENDS ON PERCEIVED VALUE: THE EXAMPLE CONTINUES

In order to estimate the impact on price response of describing the product on the box with benefits versus features, another cell was added to the concept test described previously. Half of the respondents saw a benefits-oriented concept statement, while the other half saw the original feature-oriented copy from the box. The concept statement for the benefits-oriented box is shown in Figure 3-5.

1. Looking at the photos and descriptions below, how much do you think each of these faucets sell for?

A. _____

B. _____

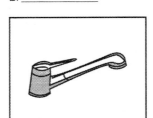

* Pull-out spray for hard-to-reach places
* Adjusts from aerated stream to powerful spray
* Can be mounted without deckplate to accommodate accessories
* Easy do-it-yourself installation
* Water-saving aerator
* Washerless, one-piece cartridge
* Lifetime limited warranty

* Pull-out spray for multi-purpose use
* European design faucet
* Matching deckplane to cover sinkholes
* Easy step-by-step installation instructions
* Flexible connector tubes fit in tight spaces under sink
* Ceramic disc cartridge/washerless design eliminates leaks, ensures maximum control
* 20-year limited warranty
* Solid brass construction for long life

If the price for Faucet A was $141 and $98 for Faucet B, which would you purchase?

Figure 3-5   Benefits-oriented concept statement

The benefits-oriented box copy was also shown to different respondents at one of the same four alternative price levels. The concept test was not only able to estimate the response of the new box copy at the four alternative price levels, but also to compare the *benefits*-oriented copy versus the existing *features*-oriented copy for the box at the different price levels. This is because the control faucet was the same for all eight versions of the concept test—two copies times four different price levels. The results when the responses to all eight versions of the concept are compared are very interesting (see Figure 3-6).

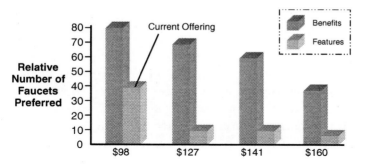

Figure 3-6   ABLE faucet demand estimates results

Keep in mind that the concept test biases, whatever they are, are not typically going to affect any one cell of the eight test cells versus any other. The results really add a lot of value and are a wonderful illustration of how important perception is to price response. They also illustrate how valuable it is to help the consumer understand product benefits that are associated with certain features. First, notice that *just by describing the product with benefit-oriented statements on its box, sales would double compared to the current box's feature-oriented statements.* Twice as many respondents chose the ABLE product versus its major competitor when it was described by relating the features to their consumer benefits. The benefits-oriented description added considerable perceived value to the customer. Approximately the same number of faucets would be sold at $160 (a 60% higher price) for the benefits-oriented box copy compared to the original features-oriented copy. Thus, just *changing the box copy to a benefits orientation added over 60% to the perceived consumer value of the same physical faucet!*

The other cells in Figure 3-3 are also quite valuable—both to ABLE and to the retailer. Notice that demand goes down much less severely for the benefits-oriented copy as the price goes up, compared to the existing features-oriented copy. When the retailer evaluated her costs and profit alternatives, the $141 price made the most sense if ABLE were to raise its wholesale price for the redesigned benefits-oriented box. At $141 with the redesigned box, the concept test shows a true win-win-win situation. ABLE gets to significantly raise its price to the retailer. The retailer sells more units of ABLE's faucets. The consumer gets a faucet that they would value at $160 for $141. Everyone is happier. It doesn't always work this way, but when it does, it is very gratifying to true entrepreneurial marketers.

PRICING, THE REST OF THE MARKETING MIX, AND PERCEIVED VALUE

As the preceding example illustrates, managing pricing really is highly dependent on how well the entrepreneur manages the *perceived value* of her product bundle. This perceived value is affected or can be affected by every element of the firm's marketing mix. The price itself can be a big driver of how potential customers will perceive your product offering bundle.

PRICE AND PERCEIVED VALUE

Sometimes, a price that is too low, particularly for a new product, can have a big impact on how valuably it will be perceived. Our next example crystallizes this phenomenon. When one of the authors was in graduate school, his professor had started an entrepreneurial company to manufacture and sell educational kit machines for helping to understand how the binary logic and arithmetic of computers worked. The machines were composed of lights, wires, and switches, so that binary arithmetic and logic could be simulated by series of light bulbs being either on or off. The first kit machine in the entrepreneur's line was the red and blue MINIVAC 601, priced at $79.95. The entrepreneur had three target market segments for the MINVAC 601—home hobbyists, high schools and colleges, and computer and technology companies (for training their employees on how computers worked). The product did very well with the first two market segments. Home hobbyists bought the product at consumer electronic stores and some higher tech hobby shops. Many colleges and some upper socio-economic high schools also bought the MINIVAC as an educational aid. However, no one in the third segment, the corporate sector, bought the product. The entrepreneur interviewed some target customers to try to find the problem. He found out very quickly. The typical description of the MINIVAC by the corporate types was: "Oh, that—it's just a toy!"

The entrepreneur was creative and he listened carefully. He also understood marketing. His next product was the same basic kit—with the switches upgraded to higher tolerances and the machine color changed from blue and red to gunmetal gray. The name was changed to the MINIVAC 6010 and he increased the price from $79.95 to $479. The MINIVAC 6010 sold very well to the corporate segment at $479. The $79.95 price was too low for the corporate buyers to take the product seriously—

at such a low price, it had to be a toy. The color and packaging of the original MINIVAC 601 amplified that perception. By changing the color, name, and packaging, and most importantly the price, the entrepreneur was able to change the perception in the corporate segment. The impact on his bottom line was just amazing! The price you put on your product offering, by itself, creates a very important part of the perceptual position.

PRICING OF INTELLECTUAL PROPERTY

One of the most difficult things to price is something that has essentially no cost associated with another copy—i.e., intellectual property. On the Internet, much of what is being sold is information, which has the property that once created (especially in electronic form), multiple copies can be recreated for no cost.

In physical goods, the price is most often related to the cost of producing the item, including some amortization of the intellectual property (research and development) used to create the design, as well as the raw materials and processing cost to turn those materials into the item for sale. Gross margins of 60–80% are not uncommon in high-tech industries, so that an Intel chip that sells for $300 may have a cost (including marketing, R&D, and production) of $50–60.

With information, the marginal cost of providing news reports on Yahoo! is effectively zero. The gross margins on the product are often above 95%, with the small cost of goods being associated with maintaining the servers that hold and transmit the information. How, then, should one select the pricing?

One price that has often been successfully used on the Internet is *free*. Give away the intellectual property so that people will come to a Web site and see the advertising, or take advantage of e-commerce opportunities. Most of the stock trading operations provide research reports and other products that way. E-Trade, DLJ Direct, and Wit Capital are all examples. They also price their actual services—for example, stock trading—as close to their real cost as possible, with only Schwab making a profit on the transaction costs.

Hotmail, ICQ (now part of AOL), and other "virally marketed" services are all vehicles that provide a free service, which is purely communications or other non-physical product, so that they can do advertising and marketing to the users.

There are some groups that can successfully charge for intellectual property, usually through some form of subscription pricing. The *Wall Street Journal* online is one of the most successful subscription-based services on the Web, with a $69.95 per year price for people who do not also get the print edition, and a lower price for those who are already print subscribers. *The New York Times* charges $9.95 per year for access to their crossword puzzles online, getting a dedicated audience to whom they can also e-sell. And, of course, playboy.com is an extremely successful subscription site, where those so inclined pay annually for the ability to access photos, editorial material, and chats about sexually explicit material.

WHAT ELSE CAN IMPACT PRICE RESPONSE?

Anything that can impact the perception of your product offering bundle can impact the price that potential customers will be willing to pay. Very simply, if the customer does not perceive that the value he or she perceives more than justifies the price, he or she will not purchase. We use the term "product offering bundle" here as we do in other places in this book in the widest interpretation possible. It includes anything that the customer can perceive impacts the value they get from the whole experience of buying and using your product or service. The first time potential customers come in contact with your firm or product or service, they begin to get impressions that will affect their value perception of the offering bundle. If it was an advertisement, did it connote the right positioning? If it was an email, did it come across consistent with a high-value positioning?

When a customer or potential customer calls in to your firm, is the phone answered in a manner consistent with a high-value perception? If potential customers get put on hold for very long, they will get bad perceptions about how fast your firm might react to any problems that need to be corrected. If the phone people are not polite, considerate, and genuinely helpful to the caller, the firm and its product's perception will suffer.

A 100+ year-old shipping company was concerned that they were losing business to competition and that their margins were continually being squeezed by what they thought was increased competitive price pressure on their routes. The firm retained a market research consultant who interviewed some of their customers and potential customers. The consultant found a number of problems that influenced how customers or potential customers perceived the firm and its product offering bundle. One pervasive problem was that the firm's telephonic interface with customers was appalling compared to competition. If someone called into a regional shipping office to either ask about a price quotation or what the status of a shipment was, there were many instances when the phone just rang and rang and was never even answered! The increased price pressure the firm was facing was not brought about by competition, but more by the reaction of their potential customers to the perceived value decline in the product offering bundle. The appalling telephone interface was just one example of the problems with customer treatment at the firm. Only after the customer sales and service operations of the firm were completely redesigned from the ground up, would the company possibly be able to command what it considered reasonable prices.

Other chapters show how all the elements of the marketing mix can affect perception that then affects price response. All of the channel management decisions affect how the end customer will perceive your product offering bundle. The environment your product is in when the customer sees it can have a large impact on its perceived value. The same product will have a higher perceived value if the consumer sees it at Tiffany's rather than at Wal-Mart. The dynamic management of distribution channels we describe in Chapter 4 has as its major objective to achieve high contribution margin and prices. Once a product has been sold at low-end channels, it typically cannot be sold at premium prices at the higher-end channels.

PERCEIVED VALUE IN USE FOR BUSINESS-TO-BUSINESS PRODUCTS

A key way that an entrepreneur can market new products and services to businesses is to show the target business that they will be more profitable if they adopt the entrepreneur's new product or service. If the potential customers *perceive* that their business will be more profitable if your product or service is used, then they will likely buy it. The key word here is *perceive*. If the customer understands and believes that your product can make the production, service, or delivery process more efficient or more valuable to the customer's customers, then the entrepreneur can make a nice sale. In order to use this value-in-use positioning, the entrepreneur must understand how the potential customers will want to calculate the value-in-use of the entrepreneur's new innovation. If there are certain measures that an industry uses to indicate efficiency or productivity, they will probably feel more comfortable if they see the new entrepreneurial innovation with data on that measure.

How does all of this relate to pricing? According to Irwin Gross of the Institute for the Study of Business Markets at the Pennsylvania State University:[2]

> "Customer Value" is the hypothetical *price* for a supplier's *offering* at which a particular customer would be at overall economic *break-even* relative to the best *available alternative* to the customer for performing a set of functions.
>
> "Customer Perceived Value" is a customer's *perception* of his/her own "customer value."

Although customer value can never be known precisely, it is a very useful idealized construct, similar to a "perfect vacuum" or a "frictionless plane" in physics.[3]

The best pricing situation occurs when there is a perceived win-win situation. The buyer perceives that he or she will have higher "customer value" when adopting the new entrepreneur's product, including the price of the new product from the entrepreneur. The entrepreneur in turn makes much higher profit margins than normal because of her understanding of how to create perceived value better than her competition.

Your competition may not be as treacherous in many business-to-business situations as it may first appear. The concept of really going into depth to understand perceived customer value is not that common. According to Gross, who has studied business-to-business markets for over 20 years: "Customers spend more effort to know supplier's costs than suppliers spend to know customer's values."[4] A really effective entrepreneurial marketer will spend her scarce time and resources to understand exactly how her target market participants develop perceptions of customer value and what methods are best for changing those values.

There are typical components that make up perceived customer value for new entrepreneurial product offerings. These can be grouped into product value, supplier value, and switching investments. According to Gross, the product value is the relative benefits delivered by the product itself, independent of the supplier, while the supplier value is the relative benefits delivered by the supplier, independent of the product itself. The switching investment is the costs and risks involved with the transition from the current practice to the implementation of the new alternative.[5] All of these benefits, of course, are as *perceived* by decision makers in the target market. Gross has categorized components of attributes that affect perceived customer value, dividing them into attributes that impact perceptions of immediate customer value versus those that will impact expected customer value in the future. Table 3-3 outlines the attributes that can impact perceived customer value.

Table 3-3 Attributes affecting perceived customer value (parentheses indicate negative attributes)

	Immediate	**Expected**
Product	Product performance Durability Serviceability Downstream performance (Current risks)	New technology Product flexibility Follow-on products (Long-run risks)
Supplier	Supplier performance— delivery technology, sales, services, etc. (Promotional values, services)	Supplier relationship Technology access Security of supply Strategic (Supplier power)
Switching	New capital Training Transitional quality Communications	

A good entrepreneurial marketer will do whatever is necessary to make sure that his or her offering's perceived customer value is higher than her competition. He or she will understand the components that are important to the members of the target market. He or she will then make sure his or her product offering and all of the marketing elements that support it are doing the best job possible in positively impacting the value perception. As reflected in Table 3-3, it is not just the product or service offering itself that needs to be impacted. It's also much of the supporting services and impressions that the entrepreneurial venture leaves. The sales force, the marketing communications, the channels used, the product packaging, the product's name, the service package, etc., are all part of what can impact perceived customer value. For business-to-business markets, real entrepreneurial marketing can enable much higher prices than competition.

THE SAS INSTITUTE, INC.—VERY EFFECTIVE MANAGEMENT OF PERCEIVED CUSTOMER VALUE

The SAS Institute, Inc. has become the world's largest privately held software company by creatively and uniquely applying many of the concepts in this chapter. The Institute provides data warehousing and decision support software to target markets in business, government, and education. The end result of this entrepreneurial marketing is a very unique software pricing strategy. All SAS Institute software products are licensed, not sold. According to their brochure: "SAS Institute's pricing strategy is designed to foster Win/Win relationships with our customers which lead to building productive long-term partnerships."[6] The Institute is not shy about the objectives of their pricing policy. "The strategy is to establish pricing consistent with the value received by SAS software customers, as they implement mission critical applications."[7]

The SAS Institute pricing model is unique among major software vendors. The other vendors typically sell a software purchase along with a maintenance contract. Their customers buy each new software release and have the option to pay ongoing fees for technical support. These other software vendors, typically public, or with objectives of going public, want to maximize the short-term revenue they obtain with each sale. The suppliers of investments for software vendors in the financial markets do not necessarily let the software firms price for value over time as SAS does.

The SAS Institute license model has the customer pay a first-year license fee and an annual fee to renew the license. According to SAS, the annual license model provides the customer with a number of valuable benefits:

1. Low cost of entry (typically less than fees paid for entering a purchase/maintenance model).
2. Rapid return on investment (ROI).
3. The most current release.
4. Technical support.
5. The most current documentation.

6. All updates during the license period.

7. Customers' investments are protected by ensuring that they always have the most up-to-date technology.[8]

The customer is never locked in to more than a one-year commitment to SAS. The company must then be perceived by their customers as continually providing excellent technical support and on-going enhancements to the software. If the customers do not perceive they are getting value from SAS, they can go elsewhere. The customers can also easily add or delete components of the SAS software as their needs change over time. SAS even comes out and says in their own literature that: "The strategy is to establish pricing consistent with the value received by SAS software customers as they implement mission critical applications."[9]

Let's compare SAS's pricing model to the typical enterprise software company. The typical company sells its software once, with a very big sales effort. They then charge annual ongoing maintenance fees of 15–18% of the initial purchase price. These maintenance fees sometimes include updates and improvements to the software. Is this pricing consistent with the customer's perceived value? Not really. The customer should receive increasing value as the software becomes implemented and tailored to the customer's specific situation and as it is improved and updated over time. The perceived value to the customer of software will almost always be higher after a successful implementation than before it. If the implementation is unsuccessful, then the reverse situation would hold. Because of these risks, customers are not willing to pay as much up-front for software as they would pay if they had continual successful experience to value. The amount the typical enterprise software company can charge up-front is thus less than the discounted present value that the customer would pay over time under the SAS Institute rental plan.

SAS's job becomes keeping its customers continually delighted so that they will continue to pay the relatively large yearly license fees. SAS does that very well. They renew 98% of their customers annually! Thus 98% of their revenue is recurring. This is an astonishing statistic for any software company. They also have used their recurring revenue as a base for expansion. The latest public statistics available show revenue of over $1.5 billion for 2004, more than double that of five years earlier.[10] SAS also has enough gross margin to spend over 30% of revenue (*revenue, not profits!*) on research and development, to enable them to provide software improvements that continually delight their customers.[11]

The SAS customer value orientation and their pricing model that captures more of that value than competition is supported by a superb employee group that is in turn supported by very marketing-oriented employee policies. SAS treats its employees in ways that foster excellent long-term performance and high loyalty. Some of the policies include 32-hour work weeks, on-site day care, unlimited sick leave, and a fully supported gym on the premises. In an extremely competitive market for software talent in the Raleigh Durham research triangle, SAS has a turnover rate lower than 5% compared to over 20% for many competitive software companies.

Why don't other software companies emulate the value-oriented pricing model of the SAS Institute? We can only speculate. One reason may be that too many U.S. companies (and their financial backers, including public shareholders) are too short-term oriented to pass up one-time purchase prices for a longer-term, but higher-value, rental revenue stream. The other reason may be lack of courage to look a customer in the eye and ask for a legitimate percent of the perceived value that your software is delivering. We note that the rise of Web-based Application Service Providers (ASPs) such as Salesforce.com have enabled value-based pricing. We hope that more entrepreneurial marketers will be encouraged by the SAS Institute example to not be afraid to set pricing policies to receive some of the perceived value they are creating.

CUSTOMER-DETERMINED PRICING

Another method for pricing at the perceived value to the customer is to let the customer set the price. This includes various auction methods, a large choice of pricing alternatives, and even riskier strategies of "pay what you think it was worth." The auction world has been completely transformed by eBay, which now helps generate sales of more than $50 billion of merchandise per year. Here, each customer believes they are getting a good deal, while the excitement of the auction often generates prices above what the same item is available for elsewhere—extra profits for the seller.

eBay has several methods for the customer to determine pricing: BuyItNow, auction, and half.com's offers. In the traditional auction, there is a seven-day period during which multiple bidders can make offers and see who is the highest bidder. The person with the highest bid when the auction closes wins—with eBay's software automatically bidding up to preset limits for customers who cannot be present in the final seconds. A set of software called sniping software has been developed to conceal bidding until the final seconds. But ultimately it is the customer who determines the price of the items on offer. The seller can insure some gross margin by having a reserve price, below which the item won't be sold. Sellers can also offer a "BuyItNow" price for those customers who cannot wait till the end of the auction. This is usually set to a price above that which previous auctions in similar items have sold, although if the seller has multiples of the same item, it may be set lower (more like a traditional store price). Finally, eBay acquired half.com, which offers books, CDs, and some other items at what was originally meant to be half of the price for new items. Because condition and seller reputation are both important to buyers, there is now a range of prices for popular items, so the buyer can choose to pay more or less for the same book, depending on condition, seller reputation, shipping date, etc.

In all the preceding cases, it is the customer who determines what he or she is willing to pay. This is much like the old days when one bargained with every merchant—before James Cash Penny posted fixed pricing in his stores. And it is much the same in many other countries in the world, where the listed price is just a starting point.

At Priceline, the customer selects the price, but not the specific merchandise. You can bid for a first-class hotel room in New York, but may be given one in any of a large selection of hotels. Similarly, Priceline has deals with Delta and other airlines that allow them to sell airline tickets at whatever price they'd like. Customers bid for tickets between a city pair, but cannot select the time of day or airline. Priceline determines if they can make money selling the user a ticket out of the inventory that the airlines have made available to Priceline at fixed prices. Here, the customer is determining price, but with time of day and airline chosen by the seller.

Often, the customer will have a different utility for money than the vendor. In this case, smart vendors will offer a range of prices that allow the customer to make the choice that is optimal for them, while increasing the profits to the vendor. Often this involves the capital/expense budget trade-off. Much of today's outsourcing of services falls into this category.

Evolution Robotics, for example, is offering their LaneHawk system, which combats supermarket losses, with three different pricing plans. LaneHawk recognizes items that are on the bottom of shopping carts but not rung up on the register, either through innocent error or deliberate fraud. Some chains are willing to pay the full capital cost upfront, in return for much lower monthly software maintenance costs. Others prefer to not pay any capital costs, and just pay a monthly rental—in this case, Evolution's cost of funds is taken into account, and customers often give Evolution much higher total margin (over three years) than if they had borrowed the money and paid the capital costs. A third choice—sharing the savings from loss prevention—is also offered. Here again, customers are determining the price they will pay based on their own preferences, capital availability, and risk tolerance.

While not all entrepreneurial ventures lend themselves to customer-determined pricing, when the products and services are new, and there is no established competition to overcome, it can often lead to much higher profits than the traditional price-testing methods. In addition, when the customers are determining the price themselves, something that is often a source of negative feelings (high prices) becomes the source of positive feelings, since it is truly a customer choice for what to pay, which is empowering.

CONCLUSION

We began the chapter by showing how common cost-based or competitive-based pricing rules may be "precisely wrong." We showed that a "vaguely right" approach is to attempt to charge the price (or prices) that maximizes your profit return over your planning horizon. It also is very important to get the initial price level at a good level, because it is much more difficult to raise prices over time than it is to lower them. Next, we described methods for in-market and pre-market (concept testing) for determining the potential relationship between alternative prices and the sales revenue that those prices would produce. The Web is the perfect in-market price-testing vehicle for many products.

We then showed a number of examples of how the price you can and should charge is intertwined with all the rest of the elements of the marketing mix. The marketing mix and the product-offering bundle all affect the perceived value for the potential customer. This perceived value in turn affects the price the consumer is willing to pay. For a consumer product, we demonstrated how a change in the product description on its box would double the sales of the product. The new box described valuable consumer benefits as opposed to the older box that described product features. We showed how perceived value in use affects the price response of business-to-business products. We showed how the SAS Institute's unique marketing mix and pricing structure captures and creates more perceived customer value than competitive software customers. Finally, we concluded the chapter by showing how it is often possible, and even desirable, to have the customers themselves determine the price dynamically. This can lead to higher gross margin, and more satisfied customers.

ENDNOTES

1. This is a disguised real example from the author's experience. The data have also been slightly altered. None of the conclusions would change because of the disguising. The disguising is to protect confidentialities.

2. Gross, Irwin, Presentation at the Wharton School, March 1999.

3. Ibid.

4. Ibid.

5. Ibid.

6. SAS Institute white paper, "SAS Institute Business Model," 1998, Cary, NC, p. 3.

7. Ibid., p. 4.

8. Ibid., p. 4.

9. Ibid., p. 4.

10. Fishman, Charles, "Sanity, Inc.," *Fast Times*, January 1999, p. 87.

11. Ibid, p. 96.

4

Distribution/Channel Decisions to Solidify Sustainable Competitive Advantage

	Products/Services	Equity/Shares	Image
Customers			
Users			
Investors			
Supply Chain/ Channel Partners			
Employees			

Nowhere has technology had a bigger potential impact than in the standard functions that used to be considered under "distribution decisions." Distribution encompasses all of the activities that need to be performed so that your product's "offering bundle" is transferred productively from you, the entrepreneurial marketer, to the customers and users who will buy and benefit from the offering. The "offering bundle" includes not only your product or service, but all of the ancillary parts of the bundle that help to mold the perception of the end customer. Packaging, how the product is placed on the shelf, what the clerk says and knows about the product, the end user price, how the end customer is treated when she has a problem or a question before or after purchase, and how easy it is for the end customer to evaluate alternative product offerings, are all just some examples of ancillary parts of the "offering bundle." The choice of which intermediaries are involved between the entrepreneurial firm and its final customers and how these intermediaries are managed has a big impact on the "offering bundle."

The distribution decisions are now much more complex than they were even 10 or 15 years ago. The alternative ways for the different parts of the offering bundle to be "distributed" have been increasing at a very rapid rate. In this chapter, we give the entrepreneurial marketer some conceptual structure to generate new, creative, and possibly productive distribution options. We describe a number of options that other entrepreneurial firms have been able to use effectively. We also show methods for evaluating the options in terms of their impact on the perceived offering bundle to the entrepreneur's target segment(s). Figure 4-1 puts the macro logic of distribution channel decisions covered in this chapter in perspective.

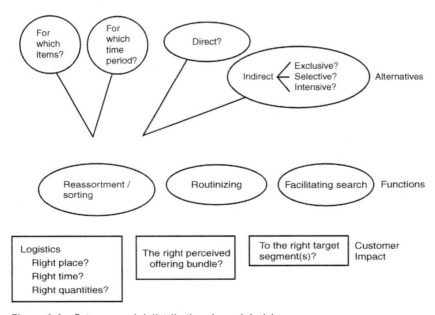

Figure 4-1   Entrepreneurial distribution channel decisions

In order to help the entrepreneur make some good distribution decisions, we first look at the required functions any distribution system must perform. We then look at additional options that need to be considered as part of the effect of the distribution channel decisions on the perceived offering bundle.

REQUIRED FUNCTIONS OF ANY DISTRIBUTION SYSTEM

First, physical distribution will almost always need to be performed. The product or service somehow has to get to the end customer or end consumer. It should be the right *product or service* at the right *place* at the right *time* in the right *quantities*. Along with physical distribution, distribution strategy also impacts the "offering bundle" that the end consumer sees. As described previously, the offering bundle can be a critical element of your success. Who the consumer is and what the consumer perceives when she is making her evaluation and purchasing decision should be the embodiment of your positioning and segmentation strategy.

Intermediaries possibly can be used to perform some of the required functions more efficiently and/or more profitably to the firm. Pitt, Berthon, and Berthon outline three basic functions that intermediaries can perform to improve the productivity of a distribution channel.[1] The functions are as follows:

1. Reassortment/Sorting
2. Routinizing Transactions
3. Facilitating Search

We outline each in turn.

Reassortment/Sorting refers to all of the typical intermediary activities that need to happen for physical distribution from a producer that likes to supply relatively large quantities of a relatively small assortment to an end consumer who will typically want relatively small quantities of a large assortment of "offering bundles." These activities may include arranging the products, sorting them into groups that are relevant to consumers, aggregating goods from different suppliers, "breaking bulk" by providing the right smaller quantities to the end customer, and putting together new packages of goods or services from different suppliers.

Routinizing Transactions are activities that standardize products and services and automate transactions so that bargaining is not needed for each small transaction; it makes it easier for the end customer to compare alternative offerings. The authors point out some instances in which re-supply of products is completely automated so that orders are entered and products replenished when inventories reach a certain minimum level.[2]

Facilitating Search is the classic aid by intermediaries to make it easier for sellers to find buyers and to make it easier for buyers to find their best alternative product or service to purchase. The traditional retailer puts products from different suppliers on the same shelf so that the consumer can make a less uncertain purchase than she would if she didn't have the alternative products right in front of her. In general, intermediaries can reduce uncertainty for both buyers and sellers. A good intermediary can help an entrepreneur do a better job of understanding and responding to customer needs, and can simultaneously help consumers to be more sure that their purchases will indeed satisfy their needs.

It is clear that the Internet is becoming a major influencer of how this search process is being performed. The search function is made to order for the Web. The Web has spawned a number of ventures that have used its capabilities to make search more effective for matching needs of buyers and sellers. These would include eBay, Google, Pricescan, Mysimon, Cnet, Expedia, and Verticalnet as examples.

EVALUATING DISTRIBUTION OPTIONS, A DISINTERMEDIATION EXAMPLE

Technology is making more alternatives available for the entrepreneurial marketer to consider for fulfilling the preceding functions. The distribution of products whose physical make-up is digital is in the process of being revolutionized by the Internet. It is now feasible (and some musicians have begun to do this) for an artist to produce a digital recording and distribute it directly to consumers over the Web. Here, "disintermediation" is replacing a record company, record distributor, rack jobber, and retailer with a direct artist-customer relationship. If the customer knows which recording of which artist she wants, direct distribution may be very attractive to her.

It would seem, at first blush, that all artists should jump aboard the disintermediation bandwagon and distribute their music directly. They would not have to pay all of the middlemen their cuts, and would be able to establish a direct relationship with their customers. This direct relationship would enable all kinds of activities to create more value (and thus make more money eventually). The artist could create loyalty programs to reward and encourage their best customers. The loyalty rewards might include special seats for concerts or special memorabilia. The artist could also reward current customers for referring new customers with similar added value offers. However, the disintermediation decision is not this simple. There are other sides to this story.

First, how will consumers find out about the artist's Web site? Many Web sites are spending tens of millions of dollars to get people to their sites. Does it make sense for each artist to go it alone to try to get customers to their site? Second, do all potential consumers know they want a particular artist's song(s), or do they want to listen to a number of options before they make a purchase? Some consumers may also be concerned about the quality of the digital recording they will download. How do they know it's of suitable quality? What about consumers who are not able to play digital music or to receive digital music over the Web? Should they be ignored? These are just some of the myriad of issues that need to be considered in developing a distribution strategy. The entrepreneurial marketer's decisions on distribution can be at the same time the most difficult and the most important decisions she makes when launching a new product, service, or business.

All the functions described previously must be evaluated as part of the evaluation of distribution options. If the entrepreneurial marketer has really done her homework on the positioning and market segmentation issues, then the distribution options to be evaluated may be self-evident. However, as technology and the environment change the characteristics of existing options and generate new options, the firm has to constantly review these options. Let's look at our digital music example in more depth to illustrate some of these issues.

Does the artist have his or her segmentation determined? Is he or she trying to reach a very small cult group, or does she want to add value to a more mass market? The answer to the targeting question will have a very big impact on the distribution strategy. However, the strategy decision is even more complex. How do the members of the alternative target groups want to buy music? Even if the cult group is the target, the direct Web site may not be appropriate. Do the "cult" consumers know where the Web site is? Do they have the technology available to download and play digital music? Do they want to buy music over the Web? How will they be reached to get the word out? All of these issues can at least be evaluated by concept testing distribution options as part of the offering bundle that is concept tested by consumers before the entrepreneurial marketer makes this decision.

The distribution decision is the one that has the most impact typically on market segmentation. With the distribution channel, the entrepreneur can implement plans with more than one target segment, if the plans are cost effective. Conceptually, it makes sense to use the distribution channel(s) that are preferred by each of the target segments. Consumers will typically find it pretty easy to tell you where they would go or look to try to find your new product or service. If it is consistent with your desired positioning and cost effective, then multiple distribution options for multiple segments may make sense. However, another big issue comes up that needs a different evaluation methodology. How will existing and parallel distribution channel members react to the new direct offering?

The existing distributors may get very upset if you try to eliminate them. If they are powerful, they may severely impact your music sales through traditional channels, if they become upset with you. They may refuse to carry music that is also available directly in digital form. If you want to sell your music on "classic" CDs as well as on the Web digitally, then you will need to have the cooperation of these distributors. To add even more complexity, if you use some distributors, they may conflict with other retailers and distributors—for example, Web based versus store based. Issues of channel conflict in which two intermediaries perceive themselves as competing needlessly can be big problem sources.

A whole set of other issues comes from your positioning. Your positioning should be embodied in the "offering bundle" that ends up being shown to the end customer. A good distribution strategy enables your "offering bundle" to be perceived by the end customer as you have planned. The distribution decisions can greatly impact how the end customer perceives you. Does the end consumer need to make a choice among a number of alternative artists, or do they feel OK just evaluating your offerings? Do they want to choose among different forms to buy the music—for example, digital downloads, compact disks, digital audiotape, and so on? How will they want to evaluate the options? Will they want to listen to everything? Will they want to read or hear unbiased reviews of the music before they buy it? How will they prefer to pay for it? Is a credit card number or PayPal on the Web acceptable? What about shipping? How fast do they want their music, if it isn't downloaded? How long will they wait for a digital download?

What typically happens is that the entrepreneur never gets exactly the "optimal" offering bundle by the distribution system she has assembled. He or she makes tradeoffs of less than optimal offering bundles versus the costs of the available distribution options. He or she is trading off potential revenue from getting the offering bundle perfect versus lower costs from less than perfect distribution options. If he or she has done a good job with his or her concept testing with target market participants and of considering the important concepts in this chapter, he or she should be able to make productive decisions on these distribution tradeoffs.

OTHER ASPECTS OF DISTRIBUTION SYSTEM DESIGN—DIRECT VERSUS INDIRECT

The earlier disintermediation example of using the Web to distribute music directly to consumers is only one example of direct distribution. Similar to manufacturers' reps and your own sales force, distribution options can run the gamut from direct to many layers of middlemen who handle your goods or services before they are bought and used by the end customer. The entrepreneurial marketer is making different tradeoffs depending on how direct or indirect her distribution system is designed. Some impacts on the business affected by distribution options include fixed and variable costs, efficiency versus effectiveness of contacts, amount of control, mass coverage versus targeting ability, and level of customization provided to the end customer. Table 4-1 shows the directions of these tradeoffs as a function of whether the distribution system is direct or indirect.

Table 4-1   Indirect versus direct distribution options

Indirect	Direct
Variable costs	Fixed costs
Efficiency per contact	Effective per contact
Control	Control
Coverage	Targeting
Customization	Customization

Because distribution intermediaries typically take title to your goods and then mark them up, or else take a fee for each item they handle, their costs are typically mostly of *variable* nature. They do not usually charge you for the fixed costs of their operations. However, some intermediaries do have minimum quantities that they may handle—effectively imposing some fixed costs. On the other extreme, direct distribution typically involves *fixed costs* for warehousing, billing, and other administrative costs. Fixed costs add more *risk* to the venture because they will be incurred regardless of what level of sales actually occurs in the marketplace. Variable costs lower risk because they are only incurred when sales are made. So direct distribution typically entails more risk than indirect distribution. However, that lower risk comes with other attributes that may or may not be worth lowering risk to achieve.

Indirect distribution is typically more *efficient* in terms of physically getting goods from the entrepreneur to the final consumer. By combining your product or service with other products and services, the middlemen are able to more efficiently perform the kinds of functions described previously. However, the middleman also takes some *control* over the offering bundle and may not provide the offering bundle that is best for your product, because she is combining your product with others. When the entrepreneurial marketer is more in control, he or she will be able to portray his or her product in the best way he or she can—this is typically more *effective* in adding perceived value to the offering bundle. The added control also enables direct distribution options to develop a more customized offering bundle for each potential customer. The indirect distributor will not typically have the flexibility or ability to make changes for each customer because the indirect distributor has to keep the needs of all of her products in her offering bundle strategy.

OWNING YOUR OWN DISTRIBUTION—THE HIGHEST CONTROL

Some of the largest sellers to end users (such as Wal-Mart and Costco to consumers, Sysco to food service intermediaries, etc.) are finding that their position in the value chain can be leveraged by introducing their own branded products. Many of their customers have learned to trust these sellers and will transfer that trust to their brands. Sam's American Choice at Wal-Mart has been very successful, for example. From a competitive viewpoint, these large sellers have the power to push their own brands at the expense of other brands in their portfolio. The other brands typically have to spend more money per customer to "pull" customers to their brands than the sellers will have to spend to "push" their brands. It is well known in the industry that a point of purchase display is typically the most impactful lever that draws customers to purchase a product. All of these point of purchase options are controlled by the sellers—not the brand manufacturers.

Thus, it is worthwhile for many manufacturers to at least consider owning their distribution channels. There are typically very significant costs for purchasing or developing distribution channels, but for very niche products, or a very broad product line, it may make sense. It has to make sense for the end customer to want to patronize your channel. There has to be enough attraction to get people to come to your store or patronize your establishment. The costs need to be weighed against the value of having the control of the end user purchasing experience.

VICTORIA'S SECRET AND THE LIMITED BRANDS' "OWN STORE" CHANNEL STRATEGY

An important element in the distinctive competence of the Limited Brands and Victoria's Secret is their ownership and complete control of all of their stores in the U.S. The consumer store experience, including sales force attention, display, and pricing, are all key elements of their positioning. Because most of the Limited Brands' stores (Victoria's Secret, the Limited, Express, Bath and Body Works, etc.) are in similar malls, they have a lot of power with mall owners to get good locations and probably good rental rates. For Victoria's Secret, it would be very hard and extremely expensive for competitors to duplicate their "own store" strategy. These stores and the consumer experience derived from them is a key source of sustainable competitive advantage for Victoria's Secret.

It is this "own store" strategy that dictates how the Limited Brands and Victoria's Secret are expanding globally. Les Wexner, the CEO, wants to use his corporate resources where they will contribute the best long-term return versus the resource costs for implementing the strategic initiatives. Going global with stores would typically involve complex relationships with intermediaries in the various countries and a loss of control to brokers, agents, and other third parties. Limited Brands feels that it has other better uses for their resources that have higher returns than global store expansion. They are starting new U.S. products that leverage their ability to very economically (compared to their competition) open new stores. For example, they are introducing a new beauty line with Henri Bendel and C.O. Bigelow—an apothecary. C.O. Bigelow was created many years ago in Greenwich, Connecticut. Limited has made it into a store concept with all of the original formulas for which C.O. Bigelow has become famous.

VS launched a new line of lingerie—Pink—for the college-age woman, which has been rolled out to all of the VS stores. The idea for the line came from a segmentation study of their customers and potential customers. They saw a need for a younger line for a more casual life style. There is a separate "Pink" room and environment in each VS store. The concept could eventually be spun off to its own stores, as was Bath and Body Works. The Pink line was first sold only in 10 stores, then modified based upon the customer reaction, then rolled out to 30 stores, modified again, then 100 stores, and then to all stores. This is a much better (i.e., valid) and cost effective way to test new products than the typical concept or in-market testing that other CPG companies that don't own stores do. Pink has become a $500 million revenue product line in less than two years! It's hard to envision any export strategy doing anywhere near that well. The ability to do these controlled, cost effective, extremely valid test markets for new store/product ideas is another sustainable competitive advantage that leverages VS distinctive competencies.

VS has found that their Internet site has been able to service demand around the world. They continue to service global customers through the Web because the incremental costs (very small) are justified by the sales generated. They also retain complete control about how the products are portrayed and how the sales process works. They also experimented with catalogs with some success in some areas of the world, but there was not enough success to justify diverting resources from other initiatives domestically that were evaluated as more productive. They will shortly be testing some of their products in the Duty Free shop channel globally. If it works in the tests to justify the resources for expansion, and the company can guarantee the integrity of the brand positions, then they will be rolled out.

The next distribution/channel option we consider and evaluate is lower on the control continuum than "owned" distribution, but retains some of the benefits—distribution exclusivity.

CLICKS AND BRICKS

Companies that own or control their own stores or other elements of physical distribution can in many cases leverage the Internet to provide increasing value to their customers and prospects at possibly lower costs. These "clicks and bricks" or "clicks and mortar" strategies are becoming increasingly common as a way to leverage distinctive competencies. For example, Barnes and Noble uses its stores and the Internet as a way to compete with Amazon.com, which has no physical stores. Borders has partnered with Amazon.com to power its Internet distribution, while retaining control of its physical stores. All prospective book or record buyers are not the same in terms of what they value when purchasing. Some people are more comfortable thumbing through a book than trying to browse parts of it or reading a blurb online. On the other hand, those same people may use the Internet for other activities and be very susceptible to coupons and other promotions that they see on the Web or that are emailed to them. The promotions can typically be used at the stores or on the Web. Amazon.com can't directly compete for those people who find the Web promotion-store purchase attractive. The countervailing issue in this example is that Amazon.com's supply and logistics costs are lower than Barnes and Noble's because they don't have to pay for all of the inventory, real estate, and personnel costs of running physical stores. Both Amazon.com and Barnes and Noble can be successful selling a similar "product"—books, but with two different offering bundles that appeal to different market segments.

Just like any other marketing resource allocation decisions, it's very important to understand and try to predict as well as possible both the incremental costs and incremental revenue (including anticipated competitive reactions) when making decisions about integrating the Internet into the sales and distribution mix. For example, Blockbuster responded to Netflix in 2004 by starting its own online DVD rental service and also eliminating late fees on its physical in-store movie rentals. Blockbuster integrated the online offering with its stores by giving online subscribers coupons for two free in-store movie rentals per month. The idea was to get the online customers into the physical store where they might purchase or rent games and used DVDs, or have opportunities to trade.[3] Blockbuster's online offering was originally priced $3 lower than Netflix per month—$14.99 versus $17.99. Because of the costs associated with the new initiatives and the slowdown in the movie rental business in 2005,

Blockbuster was facing financial pressure from creditors that it had not previously faced. According to *The Wall Street Journal*, as of September 2005, "at least one studio, News Corp's 20th Century Fox, has arranged for some sort of financial hedge to protect itself in case Blockbuster doesn't pay its bills."[4] In hindsight, it seems clear that the incremental revenue did not make up for the incremental costs of the new Blockbuster initiatives of 2004. In 2004, before the initiatives were started, Blockbuster was nicely profitable. However, by October of 2005, its stock was hitting new lows. Sometimes it may be better to let a new competitor (like Netflix) take a new market segment than to try to compete on a playing field where you don't have as many advantages. Netflix was able to stay profitable during the Blockbuster onslaught because it had a finely tuned, profitable, business model. For Blockbuster, the added incentive of free store rentals and a $3 decrease in monthly price was perhaps not attractive enough to justify the increased costs that were necessary to develop and keep the new online service running.

A good approach to dealing with these "bricks and clicks" options is to not roll out the program to the universe at once. Instead, it usually makes sense to experiment with a prototype for a sample of customers—get the offering tuned up so it works well, measure its incremental revenue and costs, and then roll it out if everything works and adds to profitability. If everything isn't working well, try to change what needs to change and re-do the experiment and the measurement until the new offering is over your profitability threshold. This process is called *adaptive experimentation*, a key concept for effective entrepreneurial marketers. Throughout this book, you will be exposed to more concepts of adaptive experimentation.

DISTRIBUTION EXCLUSIVITY ALTERNATIVES

Many firms do not even consider distribution exclusivity options. They assume that they should use the same channels in the same way as everyone else in their industry. Options regarding exclusivity are not considered nearly as often as they might be. The exclusivity options vary by how selective your distribution channel is and may vary over time. The two extremes are exclusive distribution and intensive distribution. In the middle is the selective distribution option. Exclusive distribution gives a retailer or other intermediary the exclusive right to sell your product in a defined "area" for a defined time period. Area used to mean geographical area—such as a country or metropolitan area. However, areas in cyberspace can also be exclusive to one or a select few "e-tailers." Selective distribution gives the right to distribute your product to some entities in a defined area, but limits the number to a select group. Intensive distribution lets anyone who wants to distribute your product do so. There are a number of tradeoffs that the entrepreneurial marketer needs to evaluate when she considers her choice of distribution channel exclusivity. First, as with almost all entrepreneurial decisions, creativity in terms of options is crucial. Exclusivity is just a subset of the distribution options that should be generated and evaluated as part of the venture initiation process. Table 4-2 shows elements of the tradeoffs that are involved with different levels of distribution exclusivity.

Table 4-2 Distribution exclusivity

Exclusive	Selective	Intensive
Possible easier sell in	Resellers compete	High coverage
Higher control	Less reseller loyalty	Convenience
Higher margins for all		Lower control
Less competition at point of sale		Less push in store
More push in store		More mass pull needed
Less coverage		More coverage
More association with channel members attributes		Faster sales cycle possible
Possible guaranteed minimum sales		

EXCLUSIVE DISTRIBUTION

The exclusive distribution option has a number of advantages that most firms do not realize. The first advantage is that it is usually easier to sell into a distribution channel if you are able to offer exclusivity. Exclusivity adds value to your offering bundle to most intermediaries. Using the Internet as an example, if you can offer your product to only one Web site for resale, then that Web site operator does not have to worry about any price competition from other Web sites. This price competition is made easier on the Web by the robots that automatically find the lowest price for purchasers among the competing sales sites on the Web. Not only can you sell the product easier with exclusivity, but also in many cases you can extract valuable benefits for a struggling entrepreneur. Typically, exclusivity is negotiated with either some payment in advance for it, or some guaranteed minimum sales quantities that the distributor will have to sell in order to retain the exclusivity.

INFORMATION RESOURCES, INC.—FUNDED BY EXCLUSIVITY

In the early 1980s, John Malec and Gerry Eskin had developed a potentially valuable way to help major packaged goods companies evaluate the incremental revenue impact of changes in their TV advertising. They had developed and patented technology to use to target cable television viewers in smaller markets without access to TV signals over the air. Their concept was to put boxes on the top of cable household TV sets, and to put computer systems into the "head end" where the cable system got the microwave programming signal. This technology would enable Information Resources to have viewers of the same TV show on cable get different advertisements than the other viewers of the same show. This ability to target ads was combined with a consumer panel of households who were given cards that were scanned at all of their area's food and drug stores. The Behaviorscan system was able to very validly evaluate TV advertising changes by performing the changes in an experiment where the experimental groups were matched by prior purchases of the brand and category. The matching of the experimental groups was done with the household panel data that was collected every time the household made a purchase at any of the food or drug stores in the metropolitan area.

The Behaviorscan concept was very attractive to many packaged goods advertisers, because it was the first way they had seen to validly get a handle on the productivity of their very large TV advertising expenditures. For example, if one group of matched households were given 50% more TV advertising for a brand than another group of matched households, the experiment was designed so that all other possible effects on sales were controlled for.

Information Resources leveraged the interest of these major packaged goods firms to fund their development. Before they had any of their markets instrumented, Malec and Eskin presented their design and patents to the major packaged goods firms. They offered *category exclusivity* in return for upfront payments that would pay for the development and implementation of the instrumented market technology. The packaged goods marketers were so worried that their competitors would get a competitive edge, that Malec and Eskin were able to fund their development *without any outside funding*. At the same time, Malec and Eskin were actually having problems getting funding from traditional sources. Exclusivity to potential customers turned out to be a very creative, extremely cheap, way to finance the venture.

EVALUATING CHANNEL EXCLUSIVITY

By giving exclusivity, you enable the channel member to associate your product more closely with the channel member's other products. In many cases, this can be a win-win situation for both parties. If the positioning of your product is consistent with that of other products the channel member carries, then your product will reinforce the positioning of the other products and simultaneously benefit from the association. For example, many upscale products will have exclusive retailers in each geographical area who are "authorized" to sell their product exclusively. Even the adjective "exclusive" has been used to describe this kind of product. "Exclusive," very high-priced watches and certain haute couture designer fashions are examples of products that use exclusivity as one of their distribution leverage points.

If a channel member has exclusivity, she will typically have more motivation to "push" the product to the next level of distribution, or to the final consumer. "Push" involves promotion, distribution attention (e.g., shelf space, display in store), advertising, and so on. Because she has exclusivity, the channel member can push the exclusive product and not worry about a competitive channel member capitalizing on the "push" by selling the "pushed" product without paying for any of the "push expenses." On the other hand, if the exclusive product is very attractive to consumers, advertising the exclusive product may get new people into the channel member's business and cause them to buy other products while they are there. Some very powerful retailers have begun to understand the value of having unique, high-perceived value products on an exclusive basis. Home Depot, for example, has a number of products made especially for them that can bring in new customers or cause existing customers to come visit the store more often. Home Depot's exclusive line of dehumidifiers was very well rated by a consumer magazine and thus brought new customers in. Home Depot did not have to share those new customers with any competitors because of their exclusive arrangement with the manufacturer.

Because of the lack of inter-channel competition, the margins on exclusive goods are usually higher, not only for the channel members, but also for the manufacturer. The manufacturer typically has some more control over what the channel member does with her product, if she has an exclusive arrangement. In many cases, the exclusivity contracts will not only have guaranteed minimum purchase quantities, but also stipulations about how much and what kind of "push" will be performed by the channel member. However, the granting of exclusive distribution is not a one-way street.

If you give an exclusivity contract for a long period, you may end up at the mercy of the channel member to whom you have given exclusivity. During the contracted exclusivity period, as long as all of the exclusivity contract provisions are being observed, you may have very little leverage over the channel member. This happens a lot when a firm enters a foreign country using a full service importer/distributor. These importer/distributors typically assume all responsibility for the product once the container leaves the firm's country. The firm is typically not very knowledgeable about the sales potential and/or the potential perceived value of her offering to the end consumers in the foreign country. The importer takes advantage of this by negotiating a contract that has a competitive price that the importer pays for your product, but does not specify the price or other marketing mix elements that the importer will use in his country. There are also typically annual minimum purchases that are required to retain the exclusivity. The agreements can be very long in duration—10–20 years, or even lifetime. The importer/distributor is thus free to do whatever he wants with the product as long as he buys his minimums from the firm. Sometimes, the importer will second source an inferior version of your product to distribute alongside your product and unfairly leverage your brand equity. In other cases, the importer will develop a competing version of your product and limit his competition to the minimums he has to sell of your product.

One co-author has been working with foreign companies entering the U.S. market for over 20 years, including a number of Israeli firms. He has seen a number of Israeli firms that wanted to enter the U.S. market and found someone who knew someone in the U.S. who spoke Hebrew. That person became the exclusive importer/distributor and told the Israeli firm that "standard practice" was to have very long exclusivity terms—20–30 years in many cases. The Israeli firms lost millions of dollars in opportunity costs because of the treatment of their exclusive distributors for whom they had no operational recourse. Many American firms have had similar experiences when they attempted to enter other countries—especially those with very different languages and culture. Just as it makes sense to generate and evaluate a number of alternatives for other elements of your marketing plan, it is at least as important for the distribution channel decisions.

Before getting into long-term exclusivity agreements, you should know your market, how the product offering should be perceived, and have some reasonable ideas about its perceived value and pricing options. The long-term exclusive distributor is crucial to your business—it's like a marriage. You should check out all alternatives and be sure of the ethics of your chosen distributor, if you choose the exclusive route.

ITEM EXCLUSIVITY

Some firms use exclusivity by item to help lower price competition between competing channel members or competing retailers. They will make small differences between models and give retailers or channel members' exclusive rights to one model for a geographical area. This exclusivity by item does not help as much with all of the advantages of exclusivity in Table 4-2. However, in a number of industries, it has become the way most firms go to market. For example, the medium- and high-end furniture manufacturers will have different models that are exclusive to different retailers in a U.S. metropolitan area. The biggest advantage the furniture retailers see from this tactic is that their potential customers cannot easily compare prices from one local dealer to another. Now that furniture is beginning to be sold on the Internet, it will become even more important for local retailers to attempt to insulate themselves by having exclusive items.

INTENSIVE DISTRIBUTION

Intensive distribution is the opposite extreme in the options described in Table 4-2. Anyone who wants to carry your offering is encouraged to do so. The objective is to be everywhere the end customer might be and possibly buy your product offering. Impulse purchases such as candy, snacks, and so on are typically well suited to intensive distribution. However, in order for you to be successful, the consumer needs to know your product is there and perceive its value. The product needs to be pulled off the shelves by the customer compared to all the other competitive products. The classic, non-entrepreneurial way for that pull to happen is for a company to spend millions of dollars on advertising and promotion. As entrepreneurial marketers, we know better ways. Our chapters on advertising, promotion, and public relations cover creative cost-effective ways to pull products through intensive (and other) distribution channels. One of the most creative ways to use intensive distribution is with *fad* products.

Ken Hakuta was the master user of intensive distribution to support his launch of "Wacky Wallwalkers" in concert with the rest of his ingenious, creative, lucky marketing plan that he executed in the mid 1980s. Because of the amazing demand built up by his fortuitous national public relations "Blitzkrieg," every store in the U.S. wanted to sell Wacky Wallwalkers. Wacky Wallwalkers were exactly what their name hinted. They were little plastic octopuses that if thrown against most walls, would slowly walk down the wall, one leg over the other. Every retailer wanted to sell Wallwalkers after they were featured as the "newest fad" on the CBS Evening News.

Ken knew that time was of the essence and that he should take advantage of the extraordinary consumer demand by getting as many Wallwalkers into as many storefronts as possible as fast as possible. He was aware that cheap knockoffs would soon arrive to compete, even though he had an "exclusive license" from the Japanese manufacturer. In order to accomplish mass distribution as quickly as possible, Ken authorized toy and novelty distributors to sell his product to the trade rather than have his own sales and distribution team. The distributors had the entire infrastructure in place to quickly get the product to all of the retailers who were demanding to be part of the Wallwalker action. Ken gave an additional mark-up to these distributors to compensate them for their part in the distribution chain. He thus made less on *each* Wallwalker that he sold than he would have earned had he used his own sales and distribution system. However, he correctly estimated that his total number of units sold would be much higher with the indirect distribution system. The total profits he earned by selling over 200 million Wallwalkers in less than one year were much higher than he would have earned had he struggled to develop his own sales and distribution system. He also was able to capitalize on the consumer demand before the knockoffs were able to become a big factor.

The use of intermediary sales and distribution resources was appropriate for Ken for another reason. He correctly viewed Wallwalkers as a product with limited life and did not plan to follow Wallwalkers with any other products targeted at similar mass-market customers. If he were planning a long-term business where retailer relationships were going to be important, than more direct contact between Ken's people and the mass retailers would possibly make sense. He was right to view Wallwalkers as a once in a lifetime opportunity. He made "tens of millions"[5] of dollars on the Wallwalkers—not bad for a year's work and virtually no assets before he started!

SELECTIVE DISTRIBUTION

Selective distribution is in the conceptual middle between exclusive and intensive distribution. Here, some, but not all, resellers are authorized to resell your product and/or service. By not allowing everyone to carry your product, you retain some control as to how it will be resold. The control mechanism is the implied threat to take away the product from those resellers who do not follow your rules for your product. You also may have a higher say in how the end consumer may perceive you. The selective distribution option is best if it is integrated with the rest of the marketing mix to underlie a sound positioning and segmentation plan. Brooks Sports found a way to compete with Nike that includes selective distribution as an important, integrated element of its marketing mix.

BROOKS SPORTS—INTEGRATING SELECTIVE DISTRIBUTION WITH EFFECTIVE POSITIONING AND SEGMENTATION

When Helen Rockey came to Brooks in 1994 after 11 years at Nike, Brooks was a mess. Brooks had been successful during the running boom of the late 1970s, but in the 1980s they tried to chase Nike. They expanded into other categories like basketball, aerobics, and baseball, and signed big name athletes like Dan Marino and James Worthy to sell their $70 shoes.[6] Brooks, like Superscope (discussed later) had committed the classic error of trying to move down the prestige of distribution channels to maximize revenue. According to *Forbes*:

"But in trying to become a mini-Nike, Brooks was stretched too thin. When business began to slow, it began using cheaper materials and selling its sneakers at rock-bottom prices to discount retailers like K-Mart, which sold them for as little as $20. Brooks lost credibility with joggers, and between 1983 and 1993 it lost some $60 million. 'I don't think I really knew what I had gotten myself into,' Rockey says."[7]

Rockey developed a completely different marketing strategy in order to differentiate Brooks from the rest of the competition. She went back to Brooks' running heritage and decided to be perceived as the shoe for serious running enthusiasts. This revived positioning and implied segmentation dictated all the elements of her new marketing mix, including distribution. This new strategy was consistent with what was left of Brooks' distinctive competencies—relationships with Far-East suppliers, design capability, and a new CEO who herself was a running enthusiast.

The best outlet for the newly positioned Brooks line was the specialty running store that catered to the running enthusiasts. Rockey had to make her product attractive, not only to the end purchaser, the running enthusiast, but also to the specialty running store retailers. She did that with all the elements of her marketing mix—especially her product and pricing, and very selective distribution. She first limited the Far-East suppliers from 20 to the 3 best at producing high-quality shoes and redesigned the line to be attractive to serious runners. She next boosted the suggested retail prices significantly—to as high as $120. The margin to the running specialty stores was about 45%. This was a good margin for the stores—as long as the prices were not undercut by other retail competitors. This is where Brooks' selective distribution was critical. Rockey had to control all of the retail outlets to insure that no one was undercutting each other. She did this by ensuring that only specialty running shops got the shoes and that the discounters were not able to carry the line. In the beginning of the repositioning, she had personally visited the major retail specialty running stores to convince them that she really was dedicated to having a brand that both Brooks and their partner selective retailers would make very good money on.

The other elements of Brooks' marketing mix also supported the new segmentation and positioning. Their sales force helped their retailers to offer running clinics and trained the retail sales force about how to get the right shoe for the store's runner clientele. Brooks also had an extensive and professional presence at the major running trade shows. There are no more celebrity endorsements. Instead, the company has over 200 competing runners who are given free shoes. These runners are icons within the serious running community.[8] Because the target segmentation made mass media unnecessary, Brooks was able to take advantage of media that reached its target audience very efficiently. Brooks spends less than a million dollars per year in niche publications like *Runners World* and *Running Times.* This reinvented positioning and segmentation has been very productive for Brooks. According to *Forbes* in 1999, "Brooks' sales have been growing at a 30% clip for the past 4 years and should hit $100 million by next year. Operating income (net before depreciation, interest, and taxes) last year (1998) topped $4 million, from $3 million in 1997."[9] Some brands may not be suited for intensive distribution. Brooks was one of them, as it was developed over time. Brooks does not have the potential to out compete or out muscle Nike or Reebok. However, it does have the potential to make a lot of money for its entrepreneurial owners if they continue to understand its limitations and have a marketing mix (including selective distribution) consistent with its revised positioning and segmentation.

VALUE-ADDED RESELLERS

Many business-to-business products are marketed through a form of selective distribution. They often will form relationships with *Value-Added Resellers* (VARs) who bundle their product with other products and services to solve their customer's problems. The conceptual logic that supports a decision to use VARs is very similar to that of evaluating manufacturer's reps as a sales mechanism. The VARs value added is their relationships with their customers and the other synergistic products and services that they may bundle together to solve customer problems. Many technical products that need to be used together with other products in an integrated solution are best marketed through VAR, selective, indirect distribution channels. For some component product categories, the end customer does not expect to buy directly from the manufacturer, but wants to buy an integrated solution from a VAR. In those categories, the VAR can almost become the end customer to the entrepreneurial manufacturer. The entrepreneur's job is to understand the needs of the VAR and provide more perceived added value than competitors.

NICE SYSTEMS—A VAR EXAMPLE

Nice Systems Ltd. is an entrepreneurial company started in Israel that has used the VAR channel all over the world to grow from less than $10 million in 1991 to over $270 million in 2005. Their major product line has been integrated digital recording and quality control systems for telephonic voice applications. These are systems that digitally record phone or other voice sources and provide technology so that the customer can easily search for and access conversations that were recorded over time. The markets for Nice Systems' products include call centers, trading floors, air traffic control, and public safety and security. Even though the product is very similar, or even identical for each of these markets, Nice has wisely chosen to have selective distribution with different VAR partners in each market. For trading floors, Nice has authorized firms like British Telecom, Siemens, IPC Information Systems, and so on. For call centers, they have associated with Alcatel, Aspect Telecommunications, Rockwell, Lucent Technologies, and so on. In each of these markets, their objective is for the VAR associates to integrate the Nice Systems products into their total communications offerings to their target markets. Nice could not have grown nearly as rapidly nor have as good a base of business had they not utilized a VAR strategy. The drawback to the strategy (if there is one) is that Nice must make sure that its offering bundle is not only attractive to the end customers in the call centers and air traffic control centers, but also attractive to their VARs as well.

Selective distribution is very important if aspects of the place the product is bought are important to the perceived value of the entrepreneur's offering bundle. The entrepreneur can use the concept-testing procedure to check whether the potential customer views the product offering any differently if it is carried in one store vs. another. If a product is described as available at Sharper Image or Neiman Marcus, it will be perceived differently than if it is described as available at Wal-Mart and K-Mart.

PRESERVATION HALL JAZZ BANDS—A SELECTIVE DISTRIBUTION EXAMPLE

Alan Jaffee, the entrepreneur who founded the Preservation Hall Jazz Bands in New Orleans, understood the importance of selective distribution in determining how his product offering was to be perceived. He founded the Preservation Hall Jazz Bands by personally finding old Dixie

Land jazz stars and rehabilitating them and caring for them so that they could recreate Dixie Land jazz as it was in its hey day. His objective was to have the Preservation Hall Jazz Bands perceived as art, not just as entertainment. In order to insure that potential consumers received the correct perception, Mr. Jaffee only let the bands perform in venues that were perceived as mainly artistic as opposed to entertainment. For example, the bands would perform at the Tanglewood or Wolftrap music festivals, but not at stadium rock or jazz concerts. If they performed on television, it was on the Bell Telephone hour, not on a weekly variety or entertainment show. If you saw the Preservation Hall Band perform in the late '80s or early '90s, Alan Jaffee was the rotund white man playing the tuba in the all-black band. Their home venue, Preservation Hall in the Bourbon Street district of New Orleans, also reinforces their artistic, authentic positioning. The "hall" is very simple, with benches for the audience to sit on, and no alcoholic beverages served. You are supposed to go to Preservation Hall to listen to Dixie Land jazz and appreciate it as an art form. Their home venue, their venues on the road, and their media appearances all support and are synergistic with that positioning. Perhaps it was because Alan Jaffee did marketing at Gimbels Department store before he founded Preservation Hall that prepared him to position his very successful "offering" so well.

DYNAMIC DISTRIBUTION MANAGEMENT

Many entrepreneurs need to understand that distribution channels can sometimes be more valuable if they are changed over time. This is true especially for product lines that continually have innovation and change a lot and/or have new products or models that are introduced. The distribution channels need to change because the prestige you want to associate with your newest and most innovative product may be very different from the prestige you are able to associate with an existing product. If the existing product has been sold for a length of time and is no longer considered as the state of the art, it will not command as much prestige and status as the "newest and most advanced." Consumer electronics and fashion items are those for which changing distribution *by item* over time is often an excellent strategy. If you can associate the high-prestige items with high-prestige distribution channels, and the lower-prestige items with lower-prestige (and typically lower margin) distribution channels, you can often create win-win situations for both you and the distribution channels.

The reason this item change over time works has partly to do with examining the needs and values of the various types of channel members. The high-end channel members (Sharper Image, Bloomingdales, Hammacher Schlemmer, in the U.S.) want to sell exclusive, high perceived value items. They do not want to sell the same items that the lower end, mass market channel members (Wal-Mart, K-Mart, etc.) sell. The high-end retailers do not want to have to compete on price with the same item in a lower end, lower margin store. The high-end stores perceive that their better service, the store ambiance, and so on justify higher mark-ups than their mass-market competitors. They also do not sell the kind of mass volumes that the lower end stores do. This also justifies their higher profit margins because their fixed costs are higher per unit of sales.

The lower-end channel members have just the opposite set of needs. They would like nothing better than to be able to sell the same items that the high-end stores do. They want to advertise that they have the same items as the high-end stores, but for less. Managing the delicate balancing act of the different channel hierarchies is a real challenge for many entrepreneurs. However, with careful planning and a bit of "chutzpah," an entrepreneur can successfully manage these conflicting channel priorities. We cover two examples next—one of an entrepreneurial company, Superscope, Inc., that mismanaged the balance of their distribution channels, and Franklin Electronic Publishers, which has managed the process very well for 15 years.

SUPERSCOPE, INC.—COULDN'T ACHIEVE BALANCE

In the late '80s, Superscope, Inc. bought the right to the Marantz label for high fidelity components. When Superscope bought them, Marantz was a premier manufacturer of very high-end audio components—tuners, amplifiers, speakers, and so on. Marantz distribution was consistent with their high-end image. They had a very selective distribution channel—only the most prestigious and best audio/video "consultants"/dealers in each metropolitan area of the U.S. The Marantz business had good profits, but was not very large in terms of sales volume. The Marantz positioning and pricing limited their target market to the high-income audio file market segment. With a limited, but very profitable, target market, Marantz was growing with the high-end audio market—around 10% per year.

Superscope was not satisfied with the growth potential of Marantz. They reasoned that the brand's perceived value was so high that it could sell much more if its distribution were broadened and its advertising budget increased. When Superscope talked with mass-market retailers and distributors, they got big intentions of purchasing and promoting the Marantz line. Retailers like Wal-Mart and K-Mart or Circuit City would like nothing better than to get a very high-end, high gross profit product line. Their modus-operandi would be to discount the list price to build volume and sell very large numbers of units. They might even use the Marantz line as a loss leader to build store traffic. They reasoned that middle market consumers would love to have an opportunity to buy high-end products at a good discount.

Superscope thus began a very ambitious program to sharply increase the sales of Marantz by significantly broadening the line's distribution. They began offering the line to the mass-market retailers. They encouraged them with co-op advertising programs to advertise Marantz in their weekly circulars and newspaper inserts. Most of the circulars of retailers like Circuit City or K-Mart advertise temporary price reductions and other kinds of special pricing. Initially, the sales results of the increased distribution program were extremely strong. For the next two years, Superscope's Marantz sales volume more than doubled, and their corporate profits were up even higher because of economies of scale. Superscope was a very hot stock in New York for about a year.

Then things began to unravel. The high-end, exclusive retailers got very upset that they were being undercut on price and out promoted by the mass retailers. The high-end clients were very sophisticated and were willing to go to K-Mart to buy for much less what they used to buy at the high-end specialty retailers. So the high-end retailers began to lose business. What did they do? The high-end specialty retailers began refusing to carry Marantz and changed allegiance to other audio equipment makers who would respect the selective distribution to only high-end specialty channels that would not compete with each other on price. For a while, Superscope did not care about these distribution losses, because the high-end business was more than being made up for by large orders from the mass retailers. However, once the majority of the high-end retailers stopped carrying Marantz, its cachet and prestige began to really suffer. The high-end retailers began to bad mouth Marantz as "the cheap brand" that was being sold through K-Mart. The mass marketers began to also shy away from paying good wholesale prices for Marantz because it began to no longer fly out of their stores as it used to. This wholesale price pressure made a big impact on Superscope's profit margins. Superscope then decided to increase their profit margins by making Marantz offshore at much lower costs and somewhat lower quality. This manufacturing change held up Superscope's profits for a time, but it also added even more fodder for the high-end "Marantz Bashers" who created much word of mouth about the decline in Marantz quality. The mass-market retailers then began to cut back their orders because the consumer demand for Marantz was deteriorating. Superscope's volume began to drop precipitously. They tried to introduce a line of Marantz "Gold," made domestically, that would only be sold in the high-end stores. The high-end stores turned Superscope down flat because they felt betrayed by their Marantz experience. They would not trust Superscope not to do the same with Marantz Gold that they did with Marantz. Superscope is no longer in business and the Marantz name lost most of its former value.

Superscope made a number of mistakes. They did not create long-term value for any of their distribution and retailing channels. They used the Marantz reputation partially built by the high-end retailers to hurt the same high-end retailers when they broadened distribution to price-oriented competitors. They lost the trust of the high-end retailers by not treating them with the exclusivity that they rightfully expected. They lowered the quality of the brand as they lowered the prices. They sacrificed their long-term positioning and perceived value for a short-term big revenue and profit spike. Their short-term thinking killed the company.

FRANKLIN ELECTRONIC PUBLISHERS

Franklin Electronic Publishers' core business is hand-held reference products like dictionaries, thesauruses, wine guides, and so on. Over the years, Franklin has had a spotty record with other product lines, but they have continually been able to slowly grow and make good returns on their core product line. Their dynamic distribution channel management by item is a big part of their long-term success with this core line. They use a tried-and-true formula to provide a win-win situation for all of their channel partners—from the high-end Sharper Image and Bloomingdales to the lower-end Wal-Mart and K-Mart. They give each of them what they want without alienating anybody. Sharper Image and other high-end catalog retailers, as well as the high-end retailers and e-tailers, all want exclusivity to the high end for items that they sell. Sharper Image does not get too upset if Hammacker Schlemmer sells the same new Franklin translator at the same price. However, if K-Mart or the Heartland catalog are each selling the same item at 30% lower *at the same time as Sharper Image*, the upper-end retailers get very upset.

Franklin handles this conflict by *cycling its items* through the distribution channels *over time.* Their newest models get very selective distribution to the high-end retailers for about six months. They then are released to the mid-level retailers, like Radio Shack, Macy's, and so on for another six-month period. After that period, the items are released to the mass-market retailers, the Wal-Marts and K-Marts. If Franklin has its plan working perfectly, they have new items every six months to feed into the channel to replace the items that have been released to the next prestigious levels. When they release the item that has been at Sharper Image for six months to the next level, they should have another brand-new item to take its place. Sharper Image and other high-end retailers are happy because they are always the first to have the newest and most advanced items that they can price at high margins because of their very selective distribution. The mid-level retailers are also relatively happy because they get to carry items at a discount that had just been in the Sharper Image at higher prices. The lower-level mass-market discounters are also happy because they get to carry items at a further discount that had just been in the department stores and other mid-level retailers at higher prices.

FRANCHISING: STILL ANOTHER DISTRIBUTION OPTION

Many entrepreneurial marketers have used franchising to accelerate their revenue growth. However, as is the case with all distribution alternatives, franchising is better for some product/market situations than for others. In this section, we first describe what franchises are and which types might be useful for entrepreneurial ventures. We then evaluate the advantages and disadvantages of the different types and how a decision to offer franchises should be evaluated. We also look at franchises from the point of view of buying a franchise because many entrepreneurs consider buying franchises as a way to get their venture started. We next consider the unique conflicts that occur between franchisor and franchisee and how they might be managed.

DIFFERENT TYPES OF FRANCHISING

A franchise is usually permission or a license granted by the franchisor to the franchisee to sell a product or service in an agreed-upon territory. Franchising is typically a continuing relationship in which the franchisor provides assistance in organizing, training, merchandising, systems, and management in return for payments from the franchisee. Franchises are a big part of business in the U.S. Approximately 1 in 12 businesses is a franchise and $1 trillion in revenues come from franchises.

The different types of franchises depend on what rights are licensed to whom. Different forms of franchising are cropping up all the time. The following forms are examples of those that have been used by entrepreneurial marketers. These forms are not mutually exclusive. Many franchise forms can have elements of these different prototype forms:

1. *Manufacturing franchise*—Here, the franchisor provides the right to a franchisee to manufacture a product using the franchisor's name and trademark. The most prevalent examples of this form are soft drink bottlers. Other examples include companies who manufacture private label goods that have a retailer's label on them and firms that manufacture fashion apparel under license to a designer label. The Callanen Watch company (now a division of Timex, Inc.) had a license to manufacture watches under the Guess label.

2. *Manufacturer-retailer franchise*—In this form, the manufacturer gives the franchisee the right to sell its product through a retail outlet. Examples of this form include gasoline stations, most automobile dealerships, and many businesses found in shopping malls.

3. *Wholesaler-retailer franchise*—Here, the wholesaler gives the retailer the right to carry products distributed by the wholesaler. Examples of this form include Radio Shack (which also manufactures some of its products), Agway Stores, Health Mart, and other franchised drug stores.

4. *Business format franchise*—This is the most popular form and includes elements of the other forms. It is typically more all-inclusive. Here, the franchisor provides the franchisee with a name, an identity, and a complete, "proven" way of operating a business. Examples include Burger King and McDonald's fast food outlets,

Pizza Hut and Dairy Queen restaurants, Holiday Inn and Best Western Hotels, 7-Eleven convenience stores, and Hertz and Avis car rentals.

FROM THE FRANCHISEE'S POINT OF VIEW

For the franchisee, these franchise forms can be very helpful for some entrepreneurs who want to start a business, but may not have the vision, creativity, resources, or skill to start a completely new venture. All of the forms provide for the franchisee to benefit from the market power of large-scale advertising and marketing expenditures. These large marketing budgets typically come from the collective resources of all of the franchisees. Many franchises also enable franchisees to band together and buy products and supplies at better prices than they could as individual entrepreneurs. Probably the biggest value of these franchises is the brand name value and equity that has been built up over, in some cases, many years by the franchisor. The different forms may also add unique advantages.

For *manufacturing franchises*, the franchisee may get a well-protected market that they have exclusively. Many manufacturing franchises may also permit the franchisee to obtain licenses from more than one company. For example, the Callanen Watch Company also had a license to manufacture Monet brand watches. Having multiple licenses can lower risk levels for franchisees, especially for items that may go in and out of favor. For Callanen, if the market for Monet watches was waning, perhaps the Guess brand could take up the slack.

The *business format franchise* adds a number of benefits to the franchisee that has little business experience. The best business format franchises have encapsulated all the relevant knowledge and experience of the franchisor into training and operating systems that take most, if not all, of the guess work out of operating the franchise. McDonald's is famous for its "Hamburger University" that trains its franchisees in all elements of running a successful outlet. The franchisee basically gets to leverage on all the other experience of other franchisees and the franchisor in the past. The franchisee is helped in setting accounting procedures, facility management, personnel policies, business planning, and actually starting up. Most franchisors also help with outlet location and help arrange financing. Many business format franchises are in businesses like fast food, and convenience stores that are not very sensitive to business cycles and can make it easier to weather a poor economy. This franchise form is also available for a wide range of prices. Some business format franchises can also be operated from home—like aerobics instruction or direct marketing of cosmetics.

Following are the typical advantages of becoming a franchisee:

- Lower risk of failure
- Established product/service
- Experience of franchisor
- Group purchasing power
- Instant name recognition
- Operational standards assure uniformity and efficiency
- Assistance in setting accounting procedures, facility management, personnel policies, and so on
- Start-up assistance
- Location assistance
- Help with financing arrangements
- Power of national and regional marketing

However, there is another side to being a franchisee. The franchisee is no longer his or her own boss. All of the preceding franchise benefits come at the cost of sacrificing much autonomy. For most franchises, the franchisee has little, if any, control over the product/service they sell, or the marketing decisions on advertising, public relations, or location. It may be impossible, for example, to drop or add products that may be more or less suitable to the particular needs of your market area. Local public relations may be under the franchisee's control, but with constraints from the franchisor. The franchisees may have a cooperative governing organization that decides on national advertising and promotion policies together with the franchisor. Each franchisee is limited to one vote in these organizations. There are also usually very strict rules and regulations on all aspects of operating the business.

Aside from autonomy, there are other typical disadvantages of becoming a franchisee. You pay for the privilege. There usually is an initial franchise fee, on-going royalty payments as a percentage of revenue, as well as a percentage of revenue to a cooperative marketing fund. The marketing fund is administered by the cooperative franchisee-franchisor organization.

These fees are all "off the top." The franchisor gets paid before the franchisee may make any profits. The franchise agreements may also impose restrictions on selling the franchise if things go badly, and may also restrict how the business may be passed on to your heirs. Because the business depends on the franchisor's success, there is also a risk that the franchisor may fail. Visible franchisor failures have been Arthur Treacher's Fish & Chips and Boston Market.

Following are the disadvantages of buying a franchise:

- Payment of an initial franchise fee
- On-going royalty payments "off the top"
- "Off the top" payments for cooperative marketing fund
- Cannot add or drop products unilaterally
- Little say on national marketing policies and tactics
- Must conform to operating procedures—even if you have a better way
- You depend on the franchisor for much of your success
- Some large franchisors have failed
- May be restrictions on selling the franchise
- May be difficult to pass the business to your heirs

Besides considering all of the preceding benefits and disadvantages, before selecting a franchise, the potential franchisee should carefully read the *Uniform Franchise Offering Circular* (UFOC) for each franchise being evaluated. The U.S. government requires this document. It contains the information that typically is needed to make a well-informed decision about the franchise as well as some not as useful information. The UFOC document is much like a prospectus that is required as part of an initial public offering for a company's securities. Its major purpose is to keep the company making the offering from getting sued by people who buy the securities (or in this case, the franchise). The lawyers thus make the issuing company disclose any possible risks that the franchisee might be taking when they buy the franchise. Because of this bias in the way the document is written, it should be read in a special way. If one took all of the possible risks the lawyers put in these documents literally, you would not buy any franchise or any new public security. The lawyers are like a Jewish mother. They get paid to invent risks to worry about. Most of the risk stuff is "boilerplate" that can be found in most of these documents. There is, however, much very important information in the UFOC that is crucial for evaluating a franchise. The following sidebar highlights the important information in the UFOC that should be *scrutinized* before entering into a franchise agreement.

IMPORTANT INFORMATION FOR THE FRANCHISEE IN THE UFOC

- Business experience of the franchisor and its affiliates
- Qualifications of franchisor's directors and managers
- Any lawsuits against the company and/or managers
- Any bankruptcies of the company and/or managers
- Initial franchise fee and other initial payments
- Description of all required continuing payments
- Any restrictions regarding purchasing from the franchisor or its affiliates
- Any restrictions on the quality of goods and services that the franchisee can use
- Any financial assistance available from the franchisor
- Restrictions on goods and services the franchisee is permitted to sell
- Restrictions on customers with whom the franchisee may deal
- Territorial protection for the franchisee
- Conditions under which the franchise may be
    1. Repurchased
    2. Refused renewal
    3. Transferred to a third party
    4. Modified
    5. Terminated by a third party
- Description of training programs provided
- Description of involvement of celebrities or public figures in the franchise
- Financial statements and history of the franchisor
- Basis of potential franchisee earnings projections made by the franchisor
- Percentage of franchisees that have achieved the projected results

■ Names and addresses of other franchisees to contact for their point of view
■ Statistical data on
    1. Present number of franchisees
    2. Numbers projected for the future
    3. Number of franchisees terminated
    4. Number of franchisees repurchased by the franchisor
■ Copy of the franchise contract

Because there are many "fly by night" franchisors around, it really pays to do your homework before buying any franchise. The UFOC can be very helpful. Under *no circumstances* should one buy a franchise *without scrutinizing the UFOC*. Some franchisor salespeople can be over zealous. From the franchisee's point of view, *caveat emptor* (let the buyer beware!) is the point of view that is necessary.

FROM THE FRANCHISOR'S POINT OF VIEW

Just as the consumer viewpoint is often quite different from other channel members, the franchisor's viewpoint is very different than the franchisee's in most cases.

Advantages for the Franchisor

Franchising is a distribution option that should be considered by more entrepreneurial marketers. Many of the aspects of franchising can be very attractive.[10] Franchising enables rapid expansion without large investments by the firm. The alternative ways of expanding involve both selling equity and losing some control, or borrowing money, which adds leverage and may encumber some assets. When the entrepreneurial marketer successfully franchises, she effectively leases a sliver of the business and in return receives the franchisee's capital, energy, and entrepreneurship. The more rapid expansion that franchising enables may allow the franchise to take advantage of some scale economies. Large networks mean collective buying power. Franchisees can compete with other chains because they can buy in larger quantities and vendors recognize and reward the franchise's growth. Franchisees often also set up their own advertising and promotion cooperatives to obtain scale economies.

The scale economies also increase the venture's access to real estate. Single location businesses have difficulty obtaining access and credibility with mall developers, leasing agents, and limited access locations such as stadiums and contract food feeding operations. These landlords are looking for name brands and consumer recognition, as well as repeat leasing in multiple locations. Franchising eliminates these entry barriers.

The "employees" that become franchisees are typically highly motivated to succeed because their own money is on the line. For most entrepreneurial companies, recruitment, training, and retention of great managers is key to successful expansion. The best managers are typically hard to retain unless they are offered equity. Franchising gives managers their equity with their own investment. The franchisee's investment is always at risk. This causes commitments of time and energy that typically cannot be bought with a salary. If particular skills are needed for the operation of the venture, franchisees can also be sources of highly skilled employees.

As discussed previously, the franchisor typically gets paid "off the top" as a fraction of revenue and also gets an initial franchise fee. This is typically a more predictable cash flow source than profits from an owned business. Thus, the franchisor can make profits, even if her franchises may not be profitable. It is this inherent conflict between the franchisor's incentives vs. the franchisee's that causes some of the questionable and unethical franchises to arise. Conflicts between franchisees and the franchisor also come from this potential conflict of interest. Franchising works best when the entrepreneur has a proven business model that can be replicated in different areas or venues, and in which both the franchisee and franchisor are better off financially than they would be if they were not together.

Franchises are typically easier to sell than the equivalent business that is not franchised. Think first about a traditional business with 50 managers with hundreds of employees in 10 cities with 100 leases. Contrast this with a franchise business that has 10 managers responsible for 50 franchisees with 100 locations. The franchise business is more attractive for an outsider to buy and becomes an easier exit strategy than a traditional business.

Disadvantages for the Franchisor

There are also drawbacks to franchising. In order to attract many franchisees and generate good long-term word-of-mouth, the franchisees should do well financially. These franchisee profits are sometimes sacrificed when the franchise form is chosen. Obviously, if the entrepreneurial venture is really best suited for franchising, the franchise fees should more than make up for these foregone profits as returns on resources invested in the venture. Because the franchisees are independent businesses, the franchisor has only the control given explicitly by the franchise agreement. The franchisor is thus banking the image and positioning of his franchise on the franchisees. The franchisor cannot just fire those "employees" who do not keep up the firm's image and positioning. This is the same conceptual problem that users of independent sales representatives also have. It takes constant vigilance and many programs to convince the franchisee partners to handle the image and positioning as if it were their own—which it really is. Successful franchises have reduced the fundamentals of operating their businesses to a cookbook, or operations manual. Their training programs succeed in transmitting the founder's intended positioning through the franchisee to the ultimate consumer.

The franchisor also must put in suitable systems and controls to insure that the franchisees pay the correct amount of ongoing franchise fees based on revenue of the outlet. When in doubt, the franchisee would rather report lower revenues. In many franchises where lots of cash changes hands, this control problem can be very big.

The franchisee and franchisor will typically have different incentives for pricing. For the franchisor who gets paid as a fraction of revenue, maximizing revenue becomes the objective. For the franchisee, profits are the objective. The franchisee may want to raise prices in order to increase profits at the expense of lower revenues. These pricing conflicts add a constant level of tension to many franchises.

As a franchisor, it is not as easy to change the channels of distribution because you no longer own them. Your franchisees will get very upset if they think you are going into another channel of distribution that may compete with the franchisees. For example, GNC franchises natural food and herbal remedy stores around the world. GNC has not been able to successfully use the Web as a distribution channel because their franchisees rightfully objected to the company competing with its franchisees. This is just one example of a *distribution channel conflict* that needs to be managed and planned for very carefully. We discuss management of these conflicts later in this chapter.

Another potential disadvantage of franchising is that you may be creating a new set of competitors that learn the business through your franchise and then replicate the operation under another name. In this case, it is very important for the franchisor to maintain brand positioning, image, and other proprietary assets that would make it difficult to replicate the franchise under a different name.

RITA'S WATER ICE—A SUCCESSFUL FRANCHISING VENTURE

Rita's Water Ice is an entrepreneurial venture that has succeeded very well using the franchise form. They have been able to leverage the benefits of the franchise form and minimize the impacts of most of the disadvantages. Robert Tumolo, a retired Philadelphia fire fighter, started Rita's in the summer of 1984. Bob and his mother, Elizabeth, experimented with various new recipes for Italian Water Ice—an ethnic summer refresher that was very popular in Philadelphia. Their first store was opened in Bensalem, Pennsylvania, a working class suburb of Philadelphia, in May 1984. According to Rita's Web site, "the response was overwhelming"—people really seemed to love it. Word of mouth spread like water ice on a hot summer sidewalk."[11] The next year, Bob's brother, John Tumolo, joined the business, and in 1987, they opened their second location. In 1989, the company made the decision to franchise.

For a small entrepreneurial venture begun with little capital, franchising made sense from a resource requirement point of view. Rita's could not afford to rapidly expand to more stores without going out and raising equity capital. Each franchisee invests between $135,000 and $242,000 initially to start a new Rita's outlet. That investment includes an initial franchise fee, finding and leasing a site, constructing the store layout, equipping the store, and working capital. In 2005, Rita's had over 330 outlets in the Northeast and Florida. The capital needed to open all of those outlets at minimum would have been $100,000 per outlet or $330 \times 100,000$ = $33 million dollars. In 2005, the Tumolo interests held all of Rita's assets privately and had not had to take in public funding to expand. In addition, the firm took in over 330 franchise fees from each newly opened franchise.

They also get an ongoing 6.5% of the gross sales of each franchisee. Their sales are proprietary. However, their Web site says that Rita's will sell over 30 million water ice cups. If one assumes that their total sales per water ice cup (including pretzels, and other products) is around $1, then the total gross sales across their system might be close to $30 million. 6.5% of $30 million is around $2 million. That's not bad annual revenue, with not a lot of costs that probably go with it. The franchisees also separately have to contribute 2.5% of revenue to a collective advertising fund. If one assumes that the initial franchise fee covers the costs of selling and starting up franchises, and that the cooperative advertising fee really covers the Rita's corporate marketing budget, then the $2 million of ongoing royalties that Rita's collects is probably very profitable. For this kind of operation, franchising was a very good distribution channel choice.

Rita's also developed a very smart way to collect their ongoing franchise and collective advertising fees, without having to audit or monitor their franchisee's sales. They just add a charge of 9% (6.5% royalty fee+2.5% advertising fee) of the calculated gross sales for each gallon of Rita's mix that is shipped to each franchisee. The only way a franchisee can get around paying the royalty would be to buy their mix from another supplier. All Rita's personnel need to do for control is to spot check to make sure that each outlet has only Rita's authorized mix in use. Many franchisors must put in elaborate control systems to make sure that they are getting the right amount of ongoing revenue-based franchise fees.

Another constraint for expansion of company-owned stores was the ability to find, retain, and motivate real competent help to run the stores and serve customers. The stores were not open all year—just in the spring through early fall. (Most people don't crave water ice in the winter in the Northeast U.S.) As hard as it was to get restaurant and fast food employees, it was even harder if you weren't going to be open all year. An unwritten requirement for getting a Rita's franchise is that family members want to work in the outlets. One of the neat benefits of owning a Rita's franchise is that the franchisee and her family only need to work during the late spring through early fall. The franchisee has the late fall and winter to relax. Rita's was not only selling franchisees a business. They were also selling a lifestyle.

Rita's, like most franchises, had two (at least) target markets it needed to satisfy to be successful. The first was the ultimate consumers, who bought the water ice experience at its outlets. The second target segment is the franchisee, who must invest, in many cases, their life savings to buy a Rita's franchise. It is not inexpensive to sell franchises. The first few franchises were sold by word of mouth to customers at company-owned stores who really liked the Rita's product. However, in order to expand to areas outside of metropolitan Philadelphia, Rita's had to get their franchise "offering bundle" exposed to potential franchisees. In any new area, the first Rita's to open was a company-owned store. This company-owned store attempted to replicate the original Philadelphia experience, using word of mouth to expose customers both to the end product at the Rita's outlet, but also to the possibility of becoming a franchisee. Just like most business-to-business products need a sales force to help close the big sales, Rita's required a franchise sales force to follow up and close all of the leads that came into the new areas.

Like most franchises and other distribution channels, it is very important for the franchisor to continually manage the channel relationships so that each franchisee continues to perceive the value proposition that they are getting from the franchise relationship. Rita's, like most successful franchisors, attempts to have franchisees perceive themselves as members of Rita's extended family. If you as a franchisee perceive yourself as a "family member" of a very successful family, then many conflicts between franchisor and franchisee don't seem to crop up. Franchisees who perceive themselves in this way are going to be the best source of positive word of mouth for attracting new franchisees. Good entrepreneurial marketers know that *word of mouth* is the most *powerful, cost-effective marketing lever* a venture can have.

Rita's franchise has been able to counter one possible disadvantage of franchising in the best way. Rita's is not very worried about their franchisees opening up competitive outlets for a very simple reason. According to Bob Tumolo, Rita's CEO, the average Rita's has almost twice the revenue of competitors in the same area.[12] This is because the product's reputation, the expanded product line (including gelati and crème ice), and the cooperative marketing campaign have created perceived value for consumers that is much higher than Rita's competition. Rita's has been able to create a win-win situation in which *both the franchisor and the franchisee are better off with each other than they would be if they were not together.* This synergy objective should be the essence of not only effective franchise management, but also effective management of all distribution channel relationships.

From franchising, we next turn to a different aspect of channel management—how to manage and anticipate channel conflict.

MANAGING AND ANTICIPATING "CHANNEL CONFLICT"

Entrepreneurial firms can get in major trouble if their channel members perceive the firm as beginning to compete with them when they had not been competing before. Channel members are used to relating to their competitors and usually consider it "part of the game" to compete with their channel counterparts. For example, the specialty running stores that sell Brooks running shoes are used to competing with each other on the basis of service, location, and assortment, but typically not on price. If Brooks were to try to sell directly to runners and bypass the retail channel (using a catalog or the Internet), their retailers would get really upset and many would probably stop supporting Brooks. The retailers would feel that the implicit rules by which they had been operating had changed without their consent. Like any human being, that gets them very angry.

Managing channel conflicts leverages all of the marketing concepts we discuss in this book. You need to define roles for every channel member that are not conflicting and are easily understood. These roles should be consistent with the venture's segmentation and the offering bundle that is appropriate for each segment. The benefits that are added by different channel partners will not be valued the same by all of the target segments. The channel partners will end up making the most money if they are matched with the segments that value the channel partner's benefits the highest. The channel partners also want to perceive that they are being treated fairly—which means being adequately compensated for the value that they add.

There is a big difference between channel conflict management at the beginning of a venture than when the firm wants to change the rules in the middle of the game. When a venture is beginning, the channel members should understand their role and any potential conflicts before they become a partner. If you have done your job well of marketing the role of the channel member, and the channel member signs up, then there usually will not be any conflict problems. As long as the channel member perceives that his or her role has not changed and that you have not done anything to change his role or competitive situation, he will feel that he is being treated fairly. Human beings are comfortable when their expectations are fulfilled and not changed. However, if the firm wants to change the roles of the channel members after all the expectations have been fulfilled, there can be very big problems.

For example, when vineyards began to supply firms like Virtual Vineyards and Wine.com that sold wine directly to consumers over the Internet, the existing distributors and brick and mortar retailers became incensed. They pressured state legislatures all over the U.S. to outlaw alcohol sales over the Internet. So far, Florida, Georgia, and Kentucky have made it a felony to ship alcohol directly to consumers and at least 17 other states prohibit such sales.[13] The recent Supreme Court Decision that outlawed some of these prohibitions in states that let their intrastate wineries ship to consumers may level the playing field in some states. Rumors also go around that some distributors will refuse to support those vineyards that sell over the Internet. These distributors felt that the Internet e-tailers jeopardized their positions as exclusive representatives of vineyards in each state. If the e-tailers were already part of the picture when the distributors were signed, it would not have been a problem for the vineyards. Depending on the strength of the distributors and their importance to the venture's success, the entrepreneur may have to creatively pacify the existing distribution partners in order to change or update the channels. The Internet will be causing many entrepreneurs to creatively deal with channel conflicts as they try to leverage the Internet's benefits.

The best alternative is if the entrepreneur can restructure the roles of all the distribution partners so that every member of the channel becomes more productive and adds more value. This is the best "win-win" scenario. Herman Miller, Inc. seems to have found this win-win scenario in the way it has restructured its distribution channels to take advantage of the Web to target a new segment.[14] Herman Miller's core business is selling its sleek, ergonomic premium cubicle office furniture systems to major corporations under big contracts at volume discounts. According to *Sales and Marketing Magazine*:

> "The emphasis is on **big**. The company's network of more than 250 contract dealers typically nab five-year purchasing contracts to configure, deliver, and install millions of workstation components to thousands of a single customer's employees. They also go to extraordinary lengths to serve those customers. Dealers reupholster furniture,

reconfigure workstations as needs change, move employees' workstations to new offices, and provide ergonomic consultations."[15]

These big dealers are not able to sell ones and twos of chairs or workstations very economically. The burgeoning small office-home office (SOHO) market was not being served well by the big partners Herman Miller had for its core business. In order to serve the SOHO market, beginning in 1994, Herman Miller put a few items in Office Depot and other retailers targeted at that market segment. In June 1998, Herman Miller introduced its full-fledged online store targeted at selling to the SOHO segment. Before Herman Miller management communicated with its core dealers and released its programs to help its core dealers using the Web, the dealers were furious. When the Web site was first started, the dealers' perceptions were very different than Herman Miller's. Because Herman Miller had not done the appropriate marketing with their dealers, the dealers assumed that Herman Miller was out to directly compete with them. Herman Miller, to their credit, quickly realized they had a problem and began an intense program of communicating to the dealers that the online SOHO customers were a very different market segment from the major corporations in their core dealer market. They also communicated to the dealers that the same underlying configuration engine of their Web site was also available to help corporate customers more easily and efficiently deal with their Herman Miller partner dealer. The site was designed so that corporate customers, through their own customized intranets, would be able to develop their own configurations and price them in a much more efficient and productive manner. The dealers would still handle this corporate intranet business, but it would lower their costs significantly.

"But even if they don't go after new business, the system will significantly lower operating costs, because information only needs to be entered once," says Gary Ten Harmsel, senior vice president of distribution. "A dealer's average operating expense level runs in the 16% to 18% range, and this system can help [him] lower it to 12%. If you can take six points out of your operating expenses, pass some of that on to the customer, but also keep some for your future investment purposes, it's a win for everyone."[16]

Sometimes it is not possible to segment your market clearly so that different channels can be used for the different segments. If you are changing channels, to go on the Web and sell direct for example, it may be the best policy to make your existing channel your partner in the new channel.

Ethan Allen is typical of many ventures that have been selling through very selective retail distribution and decided that the Web was too big of a potential channel to ignore. Ethan Allen owns 25% of its bricks and mortar retail outlets. The other 75% are independently owned and operated under license. In order to use the Web effectively and to not alienate their licensees, Ethan Allen had really no choice but to make their licensed retailers partners in their Web operation. If they had opened up an independent Web operation, their retailers (to whom Ethan Allen is their sole supplier) would have been very upset with the new competition. The Ethan Allen CEO, M. Farooq Kathwari, made the only reasonable decision under the circumstances. "In exchange for a cut of the Internet revenue, the store owner would deliver much of the merchandise, accept returns, and handle the minor repairs often needed when furniture comes out of the crate."[17] Stores were also to be encouraged to make contact with people in their area who visit the Web site and express an interest in having decorating help.

Mr. Kathwari also realized that his dealers needed to correctly perceive the new role of the Web in their partnership with Ethan Allen. Before the Web site was launched, he met personally with each of the dealers (in groups) to explain to them how "We'll do this in a partnership. . . We don't want to bypass you."[18]

For established ventures with existing exclusive distribution, it is very difficult to bypass them without doing something like Ethan Allen. On the other hand, if Ethan Allen did not have well-defined territories for its dealers, the preceding partnership would have been very difficult to implement. However, if Ethan Allen had multiple dealers in an area, then the dealers would be used to competing with each other, and adding a Web competitor would not have been seen as such a direct threat to each dealer. Auto companies, for example, are not having as much trouble dealing with Web retailers for this reason.

CONCEPT TESTING TO CHANNEL MEMBERS

If the entrepreneurial marketer uses all the concepts and paradigms in this chapter and decides on his or her "optimal" distribution strategy and tactics, he or she still may not be successful. If the distribution channel members you have chosen won't do the part you expect, then the plan and venture may fall apart. It is at least as important to get channel members' reactions to your new entrepreneurial product(s) or services, as it is to get the reactions of the ultimate consumers. Just like consumer concept test-ing is best when the consumer is exposed to the product in the most real-istic manner possible, concept testing to the channel members is com-pletely analogous. The channel member should be exposed to your con-cept as realistically as possible. A nice brochure mock-up and descriptions of all the services you will supply to the channel member should typically be part of the concept. You also should let the channel member know explicitly what functions you expect him to perform as well. All tentative prices and terms should also be shown. If you have done concept testing with customers of this channel member, it can be helpful to summarize those results as part of the concept. Consumer concept testing results can be powerful arguments for convincing a retailer to carry your product.

The channel member should answer a similar type of question to that the end consumer is asked: "How likely will you be to buy and carry this prod-uct or service?" "What do you like best about this concept? What about the concept could be improved?" If the channel members are all "extremely likely" to buy and carry your product, then you can feel very confident that the distribution channel plan will work as you hoped. On the other hand, if only a small fraction of the channel members are excit-ed by your offering, you have problems that need fixing before introduc-tion. Just as testing a product with real consumers can give the entrepre-neur excellent feedback that may be very different than her logic and planning, the concept testing to the channel members can be even more valuable. There may be aspects of your offering bundle that you never even considered that are very important to the channel members.

CONCLUSION

The concepts, options, and examples in this chapter should encourage you as an entrepreneurial marketer to give the attention, creativity, and resources to the distribution channel decisions that they deserve. The cre-ative juggling of different items for different time periods juxtaposed with decisions on direct, exclusive, selective, or intensive distribution can make big differences in how the firm's offering is perceived by its target segment(s). These differences in perception can have large impacts on the firm's ultimate profitability. Just as with the end customer, concept testing the offering with channel members is typically a very cost-effective way to "reality check" all of your major distribution plan assumptions.

ENDNOTES

1. Pitt, Leyland; Berthon, Pierre; and Berthon, Jean-Paul; "Changing Channels: The Impact of the Internet on Distribution Strategy," *Business Horizons*, March–April, 1999, pp. 19–28.

2. Ibid, p. 20.

3. Millman, Gregory J, "Blockbuster Bricks and Clicks," *Outlook Journal*, June 2005.

4. Flint, Joe, and Kelly, Kate, "New Signs of Strain for Blockbuster," *Wall Street Journal*, September 19, 2005, p. B5.

5. Marcus, Jillian M., "Eight Legs and an Amazing Feat," Harvard Business School, Note 394–444, 1994.

6. Gallagher, Leigh, "Runner's World," *Forbes*, Feb. 22, 1999, pp. 96, 98.

7. Ibid, p. 98.

8. Ibid.

9. Ibid.

10. Some of these advantages and disadvantages come from discussions with Craig Tractenberg, an experienced franchise attorney with Buchanan, Ingersoll in Philadelphia, 1999.

11. Ritasice.com Web site, 1999.

12. Personal communication with Leonard Lodish, 1999.

13. Garner, Rochelle, "Mad as Hell," *Sales and Marketing Management,* June 1999, p. 55.

14. Ibid, p. 58.

15. Ibid.

16. Ibid, pp. 58, 59.

17. Hagery, James R., "Ethan Allen's Revolutionary Path to Web," *Wall Street Journal*, July 29, 1999, p. B1.

18. Ibid.

5

Product Launch to Maximize Product/Service Lifetime Profitability

	Products/Services	Equity/Shares	Image
Customers			
Users			
Investors			
Supply Chain/ Channel Partners			
Employees			

The most crucial time in the marketing of a new product or service is the initial rollout. Because "first impressions last," it is essential for an entrepreneurial venture to successfully launch its product. In fact, in the world of Internet mania, the difference between an initial rollout being a success or a dud can mean literally billions of dollars in market capitalization. Much can be learned even before the launch of a new idea, using the "beta test" process to gather feedback and jump-start the customer acquisition process. This means choosing the most appropriate reference accounts, gaining those reference accounts, getting the press on board, and ironing out the bugs in the several months, weeks, or, in Internet time, days before a formal product launch. Most importantly, it means getting great referrals from delighted, influential reference accounts.

To properly plan and execute a product launch, it is imperative that marketing confirm the product availability date. Development and marketing must be in lock-step to ensure an effective launch. Unfortunately, problems do arise, bugs get discovered, and supplier commitments slip, so dates do change. Marketing must take ownership for staying in communication on the development schedule. The sidebar summarizes all of these necessary activities.

PRODUCT LAUNCH CHECKLIST

- **Confirm and monitor product development timelines.**
- **Secure initial reference customers.**
  - Identify target reference customers.
  - Create a strategy to reach these customers.
  - Establish a compelling offer for these initial customers.
    - What benefits do they receive beyond the product benefits?
    - What do you expect from them in return?
  - Determine an internal resource plan to ensure successful implementations.
    - Sales
    - Account support
    - Technical support
    - Escalation process
    - Product/experience feedback process
  - Execute.
- **Secure external support for your product.**
  - Analysts
  - Industry experts
  - Consultants
- **Define partnering opportunities.**
  - To add credibility that the product will be successful
  - To improve the opportunity for publicity
- **Include your channel/distributors in the product launch.**
  - Create supporting marketing materials and collateral.

REFERENCE ACCOUNTS

In selling any product, nothing helps as much as strong references. This is especially true for products that are highly priced, mission critical, or perceived as risky. Enterprise software is a good example. Customers take a great leap of faith to believe the value proposition that you communicate via advertising or promotional materials. For them to believe what they hear from other experienced users is merely an act of trust that those users have no incentive to lie about your product's virtues and faults. Reference accounts provide for an organized word-of-mouth campaign, so that when the press and key targeted accounts need to hear from non-company sources, there are users to call.

The benefits to the company from a good reference account are great—credibility with peers of that account, spokespeople to talk with the press, and examples to use in advertising and PR. In essence, you are trying to create "Cow Bell" accounts. "Cow Bell" accounts are those accounts that you want the world to know are your customers. You want to create as much noise as possible about the fact that they chose your product. Therefore, care should be taken to identify the ideal reference customers. The choice of who to get as initial reference accounts can have a huge impact on how fast (or whether) the product is adopted by the market. For Trust-Aid (see example later in the chapter), if the initial reference account had been a bank that other banks looked to for guidance on new technological innovations, the sales progress of Trust-Aid would have been much faster.

In most markets, there are individuals and entities that are known as early adopters and leaders in technology application. If these leaders are first to adopt your product, then the going will be much easier than if your first reference accounts are not respected as leaders. The medical market is probably the best defined in this dimension. For most new prescription drugs or new medical devices, who the first users are is crucial to whether they may become successful. Doctors have a "pecking order" of prestige and respectability. They will be much more likely to try a new innovation if it is first adopted by the physicians they perceive as highly influential in their field.

REACHING TARGET REFERENCE CUSTOMERS

Once identified, strategies need to be created to reach these companies. In addition to leveraging your existing network, don't hesitate to use your board of directors, investors, your advisors, or even your vendors such as accountants to establish introductions into your targeted companies.

While many new companies rely on these networks for introductions that lead to their first set of customers, it is amazing how many companies don't. It is not professional, nor will it be productive to ask investors or board members for a list of whom they know. The company must do the work to narrow a target list of potential reference companies. With this narrowed list, it is then appropriate to ask your network if they can assist you with introductions. This request should not be made via an email distribution list. People's relationships are typically guarded. When you ask someone to make an introduction, you are asking him or her to take a risk. They are risking that you will have something valuable to offer their contact and will be able to deliver.

Vendors such as law firms and accountants can be excellent sources of introductions. They typically organize their firm's professionals around industries and geographies. Even if the person who serves your company can't help, he might be able to find someone in the firm who can. Because you are his customer, he is usually willing to help where appropriate.

ESTABLISH A COMPELLING OFFER

Once identified, the venture must secure these initial reference customers. The targeted reference accounts themselves need a compelling reason to take the initial risk associated with being a first customer of a product. They need to understand what benefits they receive and what the company expects from them in return. Remember, the benefits received must outweigh the natural inertia to wait for someone else to try your product first, or worse, for them to use a competing product. These benefits often take the form of reduced pricing (at least for a long initial period), increased training, and far greater and more responsive support than later customers may find (although hopefully the product's bugs will have been ironed out and less support will be needed).

It is also critical to communicate, and ideally to contractually commit a targeted reference account to what you expect from them in support of your product launch. It's not helpful to have a successful implementation, only to learn your customer has a corporate policy prohibiting joint press releases with product vendors. The following is a list of examples of marketing support you can request from your customers:

- Joint press release announcing use of the product
- Use of their name as a product user in marketing materials and on the Web site
- Participation in a case study highlighting benefits of the product
- Participation in a seminar or Webinars
- Take calls from press and prospective customers

Sometimes, the value to a venture of an initial customer is important enough to make a deal with a customer that would otherwise pain the CFO. In the 1970s, an MBA student at Wharton who had developed a time-shared computer program to automate the trust accounting process for banks started what became the SEI Corp. He wanted to commercialize the software and an associated support service for bank trust departments to use. His competition during that time were in-house accounting machines and manual calculations, for the most part. Without his product (called Trust-Aid), when IBM declared a dividend, someone manually had to go into each different trust account to enter that event so it was accounted for correctly. Conceptually, adopting Trust-Aid should have been a very easy decision for any bank based on very high value in use. However, as the student quickly found out, no bank was going to put its "family jewels," its trust accounts, onto a system that no one else had shown to be reliable and to actually work. He asked his teacher, one of this book's co-authors, for advice. The advice was simple. "You need to get a very credible reference account, and even if you have to give the software and service away for free, it'll be very worth it." That is exactly what the student did to get his first customer. He gave it away for free for over a year to his first "customer." He was not very happy about not having any initial revenue for a year, but it was probably the only way the company (now with a market cap in the billions) would have gotten started.

It wasn't until that first customer had run the system for nine months without using the old manual system as a back up, that the student got his first paying customer (at still reduced "charter rates"). The first customer was really only a credible reference after he had put his trust department "family jewels" in the care of the Trust-Aid software and service and had stopped using the old manual system. Even when the reference account had both systems running (with Trust-Aid running very successfully), he was not a credible or convincing reference site until he had demonstrated his own faith in the software and service.

BUILD INTERNAL RESOURCE PLAN TO ENSURE A SUCCESSFUL LAUNCH

The SEI example highlights the importance of ensuring your first customer(s) are completely satisfied with your product and their experience with the company. This doesn't happen by accident. Spend the time upfront to establish your internal resource plan to ensure a successful implementation.

The plan starts with sales. Most companies that are willing to be first users tend to be early adopters. Because these innovators know that they are taking a risk, they prefer to work directly with the company to mitigate additional risks associated with going through intermediaries. Regardless of the distribution channel decisions you've made, the best approach is to ask the potential reference account how they want to be treated. You may have to either hire a direct sales force if the number of initial customers requires it, or as the entrepreneur, you and other senior managers may assume the sales role directly.

Geoffrey Moore, in his excellent book *Crossing the Chasm*, also recommends a small, top-level sales force as a way to deal, in particular, with those innovators he terms "visionaries,"[1] to manage their expectations during the sales and initial usage process.

"Because controlling expectations is so crucial, the only practical way to do business with visionaries is through a small, top-level direct sales force. At the front end of the sales cycle, you need such a group to understand the visionaries' goals and give them confidence that your company can step up to those. In the middle of the sales cycle, you need to be extremely flexible about commitments as you begin to adapt to the visionaries' agenda. At the end, you need to be careful in negotiations, keeping the spark of the vision alive without committing to tasks that are unachievable within the time frame allotted. All of this implies a mature and sophisticated representative working on your behalf."[2]

Once the sale is finally closed, the venture must be ready with plans to provide account support and technical support. Many times the person responsible for the initial sales takes responsibility for ongoing account support. He or she must make sure that whatever happens, the initial client's expectations are exceeded. Salespeople tend to respond directly to the financial incentives inherent in their compensation structure—i.e., they focus on the tasks that will generate the most income. During this phase, it is important that the salesperson is compensated not only for the sale, but also for customer satisfaction. This can be measured and paid when the customer agrees to be a reference. Many companies forget this step and don't understand when the salesperson is off selling the next accounts and not adequately focusing on ensuring that the current customer is being well managed.

The referrals of these initial users are what the business will live on. If this initial salesperson is not a senior manager, this person should have direct authority from the CEO to do whatever is necessary to exceed this customer's expectations. Likewise, engineering and development must be prepared to respond very quickly to technical issues or problems that arise.

One mistake that entrepreneurs sometimes make is to neglect to put in place processes for escalation of issues and for customer feedback on the product or experience with the company. Although it is important to make the product work as represented, it is equally important to solicit feedback on the overall value received and what could be done to make the product even more valuable.

A very successful Israeli high-tech company had established a very nice North American business selling products and services to call centers through VARs (Value-Added Resellers) and large equipment vendors. They had a different new product targeted toward security departments of large firms. The firm originally planned to use the same type of sales and distribution (VARs) to introduce the new security product and large equipment vendors. However, after interviewing the potential innovators, the company had to change their initial marketing plan. The innovative potential initial customers were not receptive to dealing with intermediaries. They wanted to deal directly with the company. The company used its senior managers as direct salespeople and began a very successful rollout of its new, innovative, security product. If they had not asked their initial target customers how they wanted to be treated, they would have had significant problems in penetrating the market.

THE BETA PROCESS

Most products go through many revisions between the concept and final versions. The changes are often stimulated by real user feedback to the engineering and product management teams. The process that helps this to happen is the beta process. The terminology is in common use in engineering hardware and software areas, where the first versions of a product are called "alpha" versions, the first versions that can go to customers for testing are called "beta," the almost final versions are called "release candidates," and the final versions are called the released product.

At each stage, successively more users and/or customers have the product in hand and are making comments to the product management team. This process is normally run by, and of benefit to, the engineering department. Properly managed, however, it can be a great help to the marketing of the product.

In today's Internet world, beta users provide the buzz, and amplify the presence once the service is launched openly to the world. Where in the past beta testing was usually limited to a few customers, or a few dozen, there are now cases where the number of beta users is in the tens of thousands. Microsoft Windows 95 had over 100,000 beta users, and Netscape Communicator usually has a beta version and a shipping (frozen) version available for download most of the time.

When customers agree to join a beta program, they usually agree to spend some minimum amount of time using the product, to respond to questionnaires about the features and benefits of the product, and to be available for calls from the press or other customers. In return, their questions and problems should be dealt with at high priority, and they can gain visibility to their peer groups as thought leaders, as well as the psychic income of seeing their name in print in interviews and articles about the product.

Choosing the right customers is very important since they will not only influence the press, but also provide the most cogent feedback at a key time when the offering may still be changed. Customers whose needs are not aligned with a majority of intended users could skew product features in an undesirable direction. In the software world, beta customers are often chosen from existing users of previous products. Such customers are already predisposed to a company, and can get the extra benefits of additional support and relationships to help if they have problems with any product.

On the Web, many offerings are completely new, and there is no customer tradition. In this case, make a list of the key target customers—whether they are Fortune 500 companies, Inc. 500 newcomers, consumers of certain demographics, and so on Then, network into a decision maker who is willing to listen to the benefits of a new product, and convince him or her that his or her company will benefit from being a first mover—not only through discounts, but also through having a several month advantage over any competitors. For consumer sites, there may be specific discounts, and the ability to say, "I've been there first."

iExchange.com, a site that permits people to share stock market advice and rates them on the accuracy of their predictions, needed to beta test for two reasons. The first involved the usual issues of making sure the programming was properly done and that the servers could handle the loads. Second, in order for the site to be attractive to general users, there needed to be enough predictions, about enough stocks, to give interesting content to new users. As an idealab! company, iExchange.com first called on all the people in the idealab! building (about 150) and asked them to post recommendations. The incentive offered was free pizza and T-shirts. After two weeks of building several thousand recommendations, these people were asked to virally expand the beta test to their friends and family members, by sending them emails promising prizes for their entries.

During this beta period, users were periodically asked for comments about the user interfaces, their interactions, and their overall comments about the site, including look and feel, mission, and effectiveness. Their movements through the site were tracked with software that could show each successive click, and determine when they were leaving the site. All this information was fed to the product managers and developers each day, and changes were made to improve the length of time and number of page views per visit, as well as the overall performance of the site.

As you reach the later stages of the beta process, it is important to have critics, as well as friends, test the site or the new product. People with a real need and use for the product will provide a less-filtered set of responses than those who are merely friends doing a favor. It is often the harshest critic who provides the spark for a feature change that turns him or her into a fan—and makes the site that much better for all other users.

InsiderPages.com, a Web site tagged "the Yellow Pages written by your friends," allows people to rate local merchants, either positively or negatively, and have those ratings accessible by their friends and others. In order for this type of site to be useful, it has to have a meaningful number of reviews and categories. This attracts new users, who then post their own reviews and further build the network. A beta test period was necessary to make sure it was easy for users to get their reviews in. For example, the system is designed to scour your Outlook contacts looking for words such as Doctor, Engineer, Plumber, and so on. Making that process simple and intuitive took several retries on the code during the beta process.

Users were asked for feedback throughout the process, and observed while using the system (for those users at the InsiderPages.com facility). After several weeks, the internal users were able to invite friends from outside the InsiderPages and idealab! communities. The spread of new users was carefully monitored, and comments fed to the product and development teams. This led to the creation of a marketing program that offered a $5 Starbucks card for the first three reviews posted. Once a critical mass of reviews (about 5,000) and users (about 2,000) was achieved in Los Angeles, the product was opened up from beta. The beta period allowed many adjustments to be made without the fear of a very large user community being unhappy with any particular change.

AutoDesk, an extremely successful software maker for Computer Aided Design and Manufacturing, understands how important their beta accounts are. They have a department whose responsibility is only to follow up every comment, suggestion, or problem that arises during the beta test process. This group is charged with communicating to the reference account about exactly what happened with every suggestion made during the reference, beta test process. Each reference customer is never left hanging about whether their suggestions or feedback were integrated into the released version of the product. Even if their suggestion is not implemented, the reference account is told why it wasn't. For many organizations, this step of saying what *was not implemented* in the new product is not completed. It is human nature not to want to give your important reference account bad news. However, such news is still very valuable to the account. This kind of communication adds a tremendous amount of credibility to the AutoDesk organization and gives their reference accounts a big signal that AutoDesk is trustworthy. This management of the reference, beta test process is one reason why AutoDesk has maintained the clear leadership in its marketplace for more than 10 years.

For B2B products or services, finding initial customers may be more difficult. You have to convince them to try something that may not succeed, and hence could leave them stranded if they are not careful. And the growth may be much slower. This is why it is so important to choose influential innovators and early adopters to be the initial customers. It also is critical to market to them in the best way.

The need for reference accounts is tied to a product, not to the company. The process for securing reference customers takes place with each new product introduction. Buyers don't attribute references across product lines; they want to know that others have successfully used the specific product they are considering. MetricStream, a quality and compliance software provider, had been selling software to large companies to manage their operational compliance needs, such as those dictated by the FDA, ISO9000, and Six Sigma. Despite the fact that they had customers such as Pfizer, Hitachi, and Subway successfully using their software, when they launched their Sarbanes-Oxley compliance module, they needed references for that specific module in order to successfully sell it. They established a charter customer program that provided pricing discounts, enhanced support, and consulting. This program enabled MetricStream to obtain their first few customers for the Sarbanes-Oxley module.

This practice is not limited to small companies. Companies as large as IBM establish incentives to acquire their first set of customers for a new product. These incentives are targeted at the sales force and at prospective customers. Salespeople are typically offered bonuses or accelerators to their commission plans for selling new products. Likewise, customers are offered discounts or attractive benefits for being early adopters.

SECURE EXTERNAL SUPPORT FOR YOUR PRODUCT

In addition to having strong reference customers, external support from un-biased entities is quite valuable. Many industries have analysts whose opinions are valued by potential customers when making a purchasing decision. Establishing a good review from one or more of these analysts can provide excellent credibility to your product.

Analysts can deliver real value for a company launching a product. Analysts have two main constituencies: vendors selling a product and companies who need help and assistance in selecting products. Most analysts publish research and provide a list of vendors that they have evaluated and are recommending. Getting on those lists and being included in the research can expand your visibility tremendously. Analysts are also aware of companies in the buying processes and can introduce your company into a sales process. They can also provide your company with information on purchase trends, marketing direction, and competition.

To take advantage of these opportunities, you need to educate them about your company strategy and products. You need to provide the information in the framework of the industry you serve. Analysts strive to be the expert in their area of focus. They will be less interested in hearing about why your product is so great and more interested in understanding what gap currently exists in the marketplace and your company's approach to filling it. Even when you aren't a paying customer of an analyst, you can get their attention. Analysts will typically meet with non-paying companies in their focus area once a year. Why? Because as experts, they need to be aware of what's happening in the market and who the players are.

Industry experts represent another avenue to consider. While it might be difficult to get an explicit product endorsement, there are other ways to leverage them for credibility. Invite them to speak at a key event during your launch. You can also consider recruiting them as board members, or advisory board members. NorthPoint is a classic example. NorthPoint communications was a telecommunications DSL provider that was purchased by AT&T in 2001. In the early days, following the founding of NorthPoint, they needed to establish credibility in the telecommunications industry. Their competitors were the well-established Baby Bells and other new upstart companies. To add credibility and break out of the pack, NorthPoint successfully recruited Reed Hundt, the former FCC Chairman, to join their board. His participation on the Board of Directors indirectly gave validity and notability to NorthPoint over competitors.

PARTNERING FOR LAUNCH

When Intel or Microsoft announces a new product, they release a list of companies that are "supporting" the new platform or processor. These partners help validate the eventual success, and hence make it easier for a large company customer to take a chance. Once they know that others will be using it also, they feel less afraid of being left stranded, or of being unable to convince the supplier to fix the product if it isn't working.

Smaller companies can also improve their chances of success on a product launch, by including the testimonials and support of a number of key strategic and tactical partners in their announcement

When Viewpoint.com prepared to launch its new Viewpoint 3D format, which allows low bandwidth streaming of 3D content on the Internet, it wanted the credibility that strong partners bring to a new effort. Two months prior to launch, a concerted effort was undertaken to sign up partners who could participate in the launch event. Microsoft, Intel, and AOL all had an interest in seeing 3D proliferate on the Web. For Intel, it meant a need for more processing power; for Microsoft, a leg up for its Internet Explorer 5.5 browser; and for AOL, better e-commerce. In addition, a number of companies that wanted to use the technology on their Web sites, including Nike, Sony, and CBS, all agreed.

Each of the partners got strong press exposure, the ability to add to their own leadership and forward-thinking images, and early use of the technology. Viewpoint.com, because it was linked with such powerful partners, got coverage in *The New York Times*, CNBC, and other prime media venues that probably wouldn't have covered the story, or featured it, because of the names associated with the launch.

The business development and technical organizations, rather than the straight marketing and sales forces, had to make the introductions and connections to the partners, since those organizations had to be convinced that the technology would succeed before they could approach their own marketing and public relations operations. The lead-time for such endorsements is long—typically two to three months—and it pays to create the relationships between your company and possible partners even sooner.

CHANNELS OF DISTRIBUTION

When creating your launch plan, don't forget your channel/distributors. If you've decided to leverage these entities, ensure that they are part of your launch plan. For example, they will need training, lead-time for creating their own marketing materials and go-to-market plan. They need to be brought into the planning process as early as possible so that they can be an effective sales engine when the product is ready.

These channels also represent publicity opportunities—coordinate press releases, pubic relations plans, and event participation. In some cases, your channel may be better established than your company is. Therefore they may be more likely to get extended press coverage. By coordinating, you can ensure that these opportunities are leveraged and that the messaging is on target with your strategy. These activities can create not only better reach into the marketplace, but will also strengthen your relationships with your channels.

CONCLUSION

A strong product rollout can set the tone for success, and dramatically reduce the time needed to gain customer and market acceptance. Planning for this requires sufficient time prior to launch, choosing the best reference accounts, treating them well, and sufficient feedback from a well-run beta program. Rolling out a Web site, or Web-based business, can be done more rapidly, but still requires testing and trials to see how consumers react to each piece of the Web site.

ENDNOTES

1. Moore, Geoffrey A., *Crossing the Chasm*, New York: Harper Business, 1995, p. 37.

2. Ibid, p. 37.

6

Entrepreneurial Advertising That Works—Vaguely Right or Precisely Wrong?

	Products/Services	Equity/Shares	Image
Customers			
Users			
Investors			
Supply Chain/ Channel Partners			
Employees			

Advertising is probably the most misused (and misunderstood) marketing instrument by entrepreneurial ventures of all sizes. As we discuss in this chapter, many entrepreneurs and other managers believe that advertising is too difficult to evaluate on a cost/benefit basis. Using many large, frequently purchased packaged goods companies as examples, many entrepreneurs have adopted many of those larger firms' approaches to advertising. These advertising approaches have a number of "rules" that help a firm or its advertising agencies to make some advertising management decisions. Examples of some of these "rules" include the following:

1. The incremental revenue produced by advertising is not worthwhile to measure, so don't even try.

2. If an area or market segment has x% of revenues, it should get x% of the advertising exposures—its "fair share."

3. If you want to achieve a market share of x%, you must maintain an advertising budget that is greater than x% of the amount spent by all the competitors in the category.

4. You should pulse advertising expenditures into periodic flights, which will cut through all of the competitive clutter.

5. You need at least three advertising exposures on a consumer to have an effect. Any less than three has no impact.

6. Advertising takes a long time to work, and its long-term effect is difficult to measure, but is there.

7. If you believe TV advertising works, then more TV advertising is obviously better than less.

These "rules" become mental models that many firms use as rules of thumb to make their advertising decision-making easier. Many companies have repeated these and other similar rules so often that they have become analogous to a religion. Many advertising decisions are thus made on faith.

Entrepreneurs can't run their businesses on faith. They must allocate scarce capital resources to maximize their value to the venture. Advertising is only one alternative use of scarce resources. Other marketing elements like promotion, public relations, and the sales force compete for resources with other uses such as working capital, new production equipment, and so on. We will show in this chapter that it *is* possible to evaluate the potential incremental return versus cost for advertising. These returns can then be compared with other uses of scarce capital resources to enable the entrepreneur to make the most productive use of her available resources. However, as we will show, these methods for estimating returns are imprecise, but they are the best that can be done under the circumstances. We will show that it is better to be "vaguely right" rather than using rules such as the preceding ones, which are "precisely wrong."

In order to emphasize how misunderstood advertising is, even by the large "sophisticated" firms, we first show some recently published research that analyzes the incremental sales effectiveness of their TV advertising. We then describe methodologies that entrepreneurs can use to make decisions on advertising so as to be able to at least roughly analyze advertising's return and compare it to other uses for the scarce resources.

The seismic shift to online, highly measurable advertising as represented in search engine marketing is a key arrow in the modern advertiser's quiver. Next, we discuss how this shift (over $15 billion advertising dollars in 2005) can be used to an entrepreneurial venture's advantage today.

EVEN LARGE FIRMS WASTE A LOT OF THEIR ADVERTISING EXPENDITURES

Two well-researched articles[1, 2] provide convincing evidence that even the largest TV advertisers can significantly improve the productivity of their TV advertising. The study, sponsored by all the major packaged goods marketers, analyzed almost 400 in-market, split-cable, year-long TV advertising tests using the Behaviorscan system, a service of Information Resources, Inc.

Behaviorscan is a household purchasing panel comprising approximately 3,000 demographically representative households from each of six geographically dispersed markets. All supermarket purchases are recorded via scanners and linked to individual household identification to measure precise purchasing behavior.

In addition, households receive all of their television transmissions via cable technology, and advertising can be directed to or removed from individual households on a targeted basis. This capability has allowed the execution of numerous carefully controlled advertising experiments. Media weights, media plan configuration, and many other advertising variables have been experimentally tested using this technology.

The tests that were analyzed were those in which some panelists received a different level of TV advertising than others for a year. These tests give very valid estimates of the incremental revenue impact of the tested campaigns. The study showed that only 33% of TV advertising for established brands was showing a statistically significant incremental sales response to this TV advertising. On the other hand, when TV ads worked, they produced big volume effects (a mean increase of 18% in sales), the effects lasted for a period of over two years, and they emerged surprisingly fast (within six months, in most cases). The difference between the ads that worked and those that didn't was mostly idiosyncratically related to the copy that the campaigns used. There were more frequently run smaller brands ads that worked, while ads that promoted the status quo did not work as well as ads that tried to change something or impart "news." "What you say" was much more important than "how much you say it."

These 400 in-market tests also cast much doubt on each of the "rules" in this chapter's introduction. All of these "rules" were not supported by the incremental sales response to TV advertising shown in the tests.

HOW ENTREPRENEURS CAN IMPROVE THE PRODUCTIVITY OF THEIR ADVERTISING

The key advertising decisions are typically categorized as budget (how much should I spend?), media planning (where and when should I place the advertising?), and copy (what should I say?). Many books have been written on how best to make these decisions. However, you will probably not have the luxury of trying all the different theories (most of which have not been shown to be fully validated to help entrepreneurs make more productive advertising decisions). Instead, you must do the best with what you have—little money and little time. In that spirit, the following methods and concepts should be helpful.

Typically, the entrepreneurial business gets an idea for an advertising and/or promotion campaign from someone (the owner, an employee, an agency, a customer, a friend, or an advisor). The "campaign" is typically a combination of media, copy, and budget. Examples might be—"let's run ads on the radio to announce our new line of auto accessories," or "let's put out circulars with our menu and a coupon for a free drink to the new office building that just got finished." Conceptually, what is needed is a way to evaluate whether the campaign will generate enough incremental revenue so that the incremental margin contributed by the incremental revenue will more than cover the advertising and or promotion expense. As long as this return is better than other uses for the campaign funds (including other possible different campaigns), the campaign should be continued.

The big problems are evaluating the incremental return of the campaign and generating campaigns that are even better. We first describe concepts and methods for evaluating incremental returns and next discuss methods for improving the campaigns before they are evaluated. We should emphasize here that the procedures to help with these evaluations are not as precise as evaluating some other uses for capital. However, they are the best that the entrepreneur can do in the typical circumstances in which she finds herself. This situation calls for being "vaguely right" versus being "precisely wrong." The preceding "rules" are examples of the "precisely wrong" way to approach advertising or promotion decisions. These rules are easy to apply and can be calculated very precisely, but they have been shown not to generate campaigns that are incrementally profitable. We next show some ways to handle campaign evaluation.

EVALUATING CAMPAIGNS—"VAGUELY RIGHT" VERSUS "PRECISELY WRONG"

For many entrepreneurial businesses, the incremental impact of campaigns is obvious if you are intelligently watching the daily revenues and either consciously or subconsciously relating daily revenues to the current advertising and promotion campaign. If the business is direct to the customer, you can also ask customers coming in, calling in, or logging on to the Web site if the advertising or promotion was involved in their decision to purchase. You have to estimate one number to compare to the actual achieved revenue. That number is "what would revenue have been without the advertising or promotion campaign." This number can be "vaguely" estimated by using combinations of differences in revenue in prior periods and differences in revenues from the area getting the campaign, versus the same time periods in other areas that were not subject to the campaign. If the data is available, the best comparison to use for evaluating a campaign is the difference between revenues per week during the campaign versus before the campaign started compared to the same numbers for areas in which the campaign was not used over the same time periods.

For example, if a campaign ran during May only in Cleveland, and sales per week increased by 25% in May compared to the prior three months, the first estimate you might make would be that the campaign increased sales by 25%. However, the next thing to look at would be: How did a comparable area without the campaign do in May? You could use the rest of the U.S. as a comparison, or a market you judge to be similar, perhaps Detroit or Pittsburgh. If Detroit was up 5% in May, Pittsburgh was up 7%, and the rest of the U.S. was up 3%, you could reasonably estimate that the campaign might have increased revenues by about 20% more than they would have been had the campaign not run. The big assumption you are making when using such an estimating procedure is that no *other causes were responsible for the difference between the area with the campaign and the other areas.* For example, was something else also going on in Cleveland that might have caused the sales increases—such as competitive activities, weather, public relations activities, and so on? The same questions need to be asked about the areas used for comparisons—the "pseudo" controls for this "pseudo experiment." This kind of estimating and analysis is called "pseudo experimentation" because there is not random assignment of the campaign to one area versus another. Without random assignment, one can never be sure that there wasn't some other reason than the campaign that was affecting the revenues.

It has always been amazing to see how many firms, both large and small, don't take the simple necessary steps even to attempt to analyze the impact of campaigns. If they don't keep the data, they can't do any evaluation. If you don't do any evaluation, then you can't improve the campaigns or discontinue the ones that aren't working. Businesses should keep track of exactly what is occurring daily in each campaign and put it in the same place electronically as the revenue numbers.

AN EXAMPLE

As an example, a national retailer of consumer electronics thought it was keeping track of its advertising and promotion programs. The way the data was stored could best be described as "market status reporting."[3] The data was there for managers to find out what they did in each market each day of the week. However, since the data was structured in the computers, it was impossible to do any kind of analysis of the incremental impact of the advertising or promotion programs that the firm ran. An example of how the data looked as it was stored in the computers is in Figure 6-1.[4]

ELEMENT	ADVERTISING SCHEDULE		PLAN PD		5			PAGE	
ACCOUNTABILITY	ADV DIRECTOR		MEETING		PLANNING			VERSION 12/06/89	
MARKET									

WEEK NO	1	SUNDAY 8/20/89	MONDAY 8/21/89	TUESDAY 8/22/89	WEDNESDAY 8/23/89	THURSDAY 8/24/89	FRIDAY 8/25/89	SATURDAY 8/26/89	WEEK 1
HOLIDAY									
EVENT	TY	/----SUPER SALE----				/-1 DAY SALE-/----------------			/
	LY	/----BACK TO SCHOOL ROP----			/----ENDLESS SUMMER 8 PAGE TAB----			/	
ACTIVITY	TY	AM (6X18) 6000			PM/ (6X18) C			AM (6X18) 7500	
		TV 195 PTS. 8000	RADIO (100 PTS.) 3000	TV	TV				
TOT EXP	TY	14000	3000	0	0	0	0	7500	24500
	LY	8700	0	0	0	0	19644	0	28344
SALES*	TY	50	56	43	46	30	42	58	325
	LY	40	56	32	47	25	60	84	344
	BGT								
	HPF								
A/S	TY								0.0754

WEEK NO	2	SUNDAY 8/27/89	MONDAY 8/28/89	TUESDAY 8/29/89	WEDNESDAY 8/30/89	THURSDAY 8/31/89	FRIDAY 9/01/89	SATURDAY 9/02/89	WEEK 2
HOLIDAY									
EVENT	TY	/----END OF MONTH CLEARANCE SALE----			/----LABOR DAY EOS ROP----				
	LY	/----ENDLESS SUMMER----			/ /----LABOR DAY EOS ROP W/RADIO----				
ACTIVITY	TY	AM (6X18) 9500			(6X18) C		AM/PM (6X18) 5605		
			RADIO (200 PTS.) 6000						
TOT EXP	TY	9500	0	6000	0	0	5605	0	21105
	LY	6700	0	0	0	5290	10200	0	22190
SALES*	TY	44	38	43	48	35	43	83	334
	LY	54	53	46	56	42	47	72	369
	BGT								
	HPF								
A/S	TY								0.0632

*In '000 $

Figure 6-1   The historical data as stored

After the situation was analyzed, the data was restructured into a spreadsheet that looked like Table 6-1.[5]

Table 6-1   The data restructured for analysis

Day Number	Day of Week	Sales ($)	TV ($)	Print ($)	Radio ($)
1	Sunday	50,000	8,000	6,000	0
2	Monday	56,000	0	0	3,000
3	Tuesday	43,000	0	0	0
4	Wednesday	46,000	0	0	0
5	Thursday	30,000	0	0	0
6	Friday	42,000	0	0	0
7	Saturday	58,000	0	7,500	0
8	Sunday	44,000	0	0	0
9	Monday	38,000	0	9,500	0
10	Tuesday	43,000	0	0	6,000

(continues)

Table 6-1 (*continued*)

Day Number	Day of Week	Sales ($)	TV ($)	Print ($)	Radio ($)
11	Wednesday	48,000	0	0	0
12	Thursday	35,000	0	0	0
13	Friday	43,000	0	5,605	0
14	Saturday	83,000	0	0	0

Using pretty standard regression analysis, we were able to estimate the incremental sales impacts of the firm's advertising. The software used for the analysis was Microsoft Excel, which is widely available, and very inexpensive. If doing statistical analysis is difficult for you, any statistics graduate student at a nearby university could help you out at very nominal costs. They actually *like* to do these kinds of analyses!

The regression model related each day's total sales to print, radio, and TV advertising during that day and each of the prior seven days, as well as sales during the same day last year, and the number of stores in operation that day. The analysis was able to show the impact of one dollar spent in a Sunday newspaper insert on incremental sales for each day of the following week (see Figure 6-2).

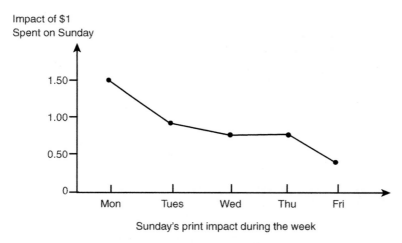

Figure 6-2 Sunday's ad impact on Monday through Friday

The analysis was able to estimate the average incremental revenue per $1 spent in all of the media options analyzed (see Table 6-2).

Table 6-2   Estimated incremental sales associated with $1 of advertising

TV Sunday	12.07**
Radio during week	5.91*
TV during week	5.27**
Print Sunday	5.06**
Print during week	Non-significant
Radio Saturday	Non-significant
Print Saturday	Non-significant

*$p < 0.10$

**$p < 0.01$

The relative impact of the various media and days of the week was very helpful to the firm in scheduling for their next campaigns. They used more TV on Sunday and cut back on other print. They did more weekday radio and less weekend radio.

The preceding example utilized naturally occurring experiments to determine the incremental revenue impact of an advertising campaign, after the campaigns had run. The statistical analysis used a multiple of last year's sales in each store as an estimate of what might have occurred had the advertising campaign not been run. A better approach to campaign evaluation is using planned experiments instead of naturally occurring experiments.

"VAGUELY RIGHT" ENTREPRENEURIAL MARKETING EXPERIMENTATION

The basic idea behind planned experiments is very simple. You want to try a campaign on subsegment(s) of the market and be able to estimate what the revenue would have been had the campaign not been run, by comparing the areas in which the campaign ran to those in which it didn't. In order to be as confident as possible that your valuation of the campaign is as "vaguely right" as possible, there are five ideal characteristics that an experiment should have. As an entrepreneur, you will not be able to execute perfect experiments, but they don't have to be. The experiments only need to help you go with the campaigns that work best and not spend money on campaigns that are not productive. The five characteristics that you should shoot for in designing market tests or experiments are the following:

1. The assignment of which areas or subjects will get the campaign or the control (nothing different) should be random. Flipping a coin or throwing dice are fine ways to fulfill this requirement.

2. Nothing else could have caused the results observed except for the campaign you are testing.

3. The results can be logically projected to the firm's real marketing situation in which the campaign would be used.

4. The experimental campaign must precede the sales effects it is supposed to cause.

5. There must be a comparison group that did not receive the campaign or received a different campaign.

The most important characteristic is number one—random assignment. If this does not happen, there is a persistent danger that those exposed to the campaign may in some ways be different from those not exposed.

EVALUATION BEFORE IS MORE VALUABLE THAN AFTER

You should realize at this point that if the evaluation of the incremental revenue attributable to the campaign is not sufficient to justify its opportunity costs, then the campaign should not have been run. The funds for that campaign would have been better used in other ways. If you can find ways to evaluate campaigns *before* they are executed in the whole market, then you can only execute campaigns that will justify their expenditures. The *planned experiments* described previously are a very good way to evaluate campaigns using a *sample* of the market instead of the whole market *before* the campaign will be executed for the entire market. You need to balance costs of the evaluation before the campaign is widely executed versus the value of only executing those campaigns that are very likely to be productive. This balancing act can be very difficult for large consumer packaged goods firms, but for the typical entrepreneur, it is relatively easy. You just have to think about evaluating the campaigns in a reasonable way before they are widely executed.

For any one-to-one marketing vehicles, such as direct mail, telesales, or the Internet, it is very feasible to test campaigns on selected samples and only broadly execute those that return more than their opportunity costs. For direct mail, for example, it is easy to test a campaign on every nth name on a list, before sending the advertisement to the whole list. For broader reach media such as radio, TV, magazines, or newspapers, more ingenuity is needed. If the firm has operations in more than one metropolitan area, then it can test campaigns in some areas, using some other areas as controls. What is very important in these experiments is to match the areas based on forecasted revenues for the test period and to *randomly* decide which areas are the test and which are the control. Flipping a coin or rolling dice to make the choice is perfectly appropriate. The use of chance makes it much more likely that the differences in revenues that are seen in each market are really due to the advertising campaign versus some other reason that caused a person to choose one market versus another. An example of how matched market experiments helped Franklin Electronic Publications, Inc. to evaluate alternative media and campaigns prior to national rollout is shown in the box.

FRANKLIN'S AD EXPERIMENT DESIGN

The following are excerpts from a presentation that describes Franklin Electronic Publications' advertising test of three alternative campaigns before a choice would be made of which, if any, was to be run. The three campaigns were spot television, cable television, and radio.

Franklin BOOKMAN Advertising Test

- **Purpose:** To evaluate the impact of advertising on retail movement of Franklin product, especially Franklin BOOKMAN.

- **Methodology:** A controlled test will be conducted to evaluate the following:

  1. **$4MM Spot TV plan.** If successful, this plan would be implemented in approximately 30% of the U.S., representing a combination of high-impact retail markets and more highly developed Franklin markets, as measured by warranty card returns. It is believed that these markets would yield a 95 reach and a 7+ frequency in the advertised markets. See theoretical plan.

  2. **$4MM Cable TV plan.** If successful, this plan would be implemented nationally. Implementation of this plan would yield a 60 reach and a 6.6 frequency in the advertised markets. See theoretical plan.

3. **$3MM Radio plan.** If successful, this plan would be implemented nationally. Implementation of this plan would run approximately 100 announcements per week.

The Franklin marketing manager had done a very careful job of developing pay back criteria.

■ **Measures of Success**

In order to be deemed a success, the adjusted unit volume increase within the test markets would need to rise sufficiently to pay back the advertising investment. Based upon current volume, this would translate to an increase of approximately 200,000 units or an 11% increase in volume on an annualized basis. Volume increases would be measured across all Franklin volume—not just BOOKMAN.

■ **Evaluative Criteria in Reading Test Results**

Adjustments must be made to data in test versus control to reflect the following:

■ Seasonality.

■ Market strength.

■ Only portion of entire media plan implemented.

■ Translation of national theoretical plan especially in cable markets: buying specs issued to deliver overall reach and frequency and not number of spots. Desired Daypart Mix would include a greater degree of prime and weekend than could be purchased on local cable basis.

■ **Payback Criteria by Market**

Sacramento ($4MM Cable):

200,000 annual units × .72% US / 1.32 Index × .60 half the schedule [lb] .60 (seasonality index for April/May) / 12 months per year × 2 (May/June)

Volume increase over two months in Sacramento would have to be 54 units over control.

Portland ($4MM Spot):

200,000 annual units × .84% US / 1.28 Index × .60 half the schedule × .60 (seasonality index for April/May) / 12 months per year × 2 (May/June) / .85 Adjustment for spot-only control.

Volume increase over two months in Portland would have to be 77 units over control.

Bakersfield ($3MM):

150,000 annual units × .25% US / 1.45 Index × .60 half the schedule × .60 (seasonality index for April/May) / 12 months per year × 2 (May/June)

Volume increase over two months in Bakersfield would have to be 13 units over control. The test design was structured with the three test areas and a control area.

The test results showed that the spot TV campaign increased sales 66% higher than the control, better than the productivity of the cable or radio options.

However, because the number of reporting stores was small and sales per week were small, there was a higher variability than the company anticipated in the sales estimated from the tests. There was still a big probability that the spot TV campaign could have been no better than the control. There was not enough upside for the company to risk its resources on such a risky payoff.

IMPROVING CAMPAIGNS BEFORE TESTING

Next we show how to improve the advertising you put into the testing process.

COPY STRATEGY

Obviously, whatever can be done so that campaigns that are developed are more likely to be productive is beneficial to the process. There are a number of steps that the entrepreneur can take to improve the campaigns as they are being developed:

First and most important, you must make sure that every campaign that you use is *supportive* and *consistent* with your *positioning* and *segmentation* strategy. At every opportunity, you should be asking, "Is this campaign going to improve our perception in the direction of our positioning strategy, and is it targeted at the right market segment?"

As long as the campaigns are consistent with the strategy, then it's your job to have the *most widely varied copies* generated and evaluated. Profitable copy generation can be compared to a lottery. The differences in incremental revenues between alternative copies and creative strategies can be very large. Some campaigns can really add large amounts of incremental sales, while other campaigns (with similar budgets) will do nothing or might even hurt sales. *Conceptually, you should generate a number of very different campaigns, evaluate the potential incremental revenue impact of each of them, and run only the best one—as long as the best one is incrementally profitable, and pays for its opportunity costs (including being more productive than the current campaign).*

However, in reality, it's just not that simple. Managing the advertising process involves a real balancing act for the entrepreneur. A number of advertising management decisions are very interrelated and should be determined simultaneously. These decisions include: How many different campaigns should I have generated? How much should I spend for the alternative campaigns? Should I retain an advertising agency? Who else should be tapped to generate new campaign alternatives? Each of these decisions depends on the answers to the other decisions. If one manages a huge organization with lots of time and resources, it is possible to think about an "optimally" profitable answer to these decisions. For the rest of us entrepreneurs, the best we can do is a "vaguely right" approach to the process. What follows is a discussion of the directional tradeoffs that exist between the alternatives.

More campaigns should be created as

- The cost of generating the campaigns is lower.
- The cost of evaluating each campaign is lower.
- The validity of the campaign evaluation method is higher.
- The reliability of the campaign evaluation method is higher.
- The variability of the sales impacts of the different campaigns that would be generated is higher.

What the entrepreneur is trying to do is only run with the most effective campaign. The more variability there is among the campaigns generated and evaluated, the more likely the best or most effective campaign will be more effective in increasing sales. However, if we chose the campaign that isn't really going to be the best, we will not do as well—thus, the reasoning for being concerned about the reliability and validity of the evaluation technique. Also, the more costly the evaluation or generation of campaigns is, it's obvious that the profitability of the process goes down faster as we generate and evaluate more campaign options.

More should be spent on evaluating campaign options:

- The more valid and/or reliable the evaluation methods are.
- The more variability in sales success the entrepreneur believes will occur among the campaign options that will be generated.
- The lower the costs of generating and evaluating each campaign option are.

Obviously, if it is very inexpensive to generate and evaluate each campaign option, and it is likely to be a big impact on revenue from one campaign to the other, and the evaluation is likely to differentiate the best campaign, then it pays to generate and evaluate a lot of different campaign options.

For the typical entrepreneur, the biggest leverage can come from increasing the variability of the campaign options he or she evaluates. Increasing the variability of the creators of the campaign option does this. The more different are the people and their approaches that create the campaign options, the more likely is it that the best of those options will have more revenue impact. How do you get more varied campaign option creators? Encourage option ideas from everyone who possibly can help in the creative process. Your employees and customers know the business and sometimes can generate very productive ideas. Also, many times, friends and relatives with whom you discuss your venture can also be a source of creativity.

This reasoning goes against the "standard" way advertising is handled by the entrepreneur. Many entrepreneurs will hire an advertising agency and give them the job of creating and placing their advertising campaign. The agency will do its own creative development and media planning. After the agency has completed its work, they make a presentation to "sell" their campaign idea to the entrepreneur. You either accept their recommendations or send the agency back to try again. This approach has been shown to generate campaigns that are not very different from each other in sales impact.

It is much more effective to *separate* the *creative* and *media* functions of advertising agencies. Our logic would imply that more than one creative agency should submit proposed campaigns to be evaluated and be paid for their time. The best campaign among those evaluated would be the one that is broadly executed. If for some reason you have trouble getting more than one creative agency to work for you, another option is to ask for separate, independent, creative teams from one advertising agency to each develop alternative campaigns to evaluate. Then run with the campaign that is evaluated as most likely to increase sales the most.

It is not necessary to have advertising developed only by traditional advertising agencies. Other sources would include freelance people who work part-time for ad agencies, advertising and marketing students at local universities, and art students at local art schools. The conception that artistic production quality for advertising has to be excellent in order for the advertising to be "great" is not borne out by the existing research. The definition of "great advertising" is where an entrepreneur and the typical advertising professional will differ. The consumer who sees or hears advertising is typically not sophisticated enough (nor cares enough) to be influenced by very subtle artistic touches in advertising. Professionals judge most advertising competitions and awards (such as the Cleo awards). Their judging criteria do not include the sales impact of the advertising. Most of the money that is spent to make advertising (especially television) artistically beautiful (and it's often a lot of money) is of very questionable productivity.

If you are typical of most entrepreneurs, you are now asking yourself, "How can I afford to spend all this money generating and testing alternative campaigns, most of which I'll never even run?" The answer is very simple—you will make more money doing that than with "normal" ways of generating and evaluating advertising. A great advertising campaign that is really effective at increasing sales may be contributing 5 or 10 times as much incremental revenue as a typical campaign. It's worth it to spend money to try to find the exceptionally productive campaigns.

For example, MetaCreations Corp. used radio advertising on Howard Stern's radio program to ask listeners to go to their Web site or call an 800 number to order a new software program for manipulating computer images. They let Howard Stern have poetic license to do whatever he wanted to advertise the product. In fact, the advertising cost was cheaper if Howard was free to extemporize his commercials.

This campaign generated more than *ten times* the incremental revenue versus the campaign cost. It was evaluated on a daily basis because it was very simple to watch the big increases in calls and Web site visits every time the "commercial" ran on Howard's show. The campaign was orders of magnitude more effective than any other campaigns the company had run. We next hypothesize that Hindustan Lever missed productivity improvement possibilities in the way they handled the successful rollout of Lifebuoy.

THE HINDUSTAN LEVER (HLL) MISSED EXPERIMENTATION OPPORTUNITY

As we discussed in Chapter 1, "Marketing-Driven Strategy to Make Extraordinary Money," we hypothesize that HLL missed an opportunity for increased marketing productivity when they repositioned, retargeted, and relaunched Lifebuoy as a health soap to combat germs that cause diarrhea and other diseases. Though they were extremely innovative in their positioning, targeting, and distribution channels, the way they handled the rural communications plan was very traditional. They basically worked with one agency, Ogilvy and Mather, and screened some options to roll out one option that everyone was happy with. The logic we developed previously would urge them to have developed a number of different communications executions using different creative sources and then tested them as part of the early rollout.

Let's look at some of the criteria we discuss for recommending that more campaigns are generated and tested. More should be developed if the cost of generating them is low. In this case, either another ad agency could develop executions based upon the research done by HLL or other "out of the box" creators could try their luck. Government workers who have been interacting with villagers may have some excellent ideas, or the villagers themselves might also be able to generate very effective communications vehicles. Given this was to be a low cost, personally delivered communication, the cost of actually developing and producing the new options would have to be quite small—especially in relation to the possible increases in revenue that more effective campaigns might generate.

The next three criteria say more campaigns should be developed if the cost of the evaluation is lower and the reliability and validity of the evaluation are higher. In the HLL case, they could randomize villages and test alternative campaigns in randomly selected villages from a set of villages matched on relevant criteria—such as current Lifebuoy revenue and competitive strength. In terms of evaluation, it could not be hard to get the sales from each of the independent sales/distributors they have in each village. They could compare sales before and after the campaigns across all the villages in each campaign treatment. Because we are measuring sales here in randomly selected villages where the only difference is the campaign used for communicating, there is a high amount of face validity. Given that there are thousands of villages that were visited by these marketing communication teams, it would be very easy to isolate samples of 200–500 villages for each treatment. This would make the evaluation extremely reliable because of the large sample size. This is typically easy to do on the Web, but because of the massive numbers of similar rural villages and relatively low implementation costs, this experimentation is very feasible.

Lastly, the preceding suggestion for multiple campaign generation would only make sense if there was room to believe that there was the possibility of higher sales that would result from different communications campaigns. Here, the company people and people from the field would be best at estimating the possibility. We find it hard to believe that the potential benefit of a better campaign that might be evaluated as better than the current one wouldn't more than pay for the small incremental costs of the additional campaign generation and testing. Given that the villagers had not seen any marketing communications, there could be some different, innovative campaign that would really excite the villagers and the independent salespeople.

We can only hypothesize why HLL didn't try alternative campaigns as they rolled out the initiative. Probably the biggest reason is that they always did their communications the same way—even for innovative programs. As a big company, many times it is difficult to change the procedures without creating significant political problems. The current agency is not going to like having competition.

This example shows how globally very progressive and innovative firms can also benefit from being more entrepreneurial and less traditional in how they manage their advertising and communication.

SYNYGY GENERATED VERY PRODUCTIVE AD OPTIONS FOR LOW COST

Sometimes, it doesn't even have to cost very much to generate productive alternatives. Synygy, Inc. is an entrepreneurial company that does administration of complex incentive compensation plans. They had an advertising agency that they used in the traditional way. The advertising that the agency came up with was run for a period of six months in print media that their target audience—senior sales force managers and administrators—would read. The objective of the advertising was to bring good leads for their sales force to follow up. Figure 6-3 shows the ad that was typical of the ads the agency ran.

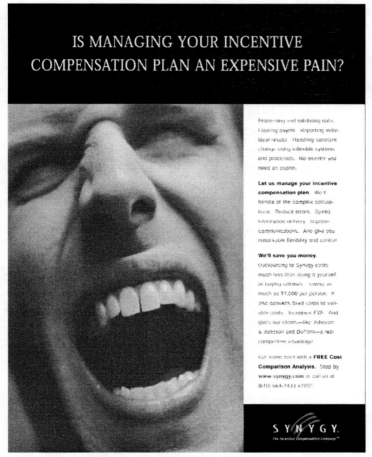

Figure 6-3   The typical ad they ran

This ad campaign brought in from 2–5 leads per week either over the phone or to the company's Web site. One of the company's employees (a graphic artist) approached Mark Stiffler, the founder and CEO, with a mock-up of a very different print ad. Mark directed the employee to make it into a print quality ad and tested the ad by running it once instead of the old ad. The new ad is in Figure 6-4.

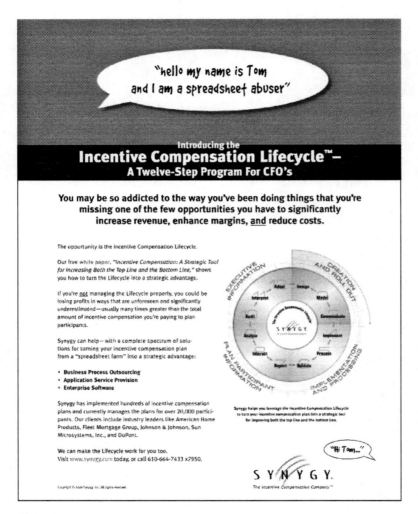

Figure 6-4 The employee-generated print ad

The ad was much better than the old ad—it was obvious by monitoring the inquiries generated that it was orders of magnitude more productive. Synygy began using the new ad exclusively, both in their print media and their direct mail brochures. In the first six months that the new campaign was running, inquiries were averaging 67 per week! With no change in media budget or media plan, the new campaign was at least 15 times more productive than the old campaign! It was certainly worth the nominal investment by Synygy to test the employee ad! The quality of the new "Tom" ad is probably not wonderful from an artistic point of view. However, *advertising for entrepreneurial companies is not an art form; it's a way to generate inquiries and sales*.

VICTORIA'S SECRET'S ADVERTISING AND TESTING STRATEGY

Victoria's Secret manages its advertising not only in relation to sales but to their pricing.

Direct mail and the Internet are big portions of VS advertising spending. They measure the incremental sales due to these media, and they are justified by the incremental profit they produce. VS's Internet site has been profitable from day one because the entire infrastructure was there to fulfill the Internet sales. It was an online extension of the existing direct mail catalog. TV advertising has been more challenging to manage.

Victoria's Secret has done a number of regional and local TV advertising tests in which some stores are in areas exposed to the advertising and others are not. They have typically not observed enough short-term incremental sales to justify a payout on the TV advertising expenditures. However, they have also measured a correlation of increases in TV advertising and their ability to increase the unit retail price. They have found that the TV advertising helps to make their customers less price responsive. The TV advertising changes and improves people's perceptions of who VS is, and it also is crucial for doing new product and product line launches. Even though there are probably opportunities for VS to fine tune its TV media, budget, and creative content, the management is spending its time more on new products and line expansion because it feels it can add more value to the company with those activities.

MEDIA PLANNING

If the discussion of campaign creativity and evaluation was not enough to get the reader's entrepreneurial juices flowing, then the next discussion of choosing media should do it. Just as there are big opportunities for increasing revenue with "non standard" campaigns, there are also big opportunities for increasing revenues by choosing the most productive among a wide variety of creative media options. The key in media planning is finding the media option that has the most likelihood of generating incremental revenue per dollar spent. We call this "bang per buck" analysis. Again, here the problem is not simple. There are a number of factors that should be considered in generating and evaluating media options. We have been able to distill experience and research over the past 30 years to develop a methodology that can guide the entrepreneur toward "vaguely right" choices.

Again, here the *market segmentation* and *product positioning strategy* of the firm needs to *drive the process*. Any options that are inconsistent with the firm's basic strategy should be eliminated. The media chosen can be an excellent way of implementing a segmentation strategy. One of the reasons for Tandem's East's success is the availability of targeted media that reach their target customers very cost effectively. Aside from reaching the targeted segment(s) cost effectively, the media options chosen should also be able to convey the firm's advertising message in an effective manner. For example, even though the audience of *Hustler* or *Playboy* magazine may be very appropriate targets for life insurance products, they would probably not be good environments for the typical life insurance ad. The male reading these magazines is probably not thinking very long term or is not very receptive to arguments against current pleasure.

The media chosen need to be evaluated not only on who will likely see or hear your ad, but on how potentially effective the option will be in motivating people who will hear or see the ad. Thus, the media options chosen will be directly related to the campaign that will be used. Some campaign options will be more effective in some media options than others. Again, this is not a simple problem. We have developed a relatively simple ranking and evaluation procedure to get right at the basic trade-offs that are essential for evaluating the relative "bang per buck" of the available options. The methodology considers the relative value of reaching different target market segments, the probabilities of members of each segment actually seeing or hearing the ads, and the appropriateness of the media vehicles as motivators of people who are actually exposed to the ads in them.

SAMPLE TEMPLATE FOR MEDIA EVALUATION

The first step in evaluating media options is to divide the market into segments that will have different value to you. This is not as simple as it seems, because you will need to estimate how those segments break out the audience of the media options you are considering. Most media audience ratings are typically only broken out by age and/or sex and sometimes other demographic variables. There is a balance between finding segmentation that is relevant to your venture and segmentation that has media audiences available. Sometimes the segments used for the media planning purposes can be as simple as "my target group" and all others. You can then estimate media audiences in the target group for all the options you are considering.

For our sample, we assume that the entrepreneur has divided his target into three segments: younger males with high income; younger females with high income; and all other adults, as illustrated in Table 6-3. The next step is to estimate the population of each segment—column A in the table. Column B in the table answers the question: "How valuable to me is reaching a person in one segment versus another?" This is an important judgment that will depend on the advertising's objectives, the potential of the segments, and so on. It is a per capita estimate that only has to be done on a relative basis. The numbers in column B could be just as easily 100, 40, and 10 instead of 10, 4, and 1. What is important is the relative judgment of how valuable reaching a person in one segment is versus reaching a person in another. Column C is just the multiplication of column A times column B to obtain a segment relative potential.

Table 6-3 Media Evaluation Data

Sample Segments	A Segment Population	B Segment Weight = Potential per Person in Segment (Relative)	C = A x B Segment Potential
25–49 Males with income > $35K	2,000,000	10	20,000,000
25–49 Females with income > $35K	2,000,000	4	8,000,000
All others	10,000,000	1	10,000,000

Table 6-4 describes some of the required numbers and estimates needed for each of the media options that are being evaluated. For our sample, we evaluate four vehicles: one Internet advertising option, a radio ad, a taxi ad on the back of the front seat of a set of taxis, and an ad in a newspaper. It is *very important* to generate *many* options to evaluate, even if you have to make rough, "vaguely right" judgments about some of the numbers needed for the evaluation. Creative media options can not only help you sell more stuff—they can position you as different from your competition.

Table 6-4 More media evaluation data

Sample Media Vehicle Options	D Cost/Insertion	E Probability of Ad Exposure Given Audience Membership	F Media Weight = Relative Value of Ad Exposure (Judgment or Experimentation)
City Internet banner ad for one week (Internet A)	$100 per week	.6	1.0
Radio 30-second spot classic rock station— drive time (Radio A)	$150 per week	.6	1.5
Taxi seat banners for one week (Taxi A)	$50 per week	.8	1.0
City newspaper ad ¼ page financial section (Newspaper A)	$800 per ad	.3	1.5

The first column (D) in Table 6-4 is just the costs per insertion for each option. The next column, E, is an estimate of the probability that someone who is counted as "in the audience" of the media will actually be exposed to the ad you would run. This estimate depends on how the "audience" number is determined for each media vehicle. It is absolutely true that your advertising can only work if the potential consumer is exposed to it. Just being in the media vehicles' audience and not seeing your ad does not help. For example, if a person reads the newspaper, but does not see your ad in the financial section, this does no good for your business. Column E estimates the fraction of audience members who will actually be exposed to your ad.

The last column (F) is probably the most *difficult* number to estimate for each media vehicle, but also the most *important*. It answers the question: How much do I care to have a good potential customer be exposed to my ad in one media vehicle versus another? This number really only needs to be estimated on a relative basis. The best way to think about this estimate is to arbitrarily assign a one-dollar value to one media option (A). For the other options, you then answer the question, If it costs one dollar for me to have a good prospect be exposed to my ad in media vehicle A, *how much more or less* than one dollar would I be willing to spend *to have my ad seen instead* in each of the other options? In the example in Table 6-4, the radio and newspaper ads are estimated as roughly 50% more valuable *per person actually exposed* than the other two media options.

Table 6-5 shows the fraction of each segment that is counted as being "in the audience" of each of the media options being evaluated. The audience numbers come from the syndicated research that is used to estimate who watches, reads, or listens, for how long. The definition that is used by each media option to define "being in its audience" is very important to understand. For example, for TV, the definition of audience is typically having the TV set in the audience member's household turned on to the channel on which your ad appears. Whether the audience member actually watches your ad is a whole other story, which is handled by column E in Table 6-4. In Table 6-5, for example, 25% of the high income younger males are estimated to be in the audience of the financial section of the newspaper, but column E of Table 6-4 says that only 30% of those audience members actually see the one-quarter page ad we plan.

Table 6-5   What fraction of each segment is counted as in the audience of each media vehicle option?

Media Vehicle	G Segment 1. High Income Younger Males	H Segment 2. High Income Younger Females	I Segment 3. All Others
Internet A	.04	.02	.01
Radio A	.08	.06	.05
Taxi A	.03	.02	.005
Newspaper A	.25	.15	.10

The next step in the evaluation is to multiply the total segment potential in column C by the audiences in Table 6-5. The mechanics of this computation is shown in Table 6-6. For each media option, column M is the total audience of each media weighted by the importance of that segment to the firm.

Table 6-6 Relative Amount of Segment Potential in Media Audiences

Segment	J= G × 20,000,000 High Income Younger Males	K = H × 8,000,000 High Income Younger Females	I = I × 10,000,000 All Others	M = J + K + L Total
Internet A	.04 × 20M = 800,000	.02 × 8M = 160,000	.01 × 10M = 100,000	1,060,000
Radio A	1,600,000	480,000	500,000	2,580,000
Taxi A	600,000	160,000	50,000	810,000
Newspaper A	5,000,000	1,200,000	1,000,000	7,200,000

The following equation puts all this together by combining the media audience potential, ad exposure probabilities, and the relative media values into the "*bang.*" This "bang" is divided by the costs per insertion of the media to get a relative "*bang per buck.*" In our example, Radio A is most productive, followed within about 17% by Taxi A. The other two options are deemed less than half as potentially productive as Radio A and Taxi A.

Total Potential in Media Audience × Individual Ad Exposure Prob. × Relative Media Value divided by Media Insertion Costs = a Relative "Bang per Buck"

$$\text{Bang per Buck} = \frac{M x E x F}{D}$$

Internet A	=	636,000/$100	=	6,360
Radio A	=	2,322,000/$150	=	15,480
Taxi A	=	648,000/$ 50	=	12,960
Newspaper A	=	3,240,000/$800	=	4,050

The preceding template for media planning should be used to screen options: to run in the marketplace and evaluate, or test in a test market and evaluate. The Franklin Electronic Publications media test described earlier is a good example.

The entrepreneur should continually be evaluating the incremental revenue performance of his advertising options as they are used in the market. Over time, the incremental revenue contribution may begin to decline because of diminishing returns. When this happens, it may be time to try some new options. This phenomenon will eventually happen even to search engine marketing, but in the meantime, it should be considered as a very plausible alternative for many entrepreneurial companies.

THE SEARCH ENGINE MARKETING REVOLUTION—EVALUATING AND MAXIMIZING ITS "BANG PER BUCK"[6]

There are very good reasons why Search Engine Marketing is by far the fastest growing advertising medium in the last few years. In 2004, online ads tied to search engine activities grew 50% over 2003 to $3.9 billion. This represented 40% of 2004's $9.63 billion in Internet advertising revenue—making search the largest single category of online ads.[7]

What exactly is Search Engine Marketing? It is a payment for appearing high on the list of sponsored search results for a particular keyword that the search engine user searches for. At this writing, the two largest players in this medium are Google and Yahoo!. The list order places are sold in an auction format. The highest bidder gets the highest spot, the second highest gets the second spot, and so on. The payment to the search engine (usually Google or Yahoo!) is an amount per click through to your site from the search engine.

Compared to other large advertising media, this "pay for performance" method is very unique. The only other large media that is comparable is the sometimes use of "per inquiry" schemes in radio and television. When a TV or radio station, network, or cable system has excess capacity, they will sometimes make "per inquiry (P.I.)" deals with direct marketers who pay for leads (typically phone calls or Web site visits) resulting from the advertising. These P.I. deals are looked upon as a last ditch, desperation tactic by the radio and TV media and viewed as better than not selling the time slot at all. Typically the revenue from P.I. deals to radio and TV is much lower than the standard price per spot. On the other hand, Search Engine Marketing is predicated on paying for performance and potentially very valuable to many advertisers.

How does Search Engine Marketing work? It depends on whether you are a direct to consumer or B2B marketer. Figure 6-5 shows the logistics of what happens in each situation.

Search Engine Marketing is the perfect complement to many of the concepts emphasized in this book. It is made for continuous adaptive experimentation and evaluation based upon marginal revenue versus marginal costs. Many successful entrepreneurial companies of all sizes will make much new profit by intelligently applying Search Engine Marketing utilizing the concepts in this book.

Business to Consumer:

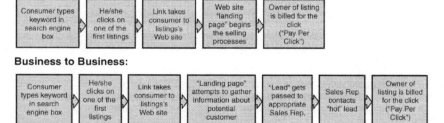

Business to Business:

Figure 6-5   Paid search—how does it work?

Source: Yosi Heber Communication, 2004

Search Engine Marketing is creating a seismic shift in how advertising is productively implemented. The reasons for its success and its even bigger potential for use by entrepreneurial entities have been elegantly portrayed by Yosi Heber in his "Heber's Advertising Relevance Matrix" (see Figure 6-6).

Figure 6-6 shows clearly how Search Engine Marketing has broken through as a new medium that has attributes that are unique and very valuable to many marketers. It reaches only potential customers to whom the message is very relevant, because the customers are searching about the issue. The consumers are spending their time to solve a problem, and the advertiser is in position to provide perceived help to the consumers.

Heber's Advertising Relevance Matrix

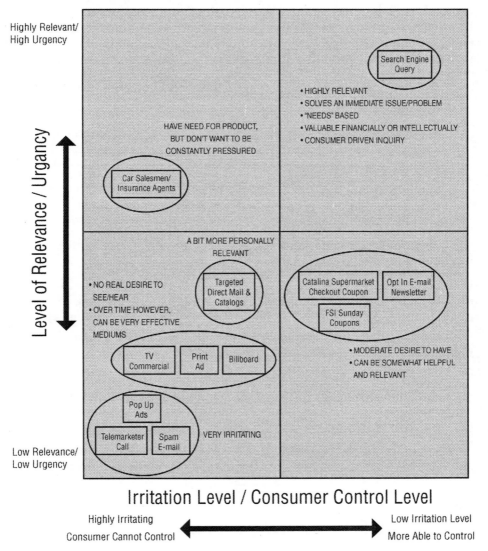

Figure 6-6 Heber's Advertising Relevance Matrix

Source: Yosi Heber Communication, 2004

The other big advantage of Search Engine Marketing is that the consumers feel much more in control than any other advertising medium. They do not feel irritated by the advertising exposure. On the contrary, they are in many cases searching for a solution to a problem that the advertiser can solve. Yosi, who until mid-2005 was the Chief Marketing Officer of Entertainment Publications, Inc. (a subsidiary of IAC/Interactive Corp.), and is now President of Oxford Hill Partners, outlined a number of benefits that he had seen from using Search Engine Marketing, as follows:

- It helps efficiently acquire new consumers and customers.
- It is measurable.
- It is relatively low cost ($.29 per lead versus $10 per lead for direct mail).
- It has a generally proven ROI.
- It is very low risk—you typically pay for performance—per "click," and you can pay as you go and stop if the returns aren't there.
- For B2B situations, it can make the sales force more efficient by providing "warm" leads versus cold calls.

In terms of the previous template for media evaluation, the target segment that is reached is extremely precise and, thus, their segment weight will typically be very high compared to other more traditional media. How much more valuable is a potential customer who has a high income and is searching for the problem you can solve on the Internet, than a typical high-income person who is not searching?

The other element of the media evaluation template that Search Engine Marketing impacts is the relative value of an ad exposure. How much more value is there in exposing a target consumer to an ad while they are searching for the product or service you are selling than when they are exposed in an unrelated setting? The neat thing about Search Engine Marketing is that the marketer doesn't have to do any elaborate experimentation or judgmental estimation—they can get the estimated revenue per $1 spent on Search Engine Marketing on an ongoing basis as they use the medium.

EVALUATING THE RETURN ON SEARCH ENGINE MARKETING

How does a marketer evaluate the productivity of Search Engine Marketing? As we recommend for all marketing resource deployment decisions and in particular other media and advertising evaluations, we need to get as close as possible to evaluating the incremental revenue to compare with the incremental costs of buying the search words and the incremental costs of fulfilling the incremental revenue that is generated. The first step is to have an estimate of the value of a new customer over that customer's lifetime.

For typical direct-to-consumer situations, for each search word and position, you then need to monitor the number of customers gotten as a fraction of the click-through population (the "clicks to customer" percentage). Then, divide this percentage by the cost per click to get the number of customers per dollar. Multiplying the number of customers per dollar times the value of the customer gets a Return on Marketing (ROM) number to compare with other search words and other alternative marketing expenditures. For example, if you bid and pay $.10 per click, 5% of those who click become customers, and the value of a customer is $10, then for each click, you will get .05 customers times $10 = $.50. So $.50 in value for $.10 spent =.50/.10 = 5.0, or a 500% return for the advertising investment. The key numbers in this analysis are the value per new customer and the clicks to customer percentage.

For typical B2B situations, the preceding analysis works with one exception. The "clicks per customer" percentage is obtained by multiplying together two component fractions—the percentage of clicks that become qualified sales leads (the "clicks to leads percentage") and the percentage of qualified leads that become customers after the sales force calls on them (the "leads to customer" percentage).

Obviously, the previous calculation can be made more precise if you keep track of the revenue patterns of the specific customers that come from each search word. Some words may attract customers who buy more than other customers. Also, the copy that you use in your sponsored search ad may have a big impact on response—either customers or leads, or both. If it can be done cost efficiently, it usually makes sense to develop information systems to capture the specific revenue response from each word and ad combination. In many cases, the learning that comes from the data will easily pay for the costs of collecting the data. It is almost always beneficial to plan for this analysis and data collection when initially designing and building your Web site.

METHODS FOR IMPROVING PRODUCTIVITY OF SEARCH ENGINE MARKETING

The basic message for improving ROM for Search Engine Marketing is very simple: Test, Test, Test!

Because the cost of testing is so low and the variability of performance is so high, it almost always pays to test a lot of different search words, different search engines, different headlines, ad copy, and various promotional offers that might be involved on your Web site. If we take the concepts from this chapter's previous section on improving copy productivity, they fit Search Engine Marketing like a glove.

More campaigns should be evaluated as

- The cost of generating the copy is lower (the sponsored search ads are typically just a few lines of copy, which can be easily changed without any professional assistance).
- The cost of evaluating each campaign is lower (the cost is negligible if the information systems are already in place).
- The validity of the campaign evaluation method is higher (revenues due to each campaign option can be isolated—as valid as can be imagined).
- The reliability of the campaign evaluation method is higher (the larger the sample size of clicks on each word and copy option, the larger the validity (repeatability) of the evaluation).
- The variability of the sales impacts of the different campaigns that would be generated is higher (in some tests that one of the authors did, he found revenue differences of 15 and 20 to 1 just depending on the ad copy used in the sponsored search ad for the same group of search words).

For the preceding reasons, it almost always very beneficial to generate a lot of varied options from different creative sources for the sponsored ads. Until you test a bunch of options that can't improve on the best current option, you should continue an aggressive program of testing, generating new options, testing, learning, generating new options, testing, and so on.

CONCLUSION

Though this chapter has discussed copy and media separately, it should be obvious that they are very interrelated. Some copy will obviously work better in some media than others. If your copy changes, you need to reevaluate your media options. Similarly, if new media options arise, you need to determine whether or not copy changes should occur.

ENDNOTES

1. Lodish, L., M. Abraham, S. Kalmenson, J. Livelsberer, B. Richards, and M.E. Stevens (1995), "How TV Advertising Works: A Meta Analysis of 389 Real-World Split-Cable TV Advertising Experiments," *Journal of Marketing Research*, 32 (May), pp. 125–139.

2. Lodish, L., M. Abraham, J. Livelsberger, B. Richardson, and M.E. Stevenson (1995), "A Summary of Fifty-Five In-Market Experimental Estimates of the Long-Term Effect of TV Advertising," Part 2, *Marketing Science*, 14 (3), pp. G133–120.

3. Little, J.D.C. (1979), "Decisions Support Systems for Marketing Managers," *Journal of Marketing*, 43 (Summer), pp. 9–26.

4. Bhattacharya, C.B., and L.M. Lodish (1994), "An Advertising Evaluation System for Retailers," *Journal of Retailing and Consumer Services*, 1 (2), pp. 90–100.

5. Ibid.

6. This section draws heavily from personal correspondence and speeches given by Yosi Heber in late 2004.

7. Perez, J.C., "On Line Advertising up in 2004; Search is Top Segment," *IDG News Service*, Miami Bureau, May 03, 2005—reported in *Computerworld*, Vol. 11, Issue 13.

7

How to Leverage Public Relations for Maximum Value

	Products/Services	Equity/Shares	Image
Customers			
Users			
Investors			
Supply Chain/ Channel Partners			
Employees			

Before people can buy your product or use your service, they have to know it exists, and how to get to it. Even more importantly, they should feel that they are going with a winner, if there is a choice among products in the category. Proper use of public relations and publicity can provide this "winner" feeling far faster, and at much lower cost, than a big national advertising campaign—one that an entrepreneurial company may not be able to afford.

In the Internet world, the key driver to quickly gaining leadership in a new category is the creation of "buzz"—the feeling that you are the winner. Yahoo!, Microsoft, Google, and others have all been beneficiaries of this. Gaining the mind share of a user—so that she routinely tries your Web page before a competitor's—quickly translates into market share. As Ann

Winblad, General Partner of Hummer Winblad Associates and an extremely successful venture capitalist, has said, "It's the cheerleader approach, where you tell the world that we're the winner even before the game has started, which is successful in the Internet space." The new world of blogging has changed the game by adding a new channel to get early information out. ePinions, for example, went with a very high profile *The New York Times Sunday Magazine* story, long before their site launched. The article made it seem as if the management team was experienced—the best and the brightest—and that they were certain to be the leader in shared opinions. The fact that About.com had thousands of users and millions of page views doing the same thing did not stop ePinions from making its claims. The perception of leadership quickly becomes the reality, allowing ePinions to be sold to Shopping.com after the crash at a reasonable price. When Netscape first made its browser available, Spry, Quarterdeck, and Spyglass all had products in the marketplace—some of which were technically superior. But a concentrated PR campaign, coupled with guerilla marketing tactics that we discuss in Chapter 10, "Entrepreneurial Promotion and Viral Marketing to Maximize Sustainable Profitability," got tremendous coverage in the trade press—which declared Navigator as the browser to beat. And it soon went to overwhelming market share to make the perception a reality.

GAINING THE PERCEPTION OF LEADERSHIP

How can you achieve this perceptual edge? First, let us understand how most users make their decision on which Web site to visit, or which high-tech product to buy. Generally, they ask someone they trust—an information gatekeeper in their organization or personal life—or they read a trusted source in a newsletter, trade, or general publication. Thus, the key to gaining the perceptual edge is to influence the influencers, or gatekeepers. And where do the gatekeepers get their knowledge? From a smaller set of influencers whom they trust. It is like a pool, where a stone thrown in the center creates waves that ripple outward, growing ever larger in diameter, until they reach the shore. You need to reach the following groups:

- **Gurus**—Key industry insiders
- **Influencers**—Key trade and business press; industry analysts

- **Decision makers**—Key bellwether buyers; those who can say yes
- **Naysayers**—People who can say no along the way
- **Mass buyers**—The masses who mainly follow what they perceive as the winning trend

In every industry, a few insiders are considered the industry experts or gurus. They are generally the ones quoted in *Business Week, Forbes, Fortune,* and the *Wall Street Journal* when key industry events occur. In the past, they mainly published high-priced newsletters and ran invitation-only conferences for CEOs of industry companies. In the personal computer industry during the 1980s and '90s, Stewart Alsop, Esther Dyson, and Richard Shaffer filled this role. At the middle of the new decade, Chris Anderson has taken over the TED Conference (TED stands for Technology, Entertainment, Design) from Richard Saul Wurman, Chris Shipley has the successful Demo conferences, John Batelle the Web 2.0, and Tim O'Reilly the influential eTech and foocamp meetings. Reaching these players, and being covered in their newsletters or appearing at their conferences, creates some immediate buzz, both with key industry buyers and partners and with key venture capitalists who can fund your entrepreneurial venture.

In today's new media world, blogs have taken an important role in this information spread. The best public relations groups try to reach out to the key bloggers on a topic, knowing that their comments will be read by other influencers and press. Selective leaking to the influential blogs may be as important as bringing in the trade press. At a recent DemoFall conference, the media list included three pages of print journalists, and one page of bloggers. Bloggers will get the word out far more quickly (often in hours) than the more thoughtful edited journalists. Technorati, Feedster, and PubSub make it easy to search and be alerted to new blog entries.

A new company, Riya, has been blogging the development of their product for the past few months, in the founder's Recognizing Deven blog. This openness has helped not only in preparing the press for their eventual launch, but also in getting the venture capital community lining up to invest. Similarly, no new cellphone product is introduced without having been seen on Engadget and Gizmodo, two key blogs for leading-edge tech products.

- **Release 1.0**—Esther Dyson
- **TED**—Chris Anderson
- **Softletter**—Jeff Tartar
- **PC Forum**—Esther Dyson
- **Venturewire conferences**—Dick Shaffer
- **Web 2.0**—John Batelle
- **eTech and foocamp**—Tim O'Reilly
- **Investment conferences**—Morgan Stanley (Mary Meeker), Goldman, TWP
- **Industry analysts**—Gartner Group for all IT matters

The telecommunications, semiconductor, database software, and applications software sectors all have additional gurus, letters, and conferences. And the same holds true for biotech, energy, and every other field we have examined. At the core of the industry are a handful of influencers, who spread the word about new ideas, products, and services, along with their opinions. These opinions are usually strong indicators of success or failure in the first year after launch.

After the gurus come the influencers—editors and writers at the key mass trade and business publications in the field. In the computer world, the Ziff Davis publications (*eWeek*, *PC Magazine*, etc.), and the IDG *Infoworld* and *Computerworld* newspapers have the broadest reach among decision makers. You must be sensitive to the lead times of each publication, in order to maximize the coincident coverage of your story. That is, if you want to launch a new product in May, you need to meet with the longer lead monthly magazines two to three months in advance of when you want the story to appear, with the weeklies two to three weeks prior, and with today's daily email zines (online magazines) a few days before the news should hit.

For products with a consumer focus, the key mass columnists can provide tremendous boost in product launch. Walt Mossberg, personal technology columnist for the *Wall Street Journal*, can make or break a product with an early review. He receives hundreds of requests each week, and has policies for filtering that good public relations agencies understand. He demands, and usually gets, to be the first to publish about your product. He likes to have them significantly in advance so that he can actually work with them and provide feedback. When Franklin Electronic Publications and Starfish Software were launching REX, Mossberg was brought in almost a year prior to launch—under appropriate embargo agreements. His input on the early betas was invaluable in making a better product. His review at the launch was a key factor in early product sales, and in helping the visibility of a product that had very little advertising dollar spending.

Newsweek's Steve Levy, *Business Week's* Steve Wildstrom, and *PC Week's* Michael Miller also have earned the respect of their readers with their insightful reviews. It is necessary to view these influencers not just as targets for getting a message out, but as highly knowledgeable users who can help to improve the design and feature set of a product or service. Clearly, in today's world, it is not only the print press, but television, radio, and the Internet that must also be attended to. It was, after all, the Internet's Matt Drudge who broke the Lewinsky story rather than *Newsweek*, which held it while awaiting further confirmations.

With the plethora of cable channels has come an opportunity for companies to provide short (30 second to 2 minute) video news releases (VNR), which are often picked up by local news or specialized cable services. The impact of such a piece shown on television, often with a voiceover by the local news or science reporter, should not be underestimated. When MetaCreations announced its Power Goo consumer image funware, the VNR was picked up by dozens of stations, and sales were noticeably increased. CNN's *Science Today* often does reports on products of interest. Energy Innovations new solar energy project had a CNN interview, and heavy Web traffic in the weeks following it.

Reaching the decision makers is best done with focused direct marketing, and with special events, which are described in Chapter 10. But the more general positive buzz you can get with a product, the less likely the naysayers are to voice negative, against-the-crowd opinions.

SPOKESPERSONS/EVANGELISTS

One of the key tasks for a public relations effort is to help one (or at most two) people in the company create personal one-to-one relationships with the gurus. Most often the CEO and chief technical person are the ones who should build and nurture these relationships. They require visiting the gurus on "press tours," getting them prerelease (beta) software or hardware, and providing oodles of technical support to ensure that any product usage goes smoothly. One should understand that this is a two-way street; the guru can't be a guru without being in on the latest product entries, and everyone likes to know a secret, or be in the know a little earlier than the next person. Often, if the relationship can be built early enough, the gurus can contribute to making the product more user friendly—and by having an emotional stake are more likely to help declare the product a winner.

The evangelists who meet with the press need to be personable, knowledgeable about the company and its products, and sensitive to what can and can't be said regarding fundraising without triggering legal obligations in the case of public companies, or concerns about "hype" in private companies. It is important not to lie to the press or influencers—although spin is certainly acceptable and common. One of the biggest mistakes is talking in the "hoped for present" tense—that is, "Yes, the product can do xxxx," when it can't. It's also important to plan the pitch in a way that is respectful of the available time of the person being wooed. Some training in public speaking—of the type that Power Presentations of San Jose provides to entrepreneurs going on road shows—can be very helpful in correcting typical mistakes. The wrong body language, too much hesitation when responding to questions, and other problems can leave a mistaken impression on the guru. Remember, in most of these cases, first impressions last.

The overall company and product pitch should be planned for at least three lengths: the "elevator story," the 15-minute demo, and the 30–45 minute road show pitch. The elevator story is meant to be told in the time it takes to go a few floors next to someone in the elevator—typically 30 seconds to two minutes. It has to convince them that they should want to hear more. There are some iconic ways to do this, the most popular current one being, "We're going to be the Amazon.com of . . .." eToys, for example, was planned to be the Amazon of toys. Unfortunately for them, Amazon allied with Toys "R" Us and remained the Amazon of toys. But this pitch needs to have some differentiation. "The REX has almost the same functionality as a Palm Pilot in a credit card-size device, and synchronizes with your laptop by being a PCMCIA card."

The 15-minute demo should be just that. No more than a minute or two to introduce the speaker and company—naming any credibility enhancers (advisory board members, directors, investors), followed by a demo that ideally allows for the person being briefed to get hands-on with the product. Most of the gurus in high tech are gadget nuts at heart—they are the epitome of early adopters—even where, like Walt Mossberg—they try to put themselves in the mindset of the more average user. This puts the evangelist, whether she is CEO or CTO or just a plain Marcom (marketing communications) person, in a position of preaching to people who want you to succeed. But they need to make the product vision their own, so that they can preach it to others.

Finally, if there is lots of time available, a slide show (PowerPoint or equivalent), which can be quickly tailored to the specific audience, should be prepared. This should include sections on company history, financing, product rollout plans, advertising plans, partnering deals (quite popular with Internet companies), and, of course, the product itself.

LINKAGE TO FUNDRAISING

For those entrepreneurial ventures that are also raising money (almost all of them), the public relations efforts serve two purposes—helping the product to be perceived and perform as a winner, and helping to fuel the fundraising. An additional set of influencers reach this community, and there is a feedback effect of strong venture capital support on the core gurus and influencers. A Kleiner Perkins funded venture has the credibility of one of the most successful partnerships behind it, and gurus take its investee company claims with somewhat less skepticism than those of an unknown company. For this field, a number of publications were started in the boom, almost none surviving. *Red Herring* has been restarted to try and recapture some of this. Having the company mentioned prominently in these publications has helped get audiences not only with influencers, but also with targeted high-profile customers who might have otherwise waited.

Similarly, having the company mentioned in *Red Herring* may open doors that have been closed on Sand Hill Road. Since most venture capitalists want to be seen as riding with a winner, the buzz which proclaims that acts like perfume to the investor.

PR AGENCIES

There is always a lot of controversy about the value that a PR agency can bring to the table. Many small companies believe that they can get to the gurus and influencers themselves, and that the often sizable cost of using an agency may not be worthwhile. Our experience is that, properly managed, PR fees gain you a tremendous multiple on your investment in them, as long as your expectations are properly set at the outset. The agency provides three basic functions:

- **Creative**—Helping to define the message
- **Execution**—Getting the message out
- **Rolodex**—Knowing who to go to, and having the ability to get them to listen

While there are dramatic quality differences among agencies with respect to how they perform the first two functions, it is the third that distinguishes the top few agencies from the next tiers. Many of the very top agencies (Alexander Oglivy, Cunningham Communications, Connors Communications, BlodgettComm) have become very selective about taking on clients, and very expensive—in much the same way as successful DC lobbyists offer access to the right people as part of their value added.

Creating the positioning and its associated message in a form best suited to reach the various types of audiences is mainly a task for the company's top management. The agency can and should, however, guide the words and "spin" of the message so that it tells the story in a memorable, quick manner. Snap.com, idealab!'s new search engine, has adopted the message "Get the search results you really want." All of management has gotten training in sticking to the message. One of the marks of great politicians is their ability to stay on the message—this is a lesson that should not be lost on entrepreneurs.

Once the press releases, press kit, and evaluation or demo software and hardware are created, the execution phase begins. The best agencies have good mailing lists of editors and other influencers. Each company must create their own contact lists, and maintain them internally so that they can continue follow-up even if they switch agencies or bring the function in-house. Agencies often have direct access to *PR Newswire*, *Business Wire*, and so on to get a story out there quickly. They are also more likely to know who has recently been assigned to which specific beats in the various periodicals, and which stock market analysts are willing to see non-public companies.

Measuring the effectiveness of PR is something that should be done in as quantitative a manner as possible. A good clipping service can let you measure how many column inches of print, and radio or TV air time, the PR efforts have generated. At HDS, we had a spreadsheet with the posted ad rates of most of the key periodicals, which allowed us to translate column inches into the equivalent cost, if we had run those inches as paid advertising. While not a perfect absolute number for value, it is quite useful if tracked over a period of time, and gives at least some handle on the advertising alternative. When possible, a good lead-tracking system can be used to tell which mentions led to actual calls, Web site visits, or customer emails. At some companies, purchases are tracked all the way back to these types of leads—showing again the true value or the PR effort.

As with most hiring, interviewing and reference checking are key in selecting the PR firm. It is imperative to check out the work they have done for similar customers. Call the CEO or marketing counterpart and ask how easy they were to work with. Be specific about the staff that will work on your account—some junior people will normally be assigned, but make sure the supervisor is someone you trust, and will actually be on the account. Too often, the name partners at these firms are mainly out marketing, not performing the actual work—although they will argue that they're keeping the influencer relationships strong, from which your company benefits.

TIMING IS ESSENTIAL

The sequencing and timing of the PR effort is crucial to getting maximum bang for the marketing dollar. Ideally you are creating a crescendo that begins with buzz about the company, moves on to create buzz about the specific product, gets industry gurus and key influencers talking off the record about the product, and culminates in a blizzard of press coverage led by the daily mass and trade press, and followed up over each of the next two or three months with additional stories in the monthly magazines, radio, and television.

PayMyBills.com began as a project at the Wharton School, and was entered into their annual business plan competition. As the judging proceeded, and the plan made it into the final eight, a leading Internet firm decided to fund it as a full-fledged business. The cofounders were brought out to idealab!'s Pasadena headquarters, and told that they had 60 days in which to launch the company and the business. The business plan competition provided the opportunity to get some buzz about the company.

Because it was covered by major media, articles appeared in *The New York Times*, *Philadelphia Magazine*, and other locations. This helped the company in its initial hiring and fundraising.

The founders moved into idealab! on May 19. Ten days later, they had hired 10 people, mainly through a job fair and contacts on the Internet, who had heard of them through the articles, and the Industry Standard Internet online newsletter. Three weeks later, idealab! used the buzz to raise more than $4 million for the company at a much more favorable valuation than would have been possible without the PR. The Alexander Oglivy agency, which has a long relationship with idealab!, was hired to get a fast track product launch. They created an interview schedule for trade press, business press, and radio that focused on a product launch date of July 19 (slipped from an original July 4 target). Meetings were held with the *Wall Street Journal*, *LA Times*, *PC Magazine*, and others, for a focused print at the launch.

In addition, spot radio was purchased in several cities, including advertising on the Howard Stern show for the first two weeks after launch. All of this orchestration led to a number of interviews, lots of customers, and acknowledgment as the leading player in this new field. This notwithstanding that the two competitors, PayTrust and CyberBills, had been in existence much longer, but had not quite launched and were staying in stealth mode. By taking the aggressive route to PR and product launch, PayMyBills.com tilted the playing field and gained 50,000 customers in less than a year. It then merged with PayTrust, and the combination was later sold to a major firm in the financial services space.

As a counterpoint, if one is going to be that aggressive, one has to deliver. Boo.com, a luxury apparel site funded by Bernard Arnaut of LVMH, orchestrated the PR campaign and got the company buzz; however, repeated delays in launching the site (more than eight months late) caused people to be skeptical. When it was launched, it was so slow and painful to use that the company developed a negative public image, which will need to be overcome as it relaunches and improves the site.

CRISIS MANAGEMENT

One key use for public relations is in the area of crisis management. Every company runs into situations that threaten its reputation and well-being.

When Intel's Pentium chip was found to have mistakes in its arithmetic computation engine, the initial publicity was horrendous. Intel was becoming the company that couldn't add two and two, a huge embarrassment. In such cases, public relations can help.

An effective PR effort at times of crisis can make sure the public knows how quickly and thoroughly the company is reacting to the crisis. It can help to provide credibility to the company actions. When a customer supposedly found a piece of a finger in Wendy's chili, the PR effort was quick and expansive. It showed how they were cooperating with police and health authorities, and why it was unlikely that this had happened through Wendy's fault. Once the perpetrator of this fraud was arrested, PR was used to show that the company was in the right, and store traffic went above prior levels.

In every case, one rule is clear: Communicate the truth. No matter the crisis, lying about it will, in the long run, certainly make things worse.

CONCLUSION

"On the Internet, no one knows you're a dog," says the famous *New Yorker* cartoon showing a dog at a keyboard. No one knows your company exists either, unless you take the proper steps to gain the perception, and then deliver the reality of leadership. Working through the various circles of influencers is the best way to quickly have that perception created. This perception of leadership will help not only in selling the product or service, but also in hiring and fundraising for the entrepreneurial venture.

8

Sales Management to Add Value

	Products/Services	Equity/Shares	Image
Customers			
Users			
Investors			
Supply Chain/ Channel Partners			
Employees			

Sales management is a key section to include in an entrepreneurial marketing book. Although sales and marketing are quite different, they are inextricably entwined. Writing about marketing without including sales management would be the same as building a house without an initial design. The challenge, of course, for these Siamese-twin disciplines is that both of them believe they are the dominant one. Without marketing, sales wouldn't have leads and collateral. Without sales, closing deals wouldn't be possible. So, there is a natural friction. Ever seen two people dance when both are trying to lead? Therefore, the role and execution plan of the sales force must be clearly defined. The organization of this chapter is as depicted in Figure 8-1.

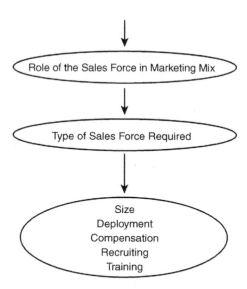

Figure 8-1 Entrepreneurial sales management issues

THE ROLE OF THE SALES FORCE

All elements of the marketing mix should be based on the marketing-driven strategy of the venture. The sales force decisions must be consistent and derived from the positioning and segmentation decisions that are the core of the strategy. In particular, the positioning and segmentation usually imply a role for the sales force in the marketing mix as part of the product's position and as a mechanism for implementing part of the market segmentation targeting.

For example, the Tandems East firm uses the owner, Mel Kornbluh, as its prime salesperson. His perceived expertise and experience with tandem bicycles and his willingness to satisfy customers is the bulk of his offering to potential customers. He also performs part of his firm's targeting functions by asking qualification questions during his first interactions with potential customers. On the other hand, some e-commerce companies have no role for personal sales in their marketing mix. Amazon.com customers have no interaction with any human salespeople when they make their purchase evaluations. However, the information and very personalized software Amazon.com has developed imitates what might happen if a customer went into a good bookstore and asked an experienced salesperson for information and recommendations. Dell Computer uses a mix of online sales and personal sales depending on customer preferences. Some Dell customers feel more comfortable interacting with a real person and value the salesperson's perceived problem-solving ability. Some bigger Dell customers feel that they deserve special prices and/or have special circumstances that need a personal touch.

The question you need to answer is: Given my positioning and segmentation strategy, what perceived value needs to be added by a personal sales force, if any, in order to most productively implement the strategy? If your thinking has been clear and your research has been good in the segmentation and positioning process, then determining the role of the sales force is usually straightforward.

The first steps are to review and understand the following:

1. How customers buy the product/service that you are offering
2. The price point of the product
3. Expected length of the sales cycle
4. Complexity of the sale

It's important to ensure that the sales approach selected is consistent with the answers to the preceding points. For example, you can't afford to pay a salesperson $200,000 a year for selling products that cost $20 apiece, such as in the previous Amazon.com example. Similarly, a customer is going to expect more than the self help of a Web site or telesalesperson when selecting a multi-million dollar enterprise software solution.

TYPE OF SALES FORCE REQUIRED

In addition to being consistent with the product and market dynamics, a company wants to deploy the most cost-effective sales model. If a product can be effectively sold over the phone, there is no reason to have external reps make in-person sales calls. Let's review the basic sales approaches to getting your product to an end user:

- **Direct to end user**—Company employees/systems sell directly to the end user of the product or service.
  - Web site—Self-serve purchasing (Amazon.com)
  - Telephone sales (L.L. Bean catalog)
  - Direct sales representatives (IBM)

- **Reseller/distributors**—Companies that resell your product in its current state to the ultimate end users (Best Buy).
- **Value-added resellers/distributors**—Companies that resell your product in an enhanced state to the ultimate end users (ATT reselling Yahoo! DSL).
- **Contract sales agents (reps)**—Individual salespeople who sell your product on your company's behalf (independent insurance agents).

Direct to end user sales represent sales models that are owned or directed by the company to sell the company's products to the entities that will use the product. Dell is an example of a company with a direct to end user sales model. Their products can only be purchased through Dell. These sales models include Web site sales, telesales, and direct sales representatives. Some of the advantages of the direct model are as follows:

1. The company can completely control the end user customer experience with the sales process.
2. Customer feedback is received directly.
3. The direct model can be more responsive to reflect changes, such as pricing, strategy, messaging, and so on.
4. The company's products are the first sales priority.

Disadvantages include the following:

1. High start-up costs.
2. It's harder to expand quickly with limited resources.
3. Personnel management.

Resellers/distributors are companies that resell your product in its current state to the ultimate end user. They typically sell products/services from multiple companies to a set of target markets. They buy the product/service from the entrepreneur and resell it to customers, keeping the margin between cost and price. An example would be Best Buy, who buys Compaq computers and resells them to consumers. The advantages of using a reseller/distributor model are as follows:

1. Faster time getting your product into the market.
2. Broader market reach to touch more customers is achieved by leveraging the marketing and sales efforts of an established company.

3. Lower start-up costs.

4. Access to the reseller/distributor's customer base.

5. The reseller/distributor has responsibility for the process and paperwork involved in closing a sale.

Disadvantages include the following:

1. Marketing and support programs must be built to support this channel.

2. The entrepreneur loses control over the customer experience during the sales process.

3. Entrepreneur still retains responsibility for training the sales force.

The reseller/distributor model requires specific sales and marketing support. This support takes on several forms: product training, tools/collateral needed to sell your product, technical support, and order placement/management support. Simply stated, much of what you need to support your own sales operation is also needed for this channel. The difference is that you need to provide modular materials that can be incorporated into a reseller/distributor's own materials—for example, providing .PDF formatted product diagrams that the channel can incorporate into their own product catalog. Likewise, you may want to have a special section of your Web site where information, collateral, self-directed training modules, and so on can be easily accessible for resellers/distributors to reduce your cost of supporting this channel. A FAQ (Frequently Asked Question) section with appropriate answers can be very helpful for your channel. The same support discussed here is required for value-added resellers/distributors as well, which are discussed next.

Value-added resellers/distributors are channels that enhance the state of your product before selling it to the end user. An example would be MetricStream. MetricStream, a quality and compliance software company, resells the Oracle database product as part of their solution. Customers buy MetricStream's Sarbanes-Oxley Compliance solution to ensure that they comply with the SEC regulation. The MetricStream software solution requires the Oracle database. Therefore, the end customer buys the Oracle product, but in a way that allows them to solve compliance problems. The strengths and weaknesses of this channel are the same as reseller/distributors.

Contract sales agents, also called manufacturers reps, are independent companies that sell on a commission basis and bear all of their own sales expenses. They are generally a local or regional entity with a defined territory that they cover. They generally do not carry competing lines and their representation contracts with their principals are not usually guaranteed for a long term. Their role is to either replace, or in some cases, supplement, the direct sales force. Reps are not a substitute for a distributor, however. They do not hold inventory or take title, invoice or ship, or take credit.

These reps provide several advantages. The assets these reps have are their relationships with their customers. In many cases, they have been providing their customers a number of products for many years. The good reps have achieved positions of perceived trust and reliability with their customers and understand their customers' needs very well. The rep may be able to achieve synergy by bundling your product with other products he or she is already selling. Also, because of the economies of combining products, a rep can typically call economically on smaller buyers or call more often on a single buyer than can the typical direct salesperson. Because their asset is their customer relationships, reps typically are more permanent and have less turnover than direct forces. Reps also pay more than direct salespeople and may retain their sales forces longer. Reps are also likely to be pretty nimble, sales focused, and very conscious of their sales costs. Reps also add a lot of flexibility—their low overhead (almost all variable costs) make it easy to forecast sales costs and provide downside cost protection if revenue is lower than anticipated. It is also much easier to terminate reps than an internal sales force.

However, reps also have disadvantages. Because they have many masters ("principals") whose products they must juggle, getting focus on your product may be difficult. The reps may also be too diversified to devote appropriate attention to the subset of their accounts that find value in your products. Some products may not have existing rep networks that are appropriate for your product. In other cases, a competitor may already take the really good reps. The biggest tradeoff that needs to be evaluated, however, is the loss of control that is part of being with a rep. The control issue applies to all the not-direct channels.

THE CONTROL ISSUE

When your firm directly employs the salesperson, theoretically you can direct the salesperson to do whatever you wish. However, in actuality, there's a continuum of realized control that depends on the kind of compensation and supervision system the entrepreneur chooses. Figure 8-2 shows this continuum.

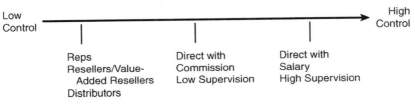

Figure 8-2 Control continuum

The figure underscores the relation between compensation method and the ability to control the salesperson. If your salespeople are on a straight commission with a low or non-existent base salary, they will also not be easy to control. If you tell a salesperson compensated by commission to do something he or she does not feel will add to his or her commissions, he or she will not want to do it. The rep is even harder to control because he or she has many masters and possibly conflicting activities he or she can do for each principal. On the other hand, if you pay the salesperson some kind of base salary, you can expect them to do some non-commission activities in return for their salary.

Control is important depending on the product positioning and segmentation and the appropriate role of the sales force. If your sales force plan requires activities that have unspecified payoff, then rep organizations (or straight commission) are probably not appropriate. If you have a product that requires single-minded dedication, then a rep may not be appropriate, but straight commission might be a viable option.

WHAT SITUATIONS FAVOR DIRECT VERSUS REP?

A very interesting study by Erin Anderson[1] analyzed how 13 firms in the electronic components industry decided on the rep versus direct decision in 159 different sales district/product combinations. These companies had a broad range of products from commodities to new, innovative, "glamour" products. The companies used reps when in doubt between reps and direct, and they used reps for the "normal," nondescript sales situations. However, there were lots of situations in which companies went direct, including the following:

1. Situations where it's difficult to evaluate salesperson's results "by the numbers," for example:

   a. Measures of sales results are inaccurate.

   b. It's difficult to assign credit for the sale because of multiple influences on the customer.

   c. Performance means much more than current sales—for example, there are long-term implications to short-term sales.

2. Situations where product and applications knowledge are difficult to learn, important, and/or complex. These include:

   a. Highly complex, unusual, or difficult to understand or explain products.

   b. Highly complex, unusual, or difficult to understand or explain applications.

3. Situations with highly confidential information in which salespeople come to learn sensitive information about their company and customers.

4. Situations where support activities are critical—for example, marketing research, trade show participation, after-sales service, and engineering support before the sale.

A situation that favors reps over direct salespeople is global expansion. When an entrepreneur is planning to expand into different countries, there are many risks that can be mitigated by leveraging local, in-country reps, to start. One of the biggest risks is hiring. Hiring an employee in a foreign company exposes you to foreign labor laws, taxation rules, and the legal and consulting expense to deal with these issues—not to mention the cost and legal risk of firing an employee in many countries if you made a mistake in the hiring process.

An in-country rep is a proven sales professional, with a Rolodex of prospects and an understanding of how local business gets done. They represent a low-cost, low-risk approach to opening sales in a foreign country.

CHOOSING REPS

If you decide to choose reps, the decision on which reps to choose is very important and should not be taken lightly. What you are buying with the rep is market reputation, relationships, and positions with complementary products. There are two criteria to tradeoff when choosing a rep. The first criterion is the rep's market position. Is he/she selling top brands in the market or do they represent the less-attractive products? The second criterion is whether the rep will have enough resources and use them to push your product or service versus the other products they sell. The best reps may not make enough time to push your new product, especially if the new product is small compared to the reps' current line. On the other hand, if your new product is really innovative and valuable, reps may use it to gain more access to their target accounts by introducing them to a new valuable product.

How can you efficiently get the information to make these tradeoffs? The way is similar to other recommendations in this book. *Talk to market participants.* Specifically, as part of the concept testing for a new product or service, ask also about which reps the target market prefers to buy from. Most market participants are quite willing to recommend people they prefer to buy from. Finding out how well the rep will push your product, if you choose them, is not so easy. Finding out how excited a rep firm will be with your product is comparable to finding out if the end customer will buy your product. Concept testing can be very helpful. You should interview rep principals from alternative rep firms and show them your product, tentative sales aids, and any possible advertisements for the product. You want to present your product to the rep in its most positive light. Then monitor the rep's reaction and compare across all the reps you interview. Your ideal rep is one who is very excited about how your product will help the rep's business, and a rep who is highly valued as a resource by the marketplace for your product. The entrepreneurial marketer's judgment, after having talked both with alternative reps and with a sample of market participants, should provide a very productive rep choice.

An important caveat—the rep choice is crucial to the financial viability of many businesses and should not be taken lightly. Above all, choosing a rep should *not* be done opportunistically. *Do not choose the first rep who approaches you.* It is almost always very productive to invest some time and money to find the best rep. Even when time and money are very scarce for the entrepreneur, it makes sense to get information *from market participants* before making a decision like choosing a rep that has a very long-term and pronounced effect on your venture.

EFFECTIVE REP MANAGEMENT

If you have decided to use reps, they will not be successful without you thinking very carefully about how they will be managed. Reps are another group that needs marketing attention. Just like the end customer, you need to understand what makes the rep tick—what her objectives and goals are and how your product offering can add perceived value for the rep. Anderson, Lodish, and Weitz studied how 71 independent reps actually allocated their time to their principals' products.[2] They found that, in general (and no surprise), reps allocated time to maximize their commission income from their principals. However, reps also deviated from solely resource allocations that maximized their commission income in order to favor principals who they perceived had similar *goals, good communication, and mutual trust.* Reps also favored principals who had *active involvement* in the rep's activities. The authors' findings imply some specific tactics that help obtain more of a rep's attention, as follows:

1. Make your products easier for the rep to sell. Make its price/perceived value better for the end user. Provide sales training for reps. Develop and implement promotions toward the end user that the rep can use to make her job more efficient.

2. Increasing commission rates will increase the sales effort toward your product, but it will have diminishing returns.

3. Reps favor products that are synergistic with other products in the rep's portfolio.

4. Principals should develop very trusting relationships with their reps.

5. Principals should improve communication through recognition programs, product training, and consultation with the reps, as well as by informing reps of plans, explicitly detailing objectives, and providing positive feedback.

6. Principals who have a hands-off approach to reps lose time for their products.

7. Even interfering in the management of the rep with negative feedback results in greater time for your product.[3]

REP MANAGEMENT AND THE PERCEIVED VALUE PROPOSITION

The entrepreneurial manager should be noticing that many of the preceding tactics cost either money (e.g., end user promotions, sales training), or margin points (e.g., improving the price/value relationship, increasing commission rates). If you have an excellent business plan that has a positioning strategy that succeeds in creating incremental perceived value to the end user compared to competition, then you should have "room" to share some of that value with your outsourced intermediaries in the channel.

Franklin Electronic Publications, Inc. is a manufacturer of electronic hand-held reference tools—spelling correctors, dictionaries, and so on. For the past 18 years, they have successfully used reps to sell their product in the consumer electronics channel. Especially when they began as an entrepreneurial company with few resources, but with a new unique product (the Spelling Ace spelling corrector), reps were a crucial part of the marketing plan. Because the Spelling Ace could be sold to the consumer at prices that gave very good manufacturing margins, Franklin was able to "share" some of those high margins with their reps and their retailers. The reps got very good commissions for selling the products, and the retailers got better margins than from comparable products that competed for scarce shelf and display space.

This Franklin example underscores the importance of including all elements of the marketing mix as part of the initial business plan. The positioning and segmentation decisions have a big impact on the viability of the venture partly because they have a big impact on what is possible for other elements of the marketing mix. The management of reps is only one element in which the positioning and segmentation decisions have a crucial impact.

DIRECT SALES: PERSONAL VERSUS TELEPHONE VERSUS THE WEB AND OTHER NONPERSONAL SALES

It is not obvious that a personal sales force is appropriate for all situations. The telephone, the Internet, and other media may be more efficient for accomplishing needed tasks in the marketing and sales process. You should first determine the tasks and activity that are required for each step in the sales process. Then you should evaluate the costs and the benefit of alternative ways to accomplish those sales tasks. Tables 8-1 and 8-2 show the evaluation of two alternative sales processes for a venture. Table 8-1 evaluates a personal sales process, and Table 8-2 evaluates how the same process might be accomplished by telemarketing instead of personal sales. These are disguised real examples.

Table 8-1   Field sales-oriented sales process

Sales Activity	Prospects Remaining	Delivery Vehicle	Elapsed Time (wks)	Activity Cost	Total Cost
1. New lead	100	Mail/Telephone	0	$25	$2,500
2. Literature fulfillment	100	Mail	1	$10	$3,500
3. Quality prospect	100	Telephone	2	$15	$5,000
4. Initial meeting	30	Field visit	4	$200	$11,000
5. Follow-up call	20	Telephone	5	$15	$11,200
6. Demonstration	10	Field visit	7	$250	$13,700
7. Proposal	5	Overnight service	8	$100	$14,200
8. Additional follow-up	3	Telephone	12	$50	$14,350
9. Approval/ Purchase	3	Telephone	16	$10	$14,380
10. Post-sale follow-up	3	Telephone	20	$30	$14,470

Table 8-2   Telemarketing-oriented sales process

Sales Activity	Prospects Remaining	Delivery Vehicle	Elapsed Time (wks)	Activity Cost	Total Cost
1. New lead	100	Mail/Telephone	0	$25	$2,500
2. Initial literature	100	Mail	1	$10	$3,500
3. Quality call	100	Telephone	2	$15	$5,000
4. Second literature	30	Mail	3	$10	$5,300

Sales Activity	Prospects Remaining	Delivery Vehicle	Elapsed Time (wks)	Activity Cost	Total Cost
5. Consult/ Sales call	30	Telephone	4	$25	$5,800
6. Payback worksheet	20	Telephone	6	$5	$5,850
7. Configuration call	10	Telephone	6	$10	$5,950
8. Proposal	5	Overnight service	8	$100	$6,450
9.–12. Additional follow-up	3	Telephone	12	$100	$6,750
13. Approval/ Purchase	3	Telephone	16	$10	$6,780
14. Post-sale follow-up	3	Telephone	20	$30	$6,870

In Table 8-1, the entrepreneur, who we can think of as Sarah in this example, has estimated the "sales funnel" for her typical personal sales process. Starting with 100 prospects, she estimates how many will remain after each stage in the process. For example, of each 100 prospects who have been qualified, 30 will remain as prospects after the telephone qualification call. She also estimates the elapsed time for each activity and the costs of each activity. It is usually pretty easy to get good estimates for the timing and costs of the various activities and sales calls. The most difficult estimate is the success rate for each activity—that is, what fraction of the people in the funnel will proceed to the next stage. For example, there is an assumption that 5 out of 10, or 50% of prospects, will ask for a proposal after a demonstration. Before one begins business, it will be pretty difficult to get good estimates for that kind of response percentage. However, once the business is going, it is conceptually easy to measure these percentages by keeping track of the number of people in the funnel at different stages, their treatment by the sales process, and the fraction who go on to the next stage after each task is performed. The challenge is to keep track of the data in the middle of launching a new product or service.

Notice that in Table 8-2, there are different activities in the telemarketing-oriented sales process. The funnel also has different costs and different fractions progressing from stage to stage. However, if the assumptions are reasonably correct, for this case, the telemarketing-oriented sales process will be much more efficient for accomplishing the sales process. The personal sales approach may convert more prospects per 100, but it costs over 50% more to get each completed sale. Only if the number of prospects is very limited does it make sense to use a personal sales approach for this example.

What these examples should illustrate is how important it is to determine all the stages of the sales process, and then to estimate the costs and benefits of performing them by different vehicles. In many cases, it will be very difficult to construct funnels like Tables 8-1 and 8-2 with no sales experience. What then makes sense is, as you begin your operations, to *experiment* with the sales process alternatives that make à priori sense. As the sales process is performed, keep track of the number of prospects in the funnel for each stage along with elapsed costs and timing. After a suitable length of time, you should be able to infer which approaches to the sales process are most efficient and use those on an ongoing basis.

It is very important to evaluate many options for accomplishing the sales process. Not every prospect should necessarily be put through the same sales process. Some market segments may respond differently to different sales processes. Depending on the costs and potential value, in many cases, it makes sense to experiment with different sales processes for different market segments. Again, depending on the circumstances, some potential prospects may wish to choose the sales process that they prefer.

The Indymac Bank has developed technology to automate the underwriting and risk-based pricing process for home mortgages. The technology is being distributed and sold in two ways to capitalize on two types of consumers that the Indymac management has defined: "low tech + hi touch" and "hi tech + low touch." The first segment is much more comfortable with a personal intermediary to help them apply for and go through the home mortgage purchase process. So a mortgage broker (personal salesperson) sits with the client and types information about the proposed loan and the loan applicant. Within five minutes, the Indymac e-MITS system comes back with an underwriting decision and a price for the mortgage that has been uniquely determined for the potential purchaser based on their credit history, and so on. The system also prints out, right at the computer, all of the closing documents that will be needed for the loan to be closed.

The same e-MITS technology is used in indymac.com, the direct-to-consumer Web site that Indymac has introduced for the other "high tech +

low touch" segment. The Web site performs almost the exact same functions as the technology available on the Web for mortgage brokers, but it is presented directly to consumers who feel confident enough to apply for and close on a mortgage without relying on a mortgage broker intermediary. These customers get to pay less for their mortgages because they are not paying the sales commissions for the mortgage brokers.

Many other creative entrepreneurial marketers have also realized that one sales/distribution system may not fit all of their customers. Just as product and service offerings should be tailored to the needs of market segments, so should the sales and distribution process that is a part of what the end consumer finally perceives. Barnes and Noble does the same thing as Indymac. They sell the same books at stores with personal assistance and over the Web at BarnesandNoble.com. Their competitor, Borders, did not take advantage of this segmentation opportunity and lost much potential business to Amazon.com and BarnesandNoble.com.

SALES FORCE SIZE, DEPLOYMENT, AND ORGANIZATION

Once you have decided to use a personal sales force, your decision making is just beginning.

SALES FORCE SIZE AND DEPLOYMENT

If you have decided to use a personal sales force, a number of questions quickly surface. How big should the force be and how should it be organized and deployed? The conceptual answer to these questions is easy. A sales force is like any other investment the entrepreneur makes. If adding resources to the sales force is the most profitable place to use the scarce capital, and if the use is more profitable than putting the money in the bank, then the funds should be added to the sales force. Funds should be added until they are no longer the most profitable place to put capital. The sales force is the right size when the "last person added" brought in more of a return on their investment than any other investment opportunity.

In many cases, the appropriate sales force size can be dictated by the market segment(s) that are being targeted and the costs and incremental benefits associated with the role of the sales force. In many cases, a salesperson is a necessary part of what the channel expects from the entrepreneur. For example, if you expect to sell through retailers such as department stores or mass merchandisers, these firms have expectations about terms of sales and service from their suppliers. It is typically not possible to change the customary way in which other suppliers have set the retailer's expectations. Interviewing buyers from the retailers as well as salespeople (or reps) who service the retailers can get you enough information to roughly estimate the sales time associated with the various activities that are required by the potential customers. You can then also estimate the incremental revenue associated with those activities. It is then straightforward to calculate the marginal revenue and marginal costs of this sales force activity.

For other sales situations, it makes more sense to evaluate the activities by estimating directly the impact of sales calls on the revenue of clients and/or prospects. For example, "What would happen to the revenue of a typical customer of type 'A' if we called four times per quarter instead of twice?" This kind of question should be asked for alternative levels of sales force size and deployment levels that you are evaluating. Once the revenue associated with the alternative levels of sales efforts has been estimated, then the incremental revenues and incremental costs can be applied to roughly determine the appropriate sales force effort to use toward each type of client and prospect.

There are three ways to estimate the sales response to alternative call frequencies. Judgment of the salesperson along with her manager (who may be the entrepreneur) has been shown to be better than deploying salespeople without considering sales response to different levels of call effort. By evaluating judgments of the sales impacts of different call effort levels to different segments of accounts, it is straightforward to allocate time to those segments where it adds the most incremental profit contribution, and then continue to add time to that segment and/or other segments until the incremental return does not justify the sales force costs. Before the business begins operations, experience is probably the only way to determine the best sales force size along with some guidelines on deployment over account segments. Without experience, competitor activity can provide a reasonable starting point. In Chapter 11, "Marketing Resource Deployment and Allocation—The Alloc Software," a resource allocation model will be discussed that can also provide guidance on sales force sizing.

Once the venture has begun and the sales process has begun, the entrepreneur can evaluate any naturally occurring experiments that may have happened. These naturally occurring experiments happen when different accounts in the same segment get different amounts of sales effort. If you have planned your information system to keep sales as well as salespeople call reports, you can evaluate to what extent different levels of sales force effort have seemed to cause sales changes. The problem with this procedure is that the sales force may be choosing who to spend more or less effort on within a segment based on other factors such as prior relationships or specific knowledge about that account's situation. The analysis may attribute sales changes to the wrong causes. The most accurate, unbiased estimates come from the third way of getting sales response to alternative levels of sales effort—experiments.

Instead of letting naturally occurring changes happen to sales force effort levels on accounts, it can be very valuable to *randomly assign* different levels of effort to different accounts within a segment. If there really is a random assignment of different levels of sales effort to accounts, then other possible causes are mitigated by the randomization. The same concerns and issues for designing experiments that we describe for advertising decisions are also appropriate for sales force experiments. See Chapter 10, "Entrepreneurial Promotion and Viral Marketing to Maximize Sustainable Profitability," for additional information.

DEPLOYMENT WITH LIMITED SALES FORCE SIZE

Many entrepreneurs do not have the luxury of evaluating many different levels of sales force sizes and appropriate deployment levels as we describe previously. They are very limited in resources and cannot afford to have many salespeople. In these cases, it is crucial to "*skim the cream*." Using the judgmental method described earlier, the entrepreneur must only spend his or her sales force effort where it contributes the highest amount of incremental revenue and profit contribution. However, keeping track of the sales effort, and associated incremental sales generated from it, can be an excellent way to show a source of financing what to expect if more resources were made available for increasing sales force effort. The resource allocation model and accompanying software in Chapter 11 will assist in applying these methods.

Travel costs and entertainment expenses also need to be considered when the size and sales force resource decisions are made. If the location of some accounts will necessitate extra trips, then these costs should be prorated over the accounts to be called on during the trips. The sales force organization decision will also impact travel costs if it means that different people will be calling on different accounts in the same geographical area.

SALES FORCE ORGANIZATION AND TRAVEL COSTS

Sales force organization typically encompasses how the force is structured vis à vis markets and geography. The tradeoff of most alternative organizations is conceptually simple. Is the specialization of sales effort achieved by having salespeople specialize in one or more market segments more beneficial to the firm than the increased costs associated with the specialization? The increased costs of segment specialization are typically travel costs and the opportunity costs of time spent traveling. For small entrepreneurial companies with their own sales forces, the organization that is appropriate is usually obvious. If there is only one target market, then a geographical sales organization is the only reasonable option. A geographical sales organization has territories that are geographically determined, with each salesperson covering accounts in one territory. If there is more than one target segment, another possible organization is to have a sales force for each segment. Each segment sales force would have its own geographical organization. It would then be possible to have more than one salesperson covering the same geographical area, with each salesperson calling on accounts in different segments. The more specialized the sales force is, the larger geographical area each salesperson's territory will cover.

COMPENSATION

Compensation is one of the topics most senior sales managers are always fretting over.

MATCHING INCENTIVES

If you as an entrepreneurial marketer remember one idea from this sales force chapter, it should be this one: People (and especially salespeople) do what they think will make them *the most money* for the time they spend at their jobs. Your compensation system should make sure that you and your salespeople have *matching incentives*. If you both are trying to do the same thing, then it's difficult to get into situations in which your salespeople do the wrong thing. The appropriate compensation also depends on the role of the salesperson. For example, if the salesperson has some control over the price she charges, then the compensation should have the salespeople negotiate as good a price as you, the entrepreneur or business manager, would negotiate. Auto dealers are classic examples of this type of compensation. The salespeople at most car dealerships who negotiate a price with each consumer have a commission that is based not on the sold car's sales price, but on the gross margin (sales price-variable costs) for the car. If the commission were on just the sales price, the salesperson would likely be selling cars to maximize revenue by selling more cars at the lowest price he or she could quote.

This same argument is very pertinent to situations in which your sales force is selling more than one product. If each product has quite different contribution margins, you want the salesperson to be incented, not on revenue, but on contribution margin (revenue-variable costs). In these multi product situations, the entrepreneur does not have to actually share her gross margins with the sales force. All the sales force needs to know (and have incentives based on) is the relative profitability of one product versus another. The entrepreneur can have sales compensation based upon "points" for each product. The points just need to be proportionally correct; that is, if product A has four points per sales dollar, and product B has two points, then product A should have twice as much gross margin per sales dollar as product B. The salespeople don't have to know the exact margin figures in order to allocate their effort to where they will get the most margin per hour of their time. Many firms have not compensated their salespeople in this way and have foregone some profit by not treating revenue differently from different products. In extreme cases, one author has seen firms give sales awards to the top revenue-producing salesperson. After some analysis, it was determined that that person was actually *losing money* for his company. He was selling products that were not profitable after his sales costs were considered.

The salespeople will visit customers who are perceived to be most likely to value the products they can sell. If the salespeople are trying to find accounts that will most likely buy the products with high contribution margin, then the salesperson and the firm both have matching incentives and the salespeople will naturally gravitate to the accounts that will be most profitable for the firm.

Outback Steakhouse—Perfectly Matched Incentives

Outback Steakhouse has been very successful in an extremely competitive restaurant industry. One reason for their success is how they compensate their store managers. Each store manager invests $25,000 in "his or her store." For that investment, they get 10% of the profits that store generates. These store managers report to regional managers who have made similar investments in return for a piece of their region's profits. The incentives here are matched perfectly. These managers will try to use the resources in their control to maximize their income—that is exactly proportional to the income of the Outback Steakhouse Corporation. By maximizing their income, the managers are simultaneously maximizing the income of their "parent" corporation. This compensation scheme is a very creative blend of some aspects of franchising with corporate control. If the managers leave, there are pre-arranged values for buying back the manager's equity interest in the restaurant.

INCENTIVES VERSUS CONTROL VERSUS TIME HORIZONS

The preceding Outback example points out one concern about matching incentives. Profit can be short term or longer term. You may have different time horizons in mind than members of your sales force. Even if you both are trying to maximize profits, a salesperson may want to maximize short-term profits, whereas you, the entrepreneurial marketer, may be more concerned with longer-term profits and building the value of the company. Some sales force activities may be very helpful to long-term profits, but take away from short-term profits. These include market research and call reporting. Our experience is that it is easier to have some portion of the fixed component of the salesperson's compensation specified as payment for these kinds of activities. You thus *tell* the sales force that they are being *paid to do market research* and/or *fill out call reports*. Most salespeople will not see the value to their future income of these kinds of activities and need to perceive that they are being directly paid to perform them.

It is important to set these expectations at the beginning of the relationship. If the salesperson is told when he or she is hired that part of his or her base salary is for call reports and other "paper work," he or she will feel that this becomes part of his or her job for which he or she is being adequately compensated. The base salary can also be used as a way to control the salesperson to do activities that may not be maximizing her short-term income. You may want the salesperson to call on some accounts that will not be ready to buy, but you need their feedback now on the next-generation product or service design.

Just as our discussion of reps had control as an issue, the same issues occur in compensation. The more straight commission you have, the lower your control. Our experience has shown that for many businesses, it makes sense to have some element of base salary as a justification for requesting the salespeople to do activities that may not be maximizing their short-term commission income. Many of the suggestions throughout this book for continually experimenting with different elements of the marketing mix will be thwarted if the sales force will not cooperate. By its nature, experimentation will show that some activities are more productive than others. You don't want your sales force to feel that they are being penalized if they happen to be in one experimental treatment that doesn't perform as well as another treatment. You need to set these expectations at the outset of the relationship. You should tell new salespeople that they are joining an entrepreneurial, adapting, learning, and continually experimenting organization. By their nature, some experiments will work better than others will, and the salespeople should expect that. If you couch their base salary as compensation for these learning and experimental activities, you will avoid possible problems later on.

COMPENSATION FOR NEW VERSUS EXISTING CUSTOMERS, A POSSIBLE FESTERING PROBLEM

Many entrepreneurs will start their businesses with a straight commission sales force. This option has the lowest variable costs. If more than one product is involved, the commission rate should be proportional to the gross profit margin of each product. However, another phenomenon is happening with straight commission sales forces that most entrepreneurs don't realize until it has begun to affect their growth and profitability. By then, it is typically too late to solve easily.

If the commission is high enough, and the product potential large enough, a straight commission sales incentive plan can result in amazing sales force effort and motivation—up to a point. The first salesperson to sell your product (let's use Sarah again as our example) will typically "bust her butt" to open up many accounts in her territory. She will view this as an opportunity to be entrepreneurial and develop these accounts as her "own little business." However, in her mind, she has an idea of what she needs to make in order to "make a good living." Once the salesperson has gotten the territory to the point where her commissions generate this "good living," the salesperson will then tend to *coast* with her established accounts and protect them from any management gerrymandering.

It is usually much easier to maintain accounts than to get new ones. The straight commission salesperson will get to a point where he or she will be content to just maintain her current accounts and not spend much effort generating new accounts. The previous scenario has been validated as typical by over 1,000 sales managers who have attended the Wharton School's executive program in sales force management.

One solution to the problem is to have *different rates* of commission for generating *new accounts* than for maintaining the business. The commission rate would thus be higher for the first year's business with an account and lower on succeeding years. Alternatively, some firms will have a different commission rate on sales until last year's level is reached and a different level on sales higher than last years.

THE SHADOW BROADCAST SERVICES EXAMPLE

The Shadow Broadcast Services story, in which one co-author (Lodish) was a minority investor and advisor, provides examples of a number of the concepts we discuss in this book. Not only are the sales force compensation issues faced by Shadow illustrative of the preceding concepts, but the business model and product-offering decisions applied some of this book's other paradigms.

SHADOW'S INITIAL BUSINESS MODEL

Shadow Broadcast Services began as an entrepreneurial organization in New York and Chicago. The business model at first was to gather traffic information using planes, helicopters, police scanners, part-time drivers, and cellphone messages from citizen volunteers. This information was then synthesized, cross-validated, and then broadcast from Shadow's studio to a radio station over high-quality communications lines. Even though Shadow's announcers were remote to the radio station, to the radio listener, the Shadow announcer sounded just like she was at the station. The Shadow announcer could banter with the disk jockeys, and participate as a member of the station's broadcast team. Depending on the station, the Shadow announcer could either say she was giving a "Shadow Traffic" report, or be reporting from the "WXXX Traffic Center." One Shadow announcer could be the traffic reporter for a number of stations. Depending on the frequency each station wanted to broadcast traffic reports, a Shadow announcer could handle as many as 10 stations.

The beginning business model was borrowed from Shadow's main competitor, Metro Traffic, that operated in over 30 major U.S. markets, almost as a monopoly in the traffic business. Shadow's beginning business model was to barter the traffic reports for advertising time in the traffic reports that Shadow would sell to advertisers. The Shadow advertising was typically a 10-second spot read at the end of the traffic report along with a lead-in. The lead-in was typically something like "this report brought to you by Chrysler." Shadow obtained most of its revenue from selling advertising time.

The attractiveness to stations of Shadow was that they didn't have to gather and report their own traffic information. Shadow took advantage of economies of scale by sharing the gathering and reporting costs over a number of stations. However, the way revenues actually occurred showed very insightful entrepreneurial marketing thinking. Another way Shadow and its competitor could have generated revenue was by selling the traffic reports to the stations for cash. There were very different perceptions of radio station managers and Shadow of the value of the 10-second spots that Shadow ended up selling. To stations, they did not feel that they could get much value from selling 10-second spots, when all of the other advertising time on their stations was sold to advertisers in units of 30 and 60 seconds. Stations were also becoming part of big, highly leveraged entities that were valued by the financial markets in terms of multiples of their broadcast cash flow. Cash flow was "king" to most radio station general managers. Thus, paying out cash had a high negative value to most station managers. They would much rather pay for the traffic reports with bartered air time that they felt they would have difficulty in selling.

Another variable to this perceived value calculation is that to the advertiser, 10-second advertisements were perceived as much more valuable when they were broadcast on a network of stations in an area versus on one or two stations. The 10-second traffic ads were great for announcing temporary promotions or very simple announcements of new features or items. Timeliness of the traffic ads as well as being able to reach large numbers of people quickly was potentially very valuable to advertisers. Shadow was able to deliver a network of stations in a city that an individual station could not match. Thus, what Shadow was bartering to the stations had different perceived value to each party—Shadow and each radio station. Both parties perceived that they were getting better value than the other side in the barter deals.

Another factor that helped Shadow in the beginning was some research they had come across by chance. This research showed that listeners paid more attention to traffic broadcasts than to any other element of a radio show. The research was actually done by a firm that was trying to determine listener preferences for all program content—mainly different music and disk jockey patter, and so on. The firm would play recordings of yesterday's radio program and ask respondents to turn a dial to indicate how much attention they were paying to what they were hearing. The dial went from 1 to 10. The researcher could then monitor the average attention "paid" to various elements of the station's programming. For different disk jockeys, their patter would get scores of anywhere from 2 to 9, the music would also get highly varied scores from 1–10, and the normal 30- or 60-second commercials would typically get low scores of 1–3. The news, weather, and sports segments were moderately well attended. Scores ranged from 3 to 8 depending on the content. The amazing thing to Shadow was that *yesterday's* traffic report always got an attention score of between 8 and 10! Because most radio listening is done in the car, evidently most listeners are conditioned to pay attention to the traffic reports as they come on. It was useful for the Shadow managers to know that their medium was likely to work for advertisers much more efficiently than the typical radio spot.

An interesting aside—over time, some of the stations began to perceive the high value of 10-second ads delivered with traffic information. These more entrepreneurial station managers started to keep some of the traffic spots to sell themselves and began to charge Shadow and Metro fees for the privilege of providing traffic services to their stations. The differences in perceived value of the 10-second spots acted like many other competitive advantages: They lose value over time if not enhanced in some way.

SHADOW'S SUBSEQUENT BUSINESS MODEL

Shadow management innovated the Shadow product in two major ways. Both innovations had much to do with entrepreneurial marketing thinking about differential perceived value to different market segments. The first innovation was a response to the increased cost pressure the radio stations were facing. One source of costs was their gathering and reporting of local news, sports, and weather. If Shadow used its already existing infrastructure to not only gather and report traffic information, but also to gather and report local news, sports, and weather, it could do it at a much lower cost per report than could a typical station. Some Shadow announcers would do traffic on one station, local news on another, and sports on still another. Shadow also bartered the news, sports, and weather reports for 10-second spots instead of selling them to the stations. The stations again perceived this as lower in cost compared to paying for the service. To Shadow, it gave them an even bigger, higher-reach network to sell to advertisers with lower incremental costs for the inventory. Because the infrastructure for reporting news, sports, and weather was already in place, the incremental costs per spot of advertising inventory from providing the newer services were lower.

The second innovation did not work out exactly as anticipated, but was pretty valuable. A major expense to Shadow was the helicopters used to gather and report the information. Not only were the helicopters expensive (over $300 per hour), but also they could not be used in inclement weather—just when you really need them. Shadow management evaluated the costs and benefits of installing remote controlled video cameras that could zoom in to observe all the major traffic arteries in a city. If the cameras could replace helicopters, it seemed that the payback on the camera investment would be less than six months! A bonus was that the cameras were to be available 24 hours per day, seven days per week. The cameras would also be useful additions to the TV news programs that had started broadcasting reports prepared in Shadow's studios. The cameras were installed and the use of helicopters curtailed.

Over time, the camera additions did not create as much cost reductions as hoped for. The radio stations were reluctant to diminish their number of helicopter broadcasts because of reactions from their listeners. Radio listeners wrongly perceive the helicopters to be the most accurate source of traffic information and prefer to listen to stations that broadcast reports directly from helicopters. An expensive educational campaign was required to convince radio listeners of the better information provided by cameras. Had Shadow concept tested the camera innovation with a sample of radio listeners *before* they made the camera investment, they would have been able to better plan for the real costs that were associated with the camera program. In planning product/service changes, it is very important to evaluate whether to *concept test* the changes with all *segments and stakeholders* who might react to the change.

Of course, after about a year, Shadow's major competitor copied these innovations. However, this just increased the profits of both competitors by increasing the size of the market and lowering the acquisition costs of advertising inventory.

THE SHADOW SALES FORCE ROLE AND COMPENSATION

The radio stations did not want to add another competitor when they took on a traffic service. Almost all stations stipulated that the advertisers that the traffic service obtained for their network should not overlap with either the radio station's current advertisers or any advertisers to whom the radio station had made a recent pitch. The stations were told that the money for traffic ads would come from different budgets than for traditional spot radio advertising—things like promotion funds or co-op vendor funds.

The Shadow sales force's role was pretty difficult. They were charged with convincing non-traditional radio advertisers to use a new kind of ad (10 second) in a new sub-medium (within live traffic reports) in a new network. This role is quintessential missionary selling—taking the gospel out to convince new people to convert. In order to attract and motivate the best people for this role, Shadow and Metro paid pretty big draws against commission and pretty high commissions (around 10%) on revenue. The really effective salespeople were making several hundred thousand dollars per year. However, many salespeople could not accomplish the job adequately and were asked to leave.

After a few years in the first two cities, New York and Chicago, Shadow managers began to see the "coasting" phenomena set in on some of the best, most experienced salespeople. Once these salespeople had gotten enough accounts so that the commission on those accounts gave them the standard of living to which they aspired, they cut down severely on their new account prospecting and spent whatever time was necessary to maintain the revenue (and commission) from their current accounts. They also spent less time selling, but maintained their income and even improved their standard of living because they had more leisure time. Maintaining revenue from current accounts typically requires less sales effort than getting an equivalent amount of new business. This was definitely true for Shadow.

To improve the situation, Shadow changed its compensation to a higher commission rate for the revenues from an account for its first year (over 12%), but a lower commission rate on succeeding year's revenue (less than 8%). Theoretically, the commission rates for new versus existing business should be roughly proportional to the effort required for each task. In this way, the salesperson should be indifferent to spending time with current accounts or trying to penetrate new accounts. A compensation system like Shadow's new one helps to control the "coasting" problem. If the salesperson coasts and just services existing accounts, she will get a lower income level. As the reader might have forecast, convincing the experienced salespeople to adopt the changed commission plan was very difficult. The salespeople rightly were concerned that their initial expectations to which they had agreed had been changed. A number of the experienced, best, salespeople had performance problems adjusting to the new arrangement. They had to work hard again!

When Shadow expanded to other cities, management initiated the tiered commission plan from the beginning—paying a higher commission for the first year of revenue and lower on succeeding years. It was no problem to get salespeople to buy in to the scheme when it was introduced *at the beginning* of their relationship with Shadow. In fact, the better salespeople were able to accelerate their compensation growth. If they ended up "coasting," they at least did it at a much higher revenue level and had to work harder to keep a compensation level. Hindsight and experience in the newer markets convinced Shadow management that it was much more productive to *introduce the differential commissions at the beginning.*

Salespeople are human beings just like any other person (or buyer of something). They are much more satisfied if their experience matches or exceeds their prior expectations than if they are told to change their expectations in the middle of an experience. This is one example of using marketing thinking to manage more than your relationships with customers. Your sales force also needs to be approached with careful marketing thinking. Just as it is crucial to manage the buyer's expectations when you or your sales force sell your product or service, it is also just as important to manage your employee's expectations when you "sell" them on working for your company.

RECRUITING, TRAINING, AND RETENTION STRATEGIES

Once you have made all of the preceding decisions about your sales force, recruiting the right people is a very difficult job. Chapter 12, "Entrepreneurial Marketing for Hiring, Growing, and Retaining Employees," looks at this process as another marketing problem to solve. For most entrepreneurial ventures, you will not be able to have the luxury of training raw recruits from scratch. You just won't have the time or available resources to train them. Raw recruits won't have the market contacts to "hit the ground running." Thus, most initial sales force hires will come from other companies that have operations in markets related to yours. Remember, the salespeople you hire will be the representatives of the company to the marketplace. The entrepreneur needs to be diligent and thoughtful in their hiring process.

B. J. Bushur, owner and president of Unlimited Results who has hired hundreds of sales reps throughout her career, has found several key factors (in addition to experience) to look for in successful sales reps:

- **Drive**—Highly motivated to excel.
- **Love of learning**—Self-improvement focused. Continually add value to their clients by sharing their knowledge and keeping up-to-date with market trends.
- **Solution-oriented**—Problem solvers who can link their customers' problems to their solutions (e.g., products and services).
- **Positive people that others like to be around**—People buy from people they like and they buy more from people they like to be around and who add value in some way to their lives: by giving them more knowledge to do their job more effectively, by helping them enjoy life more, or by making them "look good" (in many different ways).

One of the toughest tradeoffs in hiring salespeople is sales experience versus drive. If given the choice, hiring the person who may be a bit lighter or equal on experience but has the higher drive is better over the long term. In every interview, ask: "What drives you?" And, of course, money drives all salespeople. . .but you also want to hear motivations in addition to money. Chapter 12 will discuss more entrepreneurial approaches to this hiring/marketing challenge.

Training of the sales force will be very idiosyncratic to the role of the salesperson in your marketing mix and the role of the salesperson in the "product-offering bundle" that you offer. As a small, entrepreneurial company, you will typically do better with someone who already knows how to sell. Your job is to make sure that this person knows your product inside and out as well as how the market will benefit from the product. It will usually be beneficial for you to do anything you can to help the new salesperson learn about the buying process at her customers and prospects, the competition, and any other meaningful parts of the positioning of your offering bundle.

When *not* to retain salespeople is a decision that is not made nearly as well as it should be by entrepreneurs (and other managers as well). There is a tradeoff to be made that most managers and entrepreneurs rarely consider. If they have a limited sales budget and/or limited prospects on which to call, then they have a limited size of sales force to deal with. One way to possibly improve sales productivity is to fire lower-performing salespeople and replace them with new recruits who might prove to be higher performing. The tradeoff is costs of hiring and training plus the "burn in" time of the new recruit, plus the chance that the new recruit may also not be very good. In the only analysis we've seen of this phenomenon (on navy recruiting salespeople), the answer was clear. The venture was keeping mediocre people when they would have been much better off "raising the bar."

CONCLUSION

Sales management is a marketing issue. Determining the type of salesperson needed and the role and size of the sales force are decisions all driving from marketing's positioning and segmentation work. The sales force concepts and paradigms shared are useful for entrepreneurial marketers to understand and embrace, so that marketing can work with the management team to ensure good decisions are being made. These include the entrepreneurial ways to evaluate different sales approaches, handling the rep versus direct issue, and deciding which functions to do in person versus which sales functions to handle impersonally.

Once the appropriate type of sales force has been deployed, ensuring continuous improvement in productivity is important. Analyzing alternative options for sales force size, deployment, and organization are areas where marketing can assist. Because sales priorities are driven by their compensation structure—that is, sales plans—marketing needs to understand options and approaches to compensation and motivation systems. Shadow Broadcast Services was used as an example of not only a good compensation system, but also entrepreneurial thinking about its product positioning and perceived value to its different market segments. Shadow also exemplifies how much easier it can be for the entrepreneur if she gets her compensation system correct in the beginning, and manages employee expectations appropriately.

This was not meant to be a complete summary of management techniques for sales forces, but a compendium focused on key sales management ideas that have been demonstrated to help add lots of value for entrepreneurial marketers.

ENDNOTES

1. Anderson, Erin (1985), "The Salesperson as Outside Agent or Employee: A Transaction Cost Analysis," *Marketing Science*, 4 (Summer), pp. 234–254.

2. Anderson, Erin; Lodish, Leonard M.; Weitz, Barton A. (1987), "Resource Allocation Behavior in Conventional Channels," *Journal of Marketing Research*, XXIV (Feb.), pp. 85–97.

3. Ibid, p. 95.

Marketing-Enabled Sales

	Products/Services	Equity/Shares	Image
Customers			
Users			
Investors			
Supply Chain/ Channel Partners			
Employees			

Now that the sales force decisions are made, marketing needs to focus on how to best enable sales. This is a step that is frequently forgotten. Once we have a sales force and a presentation, we send the sales reps out to the market to sell and then are disappointed when sales cycles are longer than anticipated, win rates aren't as high as expected, and prices are lower than planned for. What went wrong?

Salespeople are not marketing people. Salespeople need marketing tools to support the process of selling (see Table 9-1).

Table 9-1   The sales process and marketing needs

Sales Process Steps	Marketing Needs
Identify prospective customers	Lead generation
Qualifying prospects	■ Target customer description ■ Product collateral: datasheets, brochures
Gain interest	■ Customized presentation ■ Product demonstrations ■ Relevant case studies ■ White papers ■ ROI tools
Proposal submission	■ RFP checklist ■ Proposal template
Reference checking	■ Reference customers ■ Customer testimonials/quotes
Objection handling	■ Company viability presentation ■ Detailed product spec sheets ■ Implementation methodology ■ Competitive comparisons
Close	■ Contract ■ Support materials

MARKETING TOOLS TO SUPPORT THE SALES PROCESS

Every step in the sales process can be much more productive if appropriate marketing tools are used.

LEAD GENERATION

It is marketing's responsibility to help build the sales pipeline. Lead generation can take on many forms. Therefore, it is crucial that lead generation is based upon the targeted segmentation and positioning that should have been determined first. Knowing whom you are trying to attract not only allows sales to remain focused on the right prospects, but also enables marketing to focus their activities more precisely and cost effectively. Company Web sites, online (click-through) advertising, webinars, newsletters, tradeshows, direct marketing, and so on are just some of the tactics used in lead generation.

The primary goal of lead generation campaigns is to find businesses that have an immediate need that your product can fill or to establish and maintain relationships with qualified prospects, so they will consider your products and services first when a need arises in the future. Contrary to what salespeople might demand, you don't want to create tons of leads. First of all, if you generate too many, they can't be properly processed and cultivated. Many will wither and die, which is just a waste of money, time, and effort. What you want to do is generate the right high-quality leads in numbers that can be properly handled by the company.

What is proper handling? Leads need to be captured, ideally in a system. They need to be assigned an owner responsible for qualifying and nurturing the lead. Lead data needs to be added to a marketing database so they can be marketed to in the future.

There are many ways to generate leads:

- **Company Web site**
  - To optimize your company's Web site for lead generation, you need to convince your visitors that your products/services can deliver value where they need it. Ensure that your site is "meaty"—that it focuses on what is truly important to your prospects, such as the problems that you can solve for them, costs that you can reduce, or new revenue opportunities that you can enable. These examples represent tangible benefits that you need to strongly communicate on your Web site. You want your prospects to believe that you understand their needs and can help them.
  - Navigation and layout is very important to lead generation as well. If a visitor can't quickly determine what your company can do for him or her and find valuable content, you won't generate a lead. Design the navigation so prospects can easily find the information they are looking for and easily contact the company to ask for additional information.

- **Traditional advertising**
  - Advertising is nothing more than the public promotion of your product or service. Traditional advertising occurs across a wide spectrum of media: TV, radio, outdoor, online, embedded product sponsorship, and more. The key to lead generation when using traditional advertising is getting your prospects to act. You must include a call to action. Call to actions contain the following:

- The action you want the prospect to take: call the company, sign up, register, and so on.
- The reason they should take it: free trial, free gift, discount pricing, exclusive opportunity, and so on.
- A reason why they should do it now: limited time offer, price increase coming.

- **Pay per click (PPC) advertising**
  - Pay per click advertising is one of the fastest growing advertising tools. Whereas most advertising is priced based on the number of impressions/eyeballs/exposure your ad will get, PPC only costs your company money when someone actually clicks on your ad. The ad must clearly define the value you can provide your prospect in a creative manner that encourages them to click on your ad. Don't complicate the message, but specify to the prospect the action you want them to take—for example, "Click here to reduce your cost of Sarbanes-Oxley compliance up to 25%." The example has a clear action and a clear message.
  - When prospects click on your ad, you must have a landing page that continues them on the route to becoming a prospect. It's this step that will determine if they become a lead or not. Continue the same value message. Your goal is to get them to give you their contact information if they want to save money on Sarbanes-Oxley compliance. The landing page should focus only on that. It should provide content that gives credibility to the value offered. This can be done with customer quotes or a short ROI example. It should briefly explain how you deliver the value promised—that is, cut costs. Then it should have a place to enter the minimum amount of information from the prospects and give them options for follow-up: Do they want a salesperson to call? Some product collateral? Attend a seminar?

- **Webinars**
  - A *webinar* is a Web-driven workshop or seminar where prospects can participate simply by logging in to an event via their computer versus having to travel to participate in person. Webinars offer an easy means for participants to engage with the speaker as well as one another. Using discussion

group technology, all participants are able to explore issues and share knowledge effectively. Webinars can be hosted "live" or can be taped and viewed at a prospect's convenience.

■ Webinars can therefore be excellent lead generation vehicles. Offering webinars targeted at providing valued content to your prospects will encourage them to register for the webinar and thus identify themselves and their interest. For example, MetricStream, a quality and compliance software company mentioned earlier in the book, offers weekly webinars on topics such as

- ■ Sustaining Sarbanes-Oxley (SOX) compliance at significantly lower costs

- ■ Sarbanes-Oxley, and how IT controls fit into the compliance framework

- ■ Sarbanes-Oxley, making our investment count

Each of these topics not only provides value to the participants, but people interested in these subjects may also be interested in software that automates SOX compliance while reducing risk and cost, which is what MetricStream sells.

■ **Tradeshows**

- ■ Tradeshows are gatherings of companies with similar products or companies with different products serving the same markets, to showcase their latest offerings, meet customers, learn new trends, and identify new prospects. To generate leads at a tradeshow, you must create a specific marketing plan. It's not enough to just show up. An effective plan includes

  - ■ **Targeting the right tradeshow**. There are over 10,000 tradeshows annually. Do your homework to identify those shows that will attract your ideal prospect.

  - ■ **Setting clear objectives.** We are discussing lead generation; therefore, specific objectives to support lead generation should be set. These could include building a mailing list of quality names for your offering and/or qualifying prospective buyers. Your objective will guide your execution.

- **Staffing your booth properly.** You need at least two people to staff a booth. A good rule of thumb is to add another staff person for each additional 100 square feet of exhibit space. The staff should be trained on your offering, well groomed, and friendly.

- **Focusing your message.** You have little time to make an impression. Establish one or two key messages and ensure the booth graphics, collateral, show pre-promotion, and the staff stays on message.

- **Lead follow-up.** Ensure you build a plan for following with leads generated at the show prior to the show. Leads are perishable. Timely and appropriate follow-up is critical. Also, keep all promises made at the booth. A tradeshow is one of the few times prospects actually engage with the company prior to a formal selection process. The impression you make will affect whether they consider your company in the future.

- **Electronic newsletters (e-newsletters)**
  - E-newsletters are newsletters published online and distributed through email to subscribers. The critical factor to using newsletters for lead generation is to ensure they offer consistent value to the readers. Your e-newsletter should be a soft-sell vehicle. Only include a section of the different articles in the actual newsletter. Entice the reader to click through to read an entire article. This will provide statistics and information on who's reading the e-newsletter, what they are reading, and how often. After the readers click through and have read the full article, offer them more information, offer a free trial, or invite them to a webinar or whatever is appropriate for your business.

- **Email campaigns**
  - An email campaign for lead generation is a program of sending a planned series of emails to your prospective targets with the objective of generating interest. It's more than a one-shot email. But don't be a spammer—use good lists, ones from a reputable company with contacts that fit your target profile and give recipients the ability to subscribe/unsubscribe. Make the email personal to the recipient, addressing him or her by

name and including content that is pertinent to the individual. Make the emails short and concise and always have a call to action. Like any marketing tactic, test it. Run tests against 10% of your target using different subject lines, different calls to action, and content design. Then launch the most effective result.

The key to make any lead generation approach successful is targeting. Many marketing departments spend 80% of their time on the creative aspects of a lead generation campaign, for example: collateral creation, venue, messaging, and so on. But little time is spent on the audience. An average piece of collateral directed at the right audience performs far better than an outstanding collateral piece directed at the wrong audience. Spend time to define your target and research how to reach your target.

QUALIFYING PROSPECTS

The sooner prospects are qualified out of the sales process, the better. Fewer resources are consumed, less money is wasted, and, most importantly, the more realistic the sales pipeline is. A quality pipeline enables sales management and company executives to plan and predict business results and take corrective actions when needed.

Marketing's role in qualification is twofold. First, marketing needs to provide as clear and precise a definition as possible of the target prospect. This definition should include as much detail as possible. To do this, marketing needs to analyze the product's benefits to determine what companies need it, which ones can afford it/justify it, who in the company specifically makes the buying decision for it, and so on. For example, a company selling supplier quality software with an average price point of $1 million needs to select a target market. Obviously, companies with multiple suppliers are a target, and given the outsourcing trend in manufacturing, manufacturing companies could be a target. But that is not specific enough. There are many manufacturers who would not be good prospects. By selecting a target that is too broad, marketing dollars will be wasted by delivering messages to companies that wouldn't ever need your product. Selecting U.S. discrete manufacturers with sales in excess of $500 million and more than 30 suppliers in the automotive industry is an example of a target prospect. See Table 9-2 for more examples of target market descriptors.

Table 9-2   Examples of target market descriptors

Business to Business	Business to Consumer
Industry segment	Demographics
Revenue size	Income/net worth
Employee size	Geographic location
Geographic location	Gender/age
Growth rates	Hobbies/interests
Experience	Experience
Individual titles	Profession

For each target group, marketing should create appropriate collateral to assist both the sales channel and the prospect in qualification. Examples of collateral include brochures, data sheets, Web-based demos, sample pricing sheets, and so on.

A quick note on collateral: Don't print it until you need it. Collateral design and content should evolve as your understanding of the market improves. Print only what you need so that you don't end up with stacks of unused, wasted collateral. Also, with today's technology, a good quality color printer, and premium paper stock choices, printing in-house and on demand is a very cost-effective alternative. In the business-to-business market, the PDF format is actually preferred as it can be easily shared electronically.

GAIN PROSPECT'S INTEREST

Once a prospect has been qualified, the field sales representatives need to develop the prospect's interest in the company's product. Here again, marketing needs to provide effective tools. The goal of the tools is to simply explain why a prospect should buy your product instead of buying someone else's or instead of doing nothing. It is imperative that these tools are built from the prospect's perspective. It is not effective to explain why your product is so great, although many marketing tools do just that. It is very effective to explain why a prospect should care about your product and how it benefits the prospect's company.

Marketing needs to maintain an *"outside in"* mindset versus an *"inside out"* mindset. "Outside in" means to critically evaluate all prospect communications from the prospect's vantage point. It's not important to the prospect that your product is made of high-quality components. However, it is important to them that your reliability is better than the industry norms, which results in less downtime. The latter example is "outside in"—it explains the benefit to the prospect explicitly of having high-quality components.

Marketing tools that support gaining a prospect's interest are those that answer the following questions:

- How will the product benefit me and my company?
- Why is it better than other options out there?
- How does it work?
- What do other people/companies say?
- Why should I buy now?

Customized presentations, ROI tools, and company Web sites are excellent tools for explaining benefits and differentiating your product over others. Nothing beats a demonstration in showing prospects how your product works. There are several ways to handle a product demo. Flash demos are a recorded demonstration of your product that can be viewed by prospective customers using free flash player technology, such as Macromedia. Flash demos can be created and put on the company's Web site. Then, prospects can view these demonstrations at will. Slideware demos can be created using PowerPoint software. Unlike a recording of an actual demonstration, slides would be created that show different aspects of using the product, and a sales or technical person would have to explain the process while showing the slides. For example, if selling software, the slides could include pictures of the screens that users would interact with and reports that would be generated. Sales or sales support people can do live demos, but they are risky unless personnel are well trained. As discussed in Chapter 7, "How to Leverage Public Relations for Maximum Value," a failed demo can hurt far more than no demo at all.

There are a couple of tools available to share customer references. These include press releases that contain customer quotes, case studies of a customer's experience, and inclusion of quotes in other marketing materials including the Web site. Sharing positive experiences of other customers is extremely powerful.

To answer the "Why buy now?" question takes an understanding of the individual prospect's needs and situation. However, tools that can assist sales include ROI calculators, pricing/service promotions, and special treatment programs. Special treatment programs put customers in a position to get benefits such as access to provide requirements directly to development, participation in an advisory council, joint participation in publicity events, and so on.

PROPOSAL SUBMISSION

Submitting a proposal is usually left completely up to the sales organization. It shouldn't be. For some prospects, the proposal is the most widely distributed piece of material from the company. Care needs to be taken in developing the proposal template to ensure that the company's brand and messaging come through. In addition, it's rare that prospects consider just one proposal. Your proposal should also include a checklist of key evaluation points that a prospect should consider, as well as how your company addresses those points. Obviously you want to include criteria that highlight the strengths of your product offering. The goal is to have the prospect use your criteria when evaluating other options. Table 9-3 shows an example of a checklist used by MetricStream, an enterprise quality and compliance software company that is discussed more later in the chapter.

Table 9-3   Sarbanes-Oxley checklist

Companies should look for solutions that enable them to sustain their compliance efforts, improve their internal control environment, and leverage technology to achieve a competitive advantage. This document provides a checklist of features required from a SOX-404 solution and can be used to compare solutions from various vendors.

Requirement	Vendor Support (Y/N)
1.0 Solution Overview	
1.1 Support for COSO and Enterprise Risk Management frameworks.	
1.2 Support for end-to-end management of Process Design, Assessments, Improvements, and Monitoring.	
1.3 Easy to configure and reconfigure organizational processes.	
1.4 Embedded best practices in out-of-the-box software.	
1.5 Reduction of costs and support for ongoing compliance activities.	
1.6 Can be leveraged to strengthen the internal control environment by documenting controls around other operational business processes.	

1.7   Can be leveraged to comply with other industry-specific mandates and government regulations.

1.8   Can be leveraged to provide enterprise-wide risk assessment and management.

1.9   Provides a business process management platform that can be used to improve all business processes.

1.10 Matches the phases and steps being used to organize the SOX-404 program.

2.0   *Usability*

2.1   Web-based application.

2.2   Configurable portal-based user interface.

2.3   Real-time status tracking of remediation plans via dynamic email workflows.

2.4   Email-based access to application.

2.5   Role-based menu access controls to simplify usage.

2.6   Easy to configure and customize forms, reports, and dashboards by business users.

2.7   Personalized homepage for each user that lists pending tasks in a To Do list.

2.8   Ability to add company logo on pages.

2.9   Drop-down list of values for appropriate fields.

2.10 Help function.

3.0   *Analytics and Business Intelligence*

3.1   Embedded analytics and business intelligence capability.

3.2   Built-in reporting engine.

3.3   Preconfigured standard SOX reports.

3.4   Tool to configure standard, ad-hoc, or scheduled reports.

3.5   Ability to include any field into a report.

3.6   Generate reports in printable, easy-to-read formats.

3.7   Export reports into standard formats like MS Excel, Adobe PDF, etc.

3.8   Email reports as attachments.

3.9   Executive role-based dashboards with drill-down to details.

4.0   *Compliance Platform*

4.1   Workflow and collaboration.

4.2   Document management.

4.3   Email-based access to application screens.

4.4   Built-in integration capabilities.

4.5	Integrated notification and alerts.
4.6	Built-in analytics and reporting (no additional licenses required).
4.7	Auditability.
4.8	Support for electronic signatures.
4.9	Robust authorization and authentication controls.
4.10	Highly scalable and available.
4.11	Portal-based user interface.
4.12	Support for offline access.
4.13	Multi-lingual support.
4.14	Multiple time zones support.

The checklist is just one component. The following is a proposal outline:

1. Thank you and introduction
2. Restatement of prospect's needs and checklist of evaluation criteria
3. Summary of how your company addresses the items above
4. Pricing summary
5. Details of proposal
6. References
7. Recap of proposal summary

REFERENCE CHECKING

In the business-to-business market, most customers will want to speak with reference customers. Although your existing customers may be quite happy, it does not mean that they will be willing to field frequent calls from prospects. When you receive requests for references, make sure you spread the requests around your customer base, so no one customer gets overused. Otherwise, they will stop participating. An alternative to a "live reference call" is to ask customers for a written or videotaped testimonial that can be shared. This saves them time and effort, and it can be very effective.

Prepare your reference customers prior to them taking a reference call. Let them know what kinds of questions they are likely to get. Give them background on the person calling. The better prepared they are directly correlates to how comfortable they will be during the call.

OBJECTION HANDLING

When a salesperson demonstrates a feature, talks about a benefit, or asks for the order, their customer may well respond in the negative, giving excuses or otherwise heading away from the sale. The salesperson then needs to handle these objections. Although there are numerous techniques that salespeople can use to handle these objections, in some instances appropriate marketing tools can help their effort.

Marketing needs to engage with sales to understand the current or expected sales objections and to determine what tools could be beneficial. For example, if the company is a relatively new or a small company, a prospect might be concerned with the company's viability. A viability presentation would be an appropriate tool for sales. In Table 9-4 is a list of common objections and possible tools that marketing could develop to assist sales in overcoming the objection. The key, however, is not to focus on this list, but to build your own based on input from the sales organization.

Table 9-4 Sales tools for handling customer objections

Objection	Possible Sales Tool

Viability	■ Viability presentation targeted at financial executives:
	  • Show strength of company: number of customers, financial investors.
	  • Show growth history and plans (sign non-disclosure).
	  • Show customer satisfaction data.

Lack of track record	■ Customer case study:
	  • Depict successful implementation process.
	  • Explain measurable results.
	■ Bio sheet of key implementation personnel showing experience prior to joining the company:
	  • Build confidence in the team that will support the prospect.

Competitor is cheaper	■ Total cost of ownership profile sheet:
	  • Demonstrate that the total cost of product, implementation, training, and so on is comparable or cheaper than competitor.
	■ Product benefit sheet tailored to competitor:
	  • Present argument that benefits achieved due to your superior product are greater.

Purchase risk too high	■ Trial program: • Give prospect a chance to see how the product will work and the benefits derived prior to fully committing.

CLOSING THE DEAL

A common oversight is the final contracts that a prospect sees. Your contract and subsequent support documents reflect your company's brand. Proofread, proofread, and proofread. Many times, proposals are assembled from prior proposals and multiple people are contributing content for the final product. Therefore, it's common for typos to be missed or other customer references to be accidentally left in. In addition to proofreading, take the time to make the proposal professional and consistent. Include your logo and company graphic if you have one. Print the proposal in color and have it bound. Another benefit of having professionally created customer-facing documents is that customers give them more respect. They are less likely to modify and change documents or contracts that are formal and well structured.

TRAINING IS NECESSARY

Creating the marketing tools is the first step—training the sales reps to use these tools is the second. Training sales reps on how to deliver the presentations, use the ROI tools, or walk a prospect through a demo is a step often ignored. The value proposition must come through in each presentation, conversation, or piece of collateral set before him or her. Do not skimp on the training, though it won't be easy. Salespeople want to be in front of customers; they tend to minimize the value of training. Here are a few techniques that have worked:

- For newly hired sales reps, make training outcomes part of their initial objectives. Set a date for the rep to give a product demo or sales presentation to members of senior management. Ensure that new sales reps learn from experience by being taken on sales calls that other reps are making.

- Don't call it training. There is typically a regular sales meeting; ask for 10–15 minutes of the meeting to "update" sales on marketing. Use this "update" time to review new marketing tools and how to use them.

- Leverage a "loss review." After losing a deal, good sales organizations review why the deal was lost to learn from the experience. Rolling out a tool after a review will typically meet with a more receptive audience.

■ Work with sales management to hold a quarterly or at least semi-annual sales meeting to focus sales on the objectives ahead, share best practices, educate sales on new marketing tools, and so on.

MARKETING-ENABLED SALES STRATEGY—METRICSTREAM, INC. EXAMPLE

MetricStream is a privately held enterprise software company providing enterprise-wide quality and compliance management for global corporations. Leading corporations in diverse industries such as Food, Pharmaceuticals, Manufacturing, and Electronics use MetricStream solutions to manage their quality processes, regulatory and industry-mandated compliance, and corporate governance initiatives. In early 2004, MetricStream was positioned for growth. Their value proposition, target market segments, and positioning were defined. MetricStream's product was being successfully used by a few Fortune 1000 companies who were happy. It was now time to scale sales.

MetricStream's focus was on growing sales but with a limited budget. Therefore, lead generation investment was directed toward online "click through" advertising, webinars, and email newsletters. "Click through" advertising didn't require any upfront investment in lists or databases, so it was the first method initiated. With this form of advertising, a company creates their own ads, chooses keywords that when searched upon will trigger the ad to appear, and pays only when someone clicks on the ad. Companies determine the price they are willing to pay per "click through." Yahoo! Search Marketing and Google Adwords are examples of this type of advertising program. The marketing effort required to best leverage this advertising channel is to research the keywords that would indicate a prospect's interest in your product and work to optimize the price paid for the keyword. For example, when MetricStream first began advertising in this manner, they were paying an average $80 for a "click through" that resulted in a registration on their Web site. After several months spent researching and testing different keywords at different price points and contracting the services of a consulting company, MetricStream reduced their average cost per click through leading to a Web site registration to just over $20. Note that the measurement focus was not on the pure click-through cost, but on the average cost of getting someone to click through to the ad and then register their contact information on the Web site. If someone is willing to give up their contact information, odds are they are reasonably interested in the solution, and therefore can be considered an unqualified sales lead for the solution.

Marketing through webinars and email newsletters requires investing in procuring lists and building a database of prospects. Again, focused on getting the best value for dollar spent, MetricStream leveraged India-based marketing resources to build a database of quality and compliance professionals. This was accomplished by leveraging an existing proprietary Web crawler that scanned remote sites and automatically downloaded their contents for indexing. The indexing focus was on specific role and industry titles. This technical effort was then supplemented by marketing research to create a marketing database of target prospects. After six months of effort, MetricStream had a database of approximately 10,000 quality and compliance professionals. This database was then used to promote webinars and opt-in newsletters.

Leads from the newsletters, "click through" advertising, and webinars were then qualified and nurtured by two inside sales personnel. Inside sales was measured on the number of qualified deals passed to and accepted by the field sales reps. On a weekly basis, inside sales provided feedback to marketing on the obstacles they faced. These included objections, roadblocks, tough questions, and so on. Marketing used this feedback to quickly develop specific tools and collateral. For example, progress was stalling with quality management prospects when prospects were trying to justify their project with management. Therefore, marketing created an ROI tool and held a webinar titled, "Building a Business Case for a Quality Management System." These two actions were supplemented by the creating of two case studies titled, *How to Build a Business Case for QMS* and *Supplier Quality: A Case Study*. Marketing's priorities were driven by sales needs. Likewise, marketing participated in the weekly sales conference call to get direct feedback from the field reps on what was needed to help them close deals. By the fourth quarter of 2005, MetricStream had increased the sales pipeline in the hands of the field sales reps fourfold.

THE RELATIONSHIP BETWEEN MARKETING AND SALES

The relationship between marketing and sales is usually a healthy tension. In an entrepreneurial company, the sales organization is typically being asked to grow revenues at upwards of 100–200% a year. As the pressure mounts, sales wants more from marketing—more demos, more collateral, more leads—while marketing wants to see sales do a better job of leveraging the good tools, and so on, that have already been provided. Respectful tension is normal and productive. If the relationship becomes adversarial, void of respect, or dysfunctional, then changes need to be made.

How should marketing and sales be structured? Although almost any structure can be made to work, based on experience, positive results are more likely when the following considerations are taken. The advantage of having marketing and sales report to the same senior manager is that there is someone in addition to the CEO who has the appropriate over-sight and perspective to truly optimize the cost of sale. The disadvantage of joint reporting is that sales has a short-term, quarterly focus. Marketing requires a long-term perspective. A senior staff member responsible for both can end up spending a disproportionate amount of time on sales. In early stages of an entrepreneurial venture, it's best to keep marketing and sales separate. Once the company is more mature and has senior experi-enced people in both organizations, there is strong synergy that can result from combining the organizations.

Returning to the NorthPoint example provides a case study of benefits that can be derived from combining marketing and sales. In 2000, NorthPoint had 1,000 employees and approximately 100 people in marketing and sales reporting separately to the CEO. While NorthPoint's business was growing, its cost of sale was too high. A CMO was brought in to continue to grow the top line, but to significantly reduce the total cost of sales. By combining the two organizations, eliminating duplicate work, holding marketing more accountable for the sales pipeline, and streamlining the sales process to take advantage of marketing's capabilities, in six months, the cost of sale decreased 30% and DSL line subscriber count doubled. The CMO had five direct-line reports.

In the case of Loudcloud, a Web site managed service provider (now Opsware), an executive joined the company to help the company sell its services to large enterprise customers. This EVP of Sales and CMO had both sales and marketing. At the time, Loudcloud had approximately 320 people and roughly 40 people in marketing and sales. Sales was going through a transformation, the target customer was changing, the product offering was being repositioned to better match the new target audience, and the economy was beginning to stall. In this case, the EVP and CMO had nine direct-line reports. It was too much. With the short-term quar-terly focus, sales overshadowed marketing. Marketing suffered.

CONCLUSION

Marketing plays a crucial, but often overlooked, role in properly enabling sales success. From identifying prospective customers through lead generation, to providing tools to the sales force to handle prospect objections and close deals, marketing needs to be in lock-step with sales. Marketing needs to understand the sales process and inhibitors to moving prospects through the process to close as well as sales does. Ensuring that the right tools are created to assist sales at each step is a critical responsibility of marketing. This chapter provided checklists, examples, and questions to be answered for the marketing professional to help jump start marketing's effectiveness in enabling sales. Through the NorthPoint and Loudcloud example, the issue of the relationship and reporting structure of marketing and sales was also addressed. As long as marketing and sales share a common vision and strategy, significant sales leverage can be gained and sustained by driving close working relationships between the two functions.

10

Entrepreneurial Promotion and Viral Marketing to Maximize Sustainable Profitability

	Products/Services	Equity/Shares	Image
Customers			
Users			
Investors			
Supply Chain/ Channel Partners			
Employees			

There is no substitute for the actual trial of most products or services. Promotion gets your product itself in front of the customers, influencers, or press so that they can more easily try it or see it in action. If your public relations campaign has worked, they should be eager to get their hands on it, but even if it hasn't, pushing it into their hands or onto their screens can help not just at launch, but for years afterwards. One can get products to the consumer in several ways, and this chapter discusses direct marketing promotions, viral marketing, event marketing, and other guerilla marketing techniques that entrepreneurial companies are more likely to use than long-established ones. In addition, product placement, where people see your product being used by a celebrity in a movie or television show, can be thought of as a cross between PR and promotion. Some of the methods are outlined in Table 10-1.

Table 10-1   Methods to promote products

Type	When to Use	Example
Giveaway	Low cost, viral product	Netscape
Try to buy	User needs experience to value product	Ameritrade
Credible exposure Product placement	Validate the hot product	Mini Cooper
Mass exposure Event marketing	Want large initial sales at one time	Windows 95 launch

GIVE IT AWAY

In today's Internet world, giving away the product has become a long-term strategy, not just a short-term promotion that puts a free trial bottle of shampoo in your Sunday newspaper delivery. However, as an aunt of mine was fond of saying, "Just because it's free, doesn't mean it's cheap." Users have also become more savvy about accepting free software, and understanding what it may cost them to operate and maintain it. The Open Source software revolution has even spawned companies such as Cygnus Solutions, whose slogan is "Making free software affordable."

Netscape popularized the current Internet craze for giving away software by making its Navigator browser software freely downloadable for non-profit users, and downloadable for 90-day trials for other personal or corporate use. After they had achieved very high market share, Microsoft got religion and made their Internet Explorer browser completely free—forcing Netscape to do the same for their browser. Once all the key competitors in the space had "free" as the price tag, it became almost impossible for anyone else to enter. Recently, as the backlash against security holes in Microsoft's Internet Explorer has grown, the open source spinoff of Netscape, Mozilla Firefox, has gotten over 10 million downloads in its first few months.

The Netscape strategy actually had two parts to it. The first was to encourage usage among the college and university students who had high-speed access to the Net within their dorms and schools. The word of mouth generated by this group spread rapidly to their professors, who, as consultants to industry and sources for the press, were able to certify that Netscape was the winner. At the time Netscape was launched, Spry, Quarterdeck, and Spyglass all had licensed versions from the University of Illinois NCSA (National Center for Supercomputing Activities), where the original Mosaic had been developed. Netscape had also realized that if they captured the space on the user's desktop, they could turn that into later revenue (monetize the users, in today's Internet terminology), by selling advertising and other items on their home page, which most browsers pointed to when the program was started. During their first year, they sold search buttons to companies such as Yahoo! for $5 million each. This translated into more than $100 million in advertising-related revenues in the early years. And, the user base would drive the corporations to believe that Netscape's winning position translated to their Internet servers, for which large sums could be charged.

With any advertising-supported medium, be it network television, controlled circulation magazines, or Internet searching, the true lifetime value of a user (viewer, reader) must be estimated to determine how much one can spend attracting them. If it is substantially larger than the cost, free can be made to work. Google changed the game in email with its beta of GMail, offering first 100MB, and then one gigabyte of free storage, more than ten times that of the competitors. They continue to attract a large following, which then sees appropriately targeted advertising links while reading or composing mail, and have increased it to 2.6GB and growing.

Microsoft has sometimes chosen to follow the "give it away for free" strategy with a small twist. It is only given away to those who have other Microsoft products—with the minor exception that they have free IE browsers for Unix and Macintosh operating systems. This has gotten them to 90% market share for the IE browser, and effectively stopped Netscape. The open source world is beginning to make small headway against that. Even Microsoft's loss of the antitrust suit has not changed the world—they are bundling Windows Media Player, which has hurt the RealPlayer, and caused a European antitrust commission action.

Giveaways are not limited to free software. There are now two free morning newspapers in New York (*AM* and *Metro*) that are given away to people entering the subway—a captive readership market. The *Washington Post* has also started a free morning paper to get new "users" into the habit of reading a paper. Their hope is that this leads to purchases of the flagship *Washington Post* as well.

FREE TRIALS VERSUS FREE FOREVER

Making it easy for a user to try a product or service is a key factor in creating demand. If a user takes advantage of a free trial and gets hooked, they're quite likely to be amenable to paying for the value received later on. One must take care to ensure the user realizes the true value, and doesn't perceive the product as one that should be free. *Many brokerage-only firms give you your first few trades free.* On the Internet, this leads to a number of hybrid models, where limited usage is free, while unlimited or professional versions cost money. Real has done this with the RealPlayer. A free version, with lots of limits, is available at all times. For the full features of the Real Jukebox and the Rhapsody service, you have to pay on a subscription basis. Fred Wilson has recently called this the "Freemium" model, and it continues to gain converts in the Internet world, where the costs are so low.

While free trials are especially common with software, new consumer products have done this for decades. If several software products perform similar functions, users will stick with the first one they learn, since perceived switching costs are high. It is important to get them to install and use your new service, come to your Web site, and so on. They need to play with the user interface and learn your offering's benefits so that they can make the purchase or switch decision.

America Online (AOL) achieved their large user growth by carpet-bombing the United States with diskettes (and later CDs) so that users could install and try 10 hours of their service. Even though they had far lower market share in the online world than CompuServe (which they later bought), or Prodigy (which had been supported by IBM and Sears—using IBM's technological prowess and Sears' consumer marketing skills), AOL's market research showed that if they could get people to log on and try some of their online communications (chat, message boards, and email), they could turn them into subscribers. But people who were not already online could not download software to get online. AOL decided to direct mail diskettes with the installation kit, and later not only to bind them into trade and general circulation magazines, but also to have barrels of diskettes available at many consumer stores and outlets.

The key was their knowledge that every user who logged on for their 10 free hours was equivalent to 25% of a 3-month customer and 10.5% of a "lifetime (42-month)" customer. Because those revenues were (at the early days) $9.95/month, the value of a person who actually used the disk to log in was close to $100.00. The cost of the package was around $1.00, so even a 1–2% trial rate could yield very profitable results. In addition, the stock market valuation of AOL, as a multiple of the number of subscribers, was several hundred dollars. So in terms of market capitalization and the ability to use that value to raise money for marketing programs, a much smaller trial rate was valuable to AOL. In fact, it has been such a successful promotional vehicle that its use continues to this day. As the value of dial-up Internet service diminishes because of the advance of broadband, AOL is rethinking what to give away.

Getting the disks to the users en masse was costly, so AOL went searching for an even cheaper method—having all the software preinstalled on new PCs. AOL got most major vendors to put all the software for an AOL trial on the computer in return for a bounty of several tens of dollars for each subscriber who lasted three months. This was a win-win for both AOL and such manufacturers as Dell, Compaq, and Gateway, since AOL also provided (in the pre-Web days) good support forums that could cut down on end user support calls.

Not only software can be served up free. Most newspapers and magazines offer several weeks or months of free trials, delivering their product to your door so you can read it and then subscribe. Book clubs and record clubs, and many other direct mail promotions (i.e., Gevalia coffee), give you the product and tools to use it (such as a free coffeemaker with Gevalia), in the hope of gaining a long-term customer.

VIRAL MARKETING

The rise of the Internet and the World Wide Web has given rise to even faster and cheaper forms of promotion, and the term "viral marketing." In a viral situation, each user tells his or her friends to download the software, because it will enable them to communicate or work together. Thus each new user "infects" many of her friends with the product, and an exponential growth can be achieved. The best-known early use of this technique was ICQ ("I seek you"), which made instant messaging available on the Web. It is also the AIM technology for AOL. Instant messaging had been one of the most attractive features on AOL—it permits a user to see if a friend is simultaneously online, and if so, to pop up a message on the friend's screen and get a response in real time. ICQ required Web users to download a moderately large piece of software, which took several minutes on normal modems, and to register their email and alias information with ICQ. Within a year, they had over a million users, and have since grown to almost 100 million users. As AOL moved into the Web, they purchased Mirabilis, ICQ's Israeli parent, for almost $300 million, and continued to operate it—all this before ICQ had figured out how to monetize their users.

The entire field of social networking has then followed the viral model of promotion. Each user of LinkedIn, Spoke, Friendster, Tribe, Visible Path, Orkut, Insider Pages, and other similar services is expected to get their friends to join. It is the large extended network of "friends of friends" that make these services valuable to each member. Over the past several years, tens of millions of venture capital dollars have been invested in these social networks, even before they have proven business models. The largest ones, such as MySpace (recently sold for over $650 million), have more than 14 million registered users, all gotten from a small core that invited their friends and acquaintances to join. In the case of LinkedIn, there was an early competition to have the most "friends."

An equally successful early viral marketing campaign was started when one of the Draper Fisher Jurvetson venture capitalists backing Hotmail asked them to put "Get free email with Hotmail" as a tag line on every message sent out by a Hotmail user. Within less than a year, the company had several million users, and was sold to Microsoft for several hundred million dollars. Having not only every user, but having every user of their system be an advertisement for themselves, was an extremely cheap way to spread the word. The marginal cost for increasing each email transmission by less than 50 characters was so close to zero as to be almost immeasurable. The marginal return from an extra customer was several hundred dollars in market capitalization when the company was sold.

WHEN DO GIVEAWAYS WORK?

Clearly, not every product or service is suitable for the "free" strategy. The four key elements needed to make it an efficient way to build customers are as follows:

- Low product cost
- Low switching cost
- Easy distribution
- High lifetime value relative to cost

Any software product, by its nature, has low cost of goods. Especially if the documentation is presented online, the marginal cost of reproduction is at worst the cost of a CD-ROM (under $1.00 in volume), and at best the cost of maintaining FTP or Web servers from which potential users can download the software and documentation. Services such as AOL or other Internet Service Providers have a cost in the low 10s of cents per hour. Offering 10 free hours may cost less than $2.50. And many software providers have "crippled" versions, which only work for a limited time period (usually 30 days), a limited number of uses, or have certain functions disabled (can't save files). Software.com, whose Post.Office program is one of the most successful email servers, allows people to use the software for up to 10 user accounts free of charge.

Free trials have long been used in other media, even where cost is high, as long as the customers are well qualified. Bombardier will even give you a free trial ride on a corporate jet in order to convince you of the FlexJet program's benefits. In order to qualify for this trial, however, you have to do more than send an email.

A key factor in deciding whether or not viral marketing can work is the cost to the user of switching to the new product or service. In the Internet world, this can be equated to the amount of time (or number of forms) a user must spend to set up his new account, software, and so on. For example, there are a large number of portfolio management sites, which keep you updated on your stock holdings. For someone with two or three stocks, the setup is usually very fast—but for users with extensive holdings, who may be the best customer targets, this can often take a half hour or more. This often leads to the good driving out the best; that is, the first reasonable solution a user adopts may be good enough to keep them from switching to a better, or even much better, solution.

You can help this problem by automating the switch or minimizing the user work necessary to perform such a switch. Almost all of the social networks have tools to search your existing Outlook contacts and import them. Most of the portfolio management tools can accept an exported file in Quicken or Microsoft Money format. Making the OOBE (Out of

Box Experience) as simple as possible is a key element in a promotion's success.

Broad giveaways may often reach too many uninterested users, so it is important to try and target the campaign to maximize the conversion ratio—that is, the number of users who move from trials to real (paid) users. AOL initially distributed disks within computer user magazines, since those were the people who were able to go online. After the success with that target group, disks were mailed to lists of people in the right age/economic demographic—whether or not they had a computer.

Finally, the AOL product was bundled with as many computers as possible. Computer vendors such as Dell, Compaq, and others were induced to include the AOL software and free trial offer by being paid a bounty on users who actually stayed with AOL for at least three months. In some cases, those bounties were $25–$50, and the cost to the vendors was a megabyte of software being loaded on an otherwise mostly empty drive during the burn-in phase of production. AOL's success drove others—such as Prodigy, Earthlink, AT&T Worldnet, and most notably, MSN (the Microsoft Network)—to adopt the same tactic.

EVENT MARKETING

Everyone loves a parade. The excitement of an event can create good feelings about a product or service and lead to a time-focused set of articles and press interviews that generate the all-important buzz about the new idea. Even a small company can generate a large amount of hoopla through a well-planned event—often enough to sound like a much larger company to the customers and competitors. The goal of event marketing is to have the press use editorial ink and space to promote a product, rather than paid advertising. And the press can not only write about the features and functions of the product, but also about the level of excitement surrounding the launch—which will often convince skeptical users to try it.

Steve Jobs, CEO of Apple Computer and Pixar, is one of the masters of the event. Several times each year (twice in the U.S., and once in Europe and Asia), he keynotes the MacWorld conferences. Essentially all of Apple's key product announcements are made at these events, which get large press coverage, and are Webcast to Apple enthusiasts worldwide. The iPod, iTunes, and even the U2 special edition were shown at this venue. Apple is so focused on these events that they have taken extraordinary measures to keep leaks from happening, even suing the bloggers who previewed the latest operating system releases. By controlling when the promotion and release occurs, Apple can maximize the impact. Having the CEO himself do the first public demonstrations also underscores the importance of each new release.

The Microsoft Windows 95 launch is one of the best examples of event marketing. Not only did Microsoft host some key events at their Redmond, WA headquarters, they also held major promotional events around the world, including Sydney, London, and New York. The press coverage of these events dwarfed the advertising spending that was going on in the initial launch phase and made most of the general public, as well as computer-oriented consumers, aware that something major and new was happening. Microsoft, unlike a small entrepreneurial venture, also had the wherewithal to continue the press through advertising expenditures post-launch. The Windows XP launch paled in comparison, in terms of the worldwide knowledge.

While product PR can be gained from event marketing, so can general corporate image and view. The current trend to paying for the naming of football stadiums (3COM Park) and post-season games (the IBM Aloha Bowl) is meant to associate the corporate name with certain images. This enhances the company image in many ways—as supporters of the community and supporters of sports. For smaller companies, local and charitable event sponsorships are good options to accomplish similar goals. Even companies adopting sections of highways, and helping to keep them clean, provides image and branding.

Industry conferences offer some of the best opportunities for event marketing. The key influencers and press representatives are usually present, as are many potential customers, distributors, and agents (not to mention competitors). Getting noticed above the clutter of exhibit booths and trade press ads may not be easy. Events can be as small and simple as the press conference, where company spokespeople announce a new product and invite the press to listen, or as elaborate as the big evening parties and entertainment events. Charityfolks.com provides an online method for companies to tie product launches and auctions together with a wide variety of charities, all of which can increase visibility.

MetaCreations Corp. (now Viewpoint) was a small computer graphics software company with some interesting new products. It was searching for a method of getting lots of press attention at Comdex—once the country's largest trade show—with only a small amount of money in the bank. John Wilczak, the CEO, decided to hold a large party (500 key people from the industry) at a location like the Hard Rock Café or House of Blues. He created the Digital Media Players Party, which would let several companies, including MetaCreations, showcase their newest technologies by having demo stations around the nightclub. The cost for throwing the party was a little over $250,000 that the company didn't have. Wilczak called on some of the biggest players in the industry—Kodak, Adobe, and so on—and sold them on being "sponsors" of the party. As sponsors, they would pay a fraction of the cost ($25–$50,000), and get an allocation of invitations and demo stations.

When the invitations went out, they read "MetaCreations Corporation (in big letters) invites you to the Digital Media Players Party, sponsored by Adobe, Kodak, and so on (in small letters)." This party was held at three to five major conferences a year for the next several years. MetaCreations managed it and got most of the PR credit, with a net cost to the company of zero dollars. In addition to being able to be identified with the big guns of the industry, and to get the new products in front of the press and influencer community, the fact that it was seen as the entity throwing the party caused most of the customers to assume it was a much larger company than its sales would have indicated. This increase in customer confidence definitely helped the sales effort.

CONSUMER EVENTS

Not all event marketing needs to be directed at the influencers. There can be great benefit from events focused on end consumers. The midnight launch has become a staple, not just for computer software (the Windows launches), but for *Harry Potter* books, movies (*Lord of the Rings, The Matrix*), and other new goods. The recent xBox 360 launch, where Bill Gates gave out the first xBox, generated millions of dollars of press for the company's launch.

Beer companies have certainly used summer events at beaches and student gathering places to promote their products, along with the positive messages promoting designated drivers. And the Oscar Mayer

Weinermobile, which travels to fairs and other events, adds a promotional touch to a very mundane product.

PRODUCT PLACEMENT

If you can show the most influential people in the country using your product, consumers should follow suit—hence, the dramatic rise in product placement, where a prominently logoed or identifiable product is used in a movie, television show, or other highly visible application. At a time when television shows are taped or TiVoed and commercials skipped by millions, having the product woven into the actual storyline of a series ensures at least some face time. With some recent movies, this can go quite far. *The Italian Job*, a caper movie, featured the new Mini Cooper automobile to such a great extent that many felt there would be a backlash. But in fact, the film helped awareness, and added a "coolness" factor that propelled sales for more than a year.

Richard Roeper, speaking about the Disney movie *Herbie: Fully Loaded*, said "This is a product placement movie gone wild. There's a commercial contained within every frame." Promotions appear for NASCAR, Tropicana, Volkswagen, ESPN, Goodyear (Lindsay Lohan wears a Goodyear baseball cap for 15 on-screen minutes). Of course, NASCAR itself is a master of logos, since fans can't actually see the drivers when the cars are racing around the track. Ross Johnson, writing in the *New York Times*, points out that even the Broadway musical *Sweet Charity* got Neil Simon's permission to mention Gran Centenario tequila in return for financial remuneration.

There are agencies that specialize in getting your product written into a script, or used as a giveaway. Franklin Electronic Publications, for example, offered their electronic dictionaries as a prize on *Wheel of Fortune*, a natural place. They also provide them as prizes in the National Spelling Bee. Nokia and Motorola often vie for whose phone will be the one shown in a movie or TV series, and Apple has a policy of lending Macs to any TV program that will show an office to be an all Mac office. If one were inferring computer popularity from television shows, Macs would be used in over 50% of the corporate world, quite a lot higher than their single digit percentage.

Even video games are not immune to product placement. A number of recent deals have been struck to place consumer product logos in the backgrounds of popular video games such as *Grand Theft Auto*. The hope is that the gamers, who are not watching network television, will get sufficient exposure to affect their buying habits.

WINNING THE CHOTCHKA WARS

Getting your company's name, logo, and message into the mind space of as many people for as long as possible is a major goal of any public relations effort. One way of doing this is with "chotchkas" (the Yiddish word for a small freebie)—T-shirts, key chains, coffee mugs, and so on. These are given away at trade shows, fairs, public events, and so on. After a typical computer industry trade show, I come home loaded with half a dozen T-shirts, a few key chains, some mouse pads, Post-it note pads, a logoed Swiss Army knife (not easy with airport security), and more.

The key factors for a successful chotchka are *longevity* and *visibility*. Longevity is the length of time the chotchka is likely to remain in the receiver's possession, so that it can keep making impressions. Visibility is the number of other people who are likely to actually see it, and how many times they'll see it. Each item should be chosen to maximize these factors for the specific target audience.

Articles of clothing are one of the most common classes of chotchka. Hats, T-shirts, and better shirts (such as polo shirts) get your message out to only a few people at a time, and are more effective when given to your own employees. They are likely to wear them proudly and, if asked about the company mentioned on the shirt, to provide real information. The people working a trade show should be given hats and shirts so that they are advertising the company not just at the trade show booth, but throughout their stay in the trade show location. Customers who get them often give them to the kids, diluting the multiplier value of the gift, although there is goodwill created with the prospect or customer.

For long-term mind share, mouse pads can keep a company's name, logo, URL, and 800 number continually on the desk of current or potential customers. And they have all the contact information at their fingertips, quite literally. In a similar vein, pads of various types—for example, Post-it notes, cubes with the logo on the side and top, binders that hold 8-1/2" by 11" pads, and so on—often last for a long time on the desk, and within the sight lines, of the prospect. By contrast, pens and pencils, even with the company's name, phone, and URL, are often kept in a pocket or purse, and hence do not get the number of exposures that a desk item would. If the prospect is a coffee or tea drinker, a large coffee mug or travel mug will also lend itself to staying visible on the desk for long periods of time.

There are always new items being touted as the cool new thing—water bottles in various shapes, fanny packs, Frisbees, and so on. Most of these have the same drawback that clothing does: They are not often kept around the office, where they can affect the decision and speed the ability of the prospect to get in contact with the company. And their cost is often high relative to their value.

On the other hand, using a chotchka to get a more detailed prospect form, either on the Web, over the phone, or at a trade show, is a time-honored tradition. "Fill this out and get a free . . ." still works better than a plea without the bribe. Again, items with longevity such as a small flashlight, a key chain that would be used and seen quite often, or a telephone rest, are better than the classic T-shirt or hat.

CONCLUSION

Creative methods to get your product into the hands of, or in front of, your intended purchaser or user burgeon every day. You should not just attempt to repeat the methods described in this chapter. The entrepreneurial breakthroughs will occur when you become the first to use a new method or trick. Although many of the tried-and-true techniques remain valuable, the public does become inured to some of the methods. Your job is to develop a number of possible promotion and marketing options, evaluate their potential cost and lifetime margin impact, and choose those with the highest returns on the marketing dollars. As with advertising, when there is a lot of uncertainty, testing before widespread rollout can point you to the most efficacious methods at any particular time. The entrepreneurial marketer needs to always keep in mind that any promotion must be consistent with the firm's positioning and target market.

11

Marketing Resource Deployment and Allocation— The Alloc Software

From previous chapters on advertising, sales force, and promotion, it should be clear that in many firms, the allocation of resources to these activities can be improved significantly. In this chapter, we describe and structure the general resource allocation problem that all marketers continually face. We discuss how to solve the problem conceptually using a simple example. We then show how a relatively simple Web-based software program can make this model practical and easy to use to help you improve the profitability of your resource allocation decisions for sales forces, advertising, promotion, and other marketing resources.

In most firms, the allocation of resources to products, markets, or other "buckets" is not done by explicitly evaluating where the resources will add the most to short-term and/or long-term profits. Our experience and other literature have shown that there are typically significant opportunities to reallocate dollars or other resources among alternative "buckets." In order to take advantage of these profit opportunities, it is necessary to evaluate the myriad of options for either increasing or decreasing the resources applied to each "bucket." Managers want to perform this evaluation task, but just find it too hard and don't know where to start. This chapter's problem structure and the Web-based software should make it a lot easier.

We first solve a very simple illustrative sample problem to illustrate many of the conceptual issues, and then we describe the conceptual problem, and finally we show how the included Allocation Tool Software implements the conceptual structure in the "real" world. It will be very valuable to you to *actually try to solve the sample problem and then go through the detailed solution*. We have used this problem in a number of executive education classes, and it is an excellent learning vehicle.

A SAMPLE SIMPLIFIED ILLUSTRATIVE PROBLEM

In Table 11-1, we display a matrix describing a simple problem of allocating sales hours to accounts. Conceptually, the problem is similar to any of the allocation problems described previously. The matrix shows the predicted yearly revenue in thousands of dollars in response to different levels of sales effort to each account A through H.

The issue of how to estimate these response relationships will be covered later. The purpose of this example is to show that they are essential to answering any marketing resource deployment or allocation problem. Please keep in mind that this illustrative problem is just a very useful example, but *is not indicative of all of the uses of this allocation paradigm* and methodology. Instead of hours, we could be allocating marketing support dollars, advertising dollars, trade promotion dollars, and so on. Instead of accounts, we could be allocating to countries, regions, product lines, markets, and so on. The conceptual structure of all of these allocation problems is identical to our illustrative sample problem.

Table 11-1 Yearly sales in response to sales calling hours/month

Account	0	1	2	3	4	5	6
A	20	200	205	208	213	(217)	220
B	10	(30)	50	68	80	90	95
C	0	5	(40)	45	50	55	55
D	0	100	250	(300)	340	375	400
E	0	(5)	10	15	20	25	26
F	200	220	230	240	245	(250)	260
G	0	10	(20)	30	35	40	45
H	0	(50)	110	150	180	200	215

= Present hours allocated
Total hours allocated: 5+1+2+3+1+5+2+1= 20
Sales of present allocation: 217+30+40+300+5+250+20+50= 912

For our sample problem, we are trying to maximize revenue. However, for most real problems, it is typically maximizing contribution to fixed costs (revenue-variable costs) that should be the objective.

The sales effort to each account can be decided between 0 and 6 hours per month. The numbers in the matrix are the yearly sales revenue associated in response to the different effort levels of from zero to six hours per month. For example, for account C, zero hours of sales effort per month will generate 0 in yearly revenue, one hour of sales effort per month will generate $5(000) in incremental profit per year, two hours will generate $40(000), and six hours per month will generate sales of $56(000). The revenue numbers circled in the matrix indicate the present sales effort allocation to each account—for example, Account A is being called on five hours per month, Account B is being called on one hour per month, and Account H is being called on one hour per month. As the figure shows, the total hours per month being allocated to these 8 accounts is 20, with predicted revenues of $912,000 associated with this effort allocation policy.

The question to answer is: Is the allocation of the 20 hours per month the best way to allocate them? An even more interesting question is: Is 20 hours the best amount of time to allocate to these 8 accounts? Let's try to answer the first question. If you want to get the most learning out of this exercise, we suggest you *try to find a better allocation of the 20 hours to maximize the yearly revenue.* Please keep track of what you are doing as you try to find a better allocation. We recommend you stop reading now and try to solve the problem. When you are done trying, please continue reading.

The first thing that you should be thinking about is incremental revenue versus the incremental hours you are spending to get it. You always want to use each hour to get the most incremental revenue. However, it is not quite that simple. Look at Account C, for example. The first hour gets an incremental 5(000) in revenue, the second hour gets an incremental 35(000), the third hour gets 5(000), and so forth. For this account, if it makes sense to allocate one hour, the second hour is much more valuable. There are increasing returns to scale for the first two hours allocated to this account and then diminishing returns to scale for additional hours spent. Conceptually, it only makes sense to allocate zero, two, or more hours to this account—not one hour.

The reason for the preceding is because an optimal effort allocation here will allocate hours to accounts so that no allocation will have any incremental revenue that can give more response to any hour than the optimal allocation. A property of the optimal allocation is that no tradeoffs can be made of taking time away from one account to give to another account and add incremental revenue. So for Account A (based on other possible uses of the hours), if you can optimally add one hour, you can even more afford to allocate two hours. The response *per hour* of one hour is 5(000) per hour; two hours allocated to Account C has a revenue response *per hour* of 40(000)/2 = 20(000). For three hours allocated, the average incremental revenue per incremental hour goes down to 45(000)/3 = 15(000). The amount of hours where increasing returns stops is where the average incremental revenue per hour stops increasing and begins to decrease.

So the way to solve the problem is to start from zero hours and to add hours where they can get the most incremental revenue. However, for each account, if it pays to allocate hours at all, you should not stop adding hours until you reach diminishing returns to scale, and then stop and look to see if other places have more incremental revenue per incremental hour. Table 11-2 makes operational this logic for solving this allocation problem. It shows the "rational" hours to consider allocating to each account and the incremental revenue if that (those) incremental hours are added.

Table 11-2   Incremental revenue per incremental hour (taking advantage of increasing returns to scale)

Account	1	2	3	4	5	6
A	180	5	X	X	X	5
B	20	20	18	12	10	5
C	X	20*	5	5	5	5
D	X	125*	50	40	35	25
E	5	5	5	5	5	1
F	20	10	10	X	X	6.7
G	10	10	10	5	5	5
H	X	55*	40	30	30	15

X = Irrational allocations, not taking advantage of scale economies.
* = The average per hour revenue for the hours with increasing returns.

For Account A, it's OK to add the first hour and get 180 in incremental revenue (200–20), or the second hour to get incremental revenue of 5 (205–200). However, because there are slight increasing returns from the third hour to the sixth, it only makes sense to add four hours at an average revenue of 5 per hour (225–205)/4. For the third to the sixth hour added, there are increasing returns to scale, so that if it pays adding any hours, four more should be added to generate average incremental revenue of five per average incremental hour. For Account C, again because of increasing returns, if it pays to add any hours to it, two hours should be added for incremental revenue per incremental hour of 20 (40–0)/2. After those hours are allocated, then each additional hour brings in incremental revenue of 5.

Now, with Table 11-2, it is very straightforward to solve the allocation problem. We use something similar to "zero-based budgeting." We start with zero hours and get the revenue associated with all of the zero levels = 20 + 10 + 200 = 230. We look for the highest number in Table 11-2, which is 180, associated with the first hour allocated to Account A. As our first step, we allocate one hour to Account A and add 180 to our revenue to total 230 + 180 = 410. We then look for the next highest unallocated number in Table 11-2, which is 125 and associated with the first two hours of sales effort expended on Account D. We allocate two hours to Account D and have added 125 revenue per hour for two hours = 250 to our current total of 410 to get 660 revenue for our first three hours. Please note that if we could afford to allocate two hours to these eight accounts, it is even more efficient on a revenue per hour basis to use three hours. Thus, the allocation will not show an allocation for two hours—just one and three hours. Continuing, after allocating three hours, we look to the next highest unused number in Table 11-2, 55, which is associated with two hours allocated to Account H. We thus allocate the next two hours to Account H, making five total hours allocated and adding 2 × 55 = 110 to our revenue to obtain 660 + 110 = 770 total. Again here, it is "irrational" to allocate four hours to these accounts, because the fifth hour will be more productive than the fourth. The next highest unused number is now 50, associated with the third hour allocated to Account D. Thus, we allocate the next hour to Account D, making three hours allocated to Account D, and adding revenue of 50 to our total to obtain 770 + 50 = 820 for six total hours allocated. Table 11-3 chronicles the logic of adding hours where they add the most incremental revenue until we finish allocating 20 hours.

Table 11-3 "Zero-based" incremental solution to the sample allocation problem

(1) Step	(2) # Hours (Per Month) Added	(3) To Which Account?	(4) Total # Hours Allocated	(5) Incremental Revenues for Those Incremental Hours	(6) Total Revenue
0	0		0	—-	230
1	1	A	1	180	410
2	2	D	3	125	660
3	2	H	5	55	770
4	1	D	6	50	820
5	1	D	7	40	860
6	1	H	8	40	900
7	1	D	9	35	935
8	1	H	10	30	965
9	1	D	11	25	990
10	1	H	12	20	1010
11	2	C	14	20	1050
12	1	B	15	20	1070
13	1	B	16	20	1090
14	1	F	17	20	1110
15	1	B	18	18	1128
16	1	H	19	15	1143
17	1	B	20	12	1155

Column 5 of Table 11-3 is very relevant for determining the best total amount of hours to allocate to the eight accounts. For each level of total hours allocated, it represents the marginal revenue that is obtained by adding the last hour if all hours are allocated optimally. Every hour is at least as productive as the number in column 5. Notice that the value decreases as more hours are allocated. Conceptually, hours should be added to these accounts until *the marginal revenue is equal to the marginal costs* of the hours. The marginal costs of the hours should also include the opportunity costs of spending resources in other areas or possible corporate "buckets."

We can relatively easily use the data in Table 11-3 to not only find the best allocation solution for 20 hours, but also any other number of hours up to 20. For example, if we have somehow made a decision that (perhaps because of opportunity costs), we should only spend monthly hours of sales effort that bring in at least 50(000) in yearly revenue, Table 11-3 shows that at six hours per month, the marginal revenue is 50(000). To find the best allocation of these six hours, we just need to add up the hours allocated to each account in column 2 up through Step 4. This results in one hour to A, three hours to D, two hours to H, and zero to all other accounts. If we then apply the expected revenue for these accounts at those hour levels from Table 11-1, we get the allocation and revenues in Table 11-4a.

Table 11-4a   The best allocation of six hours

Account	# Hours Per Month	Yearly Revenue
A	1	200
B	0	10
C	0	0
D	3	300
E	0	0
F	0	200
G	0	0
H	2	110
TOTAL	6	830

Note that with 30% of the effort allocated to these accounts (6/20), we can obtain 91% (830/912) of the revenue we are now getting with 20 hours that are not allocated correctly.

For our original problem with 20 hours to allocate, using similar logic, we end up with the allocation in Table 11-4b and marginal revenue for the last hour of 12(000).

Table 11-4b The best allocation of 20 hours

Account	# Hours Per Month	Yearly Revenue
A	1	200
B	4	80
C	2	40
D	6	400
E	0	0
F	1	220
G	0	0
H	6	215
TOTAL	20	1155

Note that if the 20 hours are better allocated, revenue with the same amount of sales effort goes up by 27% (1155/912).

ALLOCATION INSIGHTS AND FALLACIES ILLUSTRATED BY THIS SAMPLE PROBLEM

We can show the fallacies of some very popular allocation methodologies with the preceding sample problem. The first allocation methodology is to *allocate resources based on current revenue*. For sales force allocations and deployments, it is usually done by dividing accounts into classes based upon their current sales: that is, A accounts have revenue of over $1 million and get called on once per month; B accounts are between $.5 million and $1 million and get called on once every two months; C accounts are between $.25 million and $.5 million and get seen every three months; and D accounts are less than $.25 million and get seen once every six months. Once you know how many calls a salesperson can make in a year, and how many A, B, C, and D accounts there are, it is very straightforward to decide on how many salespeople you need and how they should be allocating their time.

The preceding problem and its solution demonstrate the fallacy of this method. Let's compare the current revenue of each account with the optimal number of hours to spend based upon Table 11-4b. The highest current revenue account is Account D with 300(000) in current revenue. It gets an optimal six hours per month, so the rule works so far. However, the next highest current revenue, Account F at 250(000), gets only one hour for the optimal policy. Account H, which has very small current revenue of 50(000), gets six hours per month under the optimal strategy. It is clear that the optimal allocation is *not proportional to current revenue*.

A second common deployment method is similar to the first one, but allocates *proportional to potential* instead of current revenue. The A, B, and C accounts are grouped by potential instead of current revenue. We can use the revenue at the highest call level of six hours per month in Table 11-1 as an indicator of potential to see if this proportional to potential allocation is close to optimal. The highest potential account in Table 11-1 is D with 400. In the optimal solution of Table 11-4b, it does get the maximum number of hours, which is six, allocated. However, the second highest potential account is F at 260. In the optimal allocation, F only gets one hour per month. Account B, with a much smaller potential of 95, gets four hours per month allocated by the optimal policy, as shown in Table 11-4b. It is then also clear from this example that the optimal allocation is also *not proportional to account potential* either.

What should be clear from this example and its solution is that the optimal solution *does depend on the incremental revenue (or really incremental profit)* associated with *incremental changes in the resources* deployed to the account. An *optimal allocation* is defined as one in which any changes made will be less profitable. In order to solve for an optimal allocation, some kind of response relationship (like Table 11-1) is necessary. Either implicitly or explicitly, one needs to evaluate the profitability of all allocations to know that the one chosen is optimal. In order to perform that evaluation, these response relationships are required.

Even if the typical executive who tries to solve an allocation problem *doesn't use the response relationships explicitly*, implicitly, he or she is making some *extremely heroic assumptions* about them. When an executive decides one allocation or deployment of resources is right, he or she is implicitly assuming that any other allocations won't be more profitable. The only way to verify that assumption is to evaluate the profit response of other allocations, which requires the response relationships that the executive tried to ignore in the first place. Everyone who decides on any Marketing Resource Allocation has implicitly assumed that they have evaluated the profitability of all feasible allocations.

Much research and 30+ years of experience shows that executives will make *much more profitable* deployment and allocation decisions if they do *the best they can at estimating the required response relationships* and then *let a computer help them evaluate all of the options* similar to the procedure we used in Tables 11-2, 11-3, and 11-4. The Web-based software that is included with this book enables this activity to be done quite efficiently. In the chapter Appendix, we first describe the general problem that the software solves and then show how the software works. We next give some practical direction on how to use this methodology in the real world, especially on how to estimate the sales and profit response relationships. If you have no experience with the Alloc software, you may want to read this chapter's Appendix before continuing.

HOW TO ESTIMATE THE SALES RESPONSE TO ALTERNATIVE EFFORT OR RESOURCE LEVELS

The astute reader should now be asking himself or herself, "Okay, I see how allocating resources can be done more efficiently, but it all depends on these estimates of sales response to changes in effort or resources applied. How do I get those to be reliable enough to use these techniques?" The answer is very simple. The allocations that a manager will make if he or she goes through the effort of estimating each of the required response estimates will be more profitable than not doing it. There are a number of field studies that document this assertion. There are three ways of generating these response estimates, which should all be considered and used together because they are complementary:

1. Managerial judgment by those familiar with the allocation problem.
2. Analysis of historical naturally occurring allocation differences.
3. Planning and analyzing experiments where allocations are purposely changed.

It is always worthwhile to get any people who can shed some insight into how different "buckets" respond to effort or resources. They together can estimate the responses to different levels of effort. The group should include people who can from their experience help the rest of the group to understand how different buckets might respond. The wrong way to get these estimates is to have a meeting and ask volunteers for their ideas of what would happen to revenues at the four alternative levels (0%, 50%, 150%, and saturation) of effort or resources. What will happen is that the most senior or powerful person in the room will have her estimate given too much weight by the group. The most productive way to get these estimates is to use a modified "Delphi" technique. In this technique, each person first puts down their estimate on a piece of paper or into an interactive computer system. Then all the answers to each question are put onto a screen with measures such as the mean, median, and extremes (highest and lowest). The moderator (the Delphi) then asks the people who have outlier estimates from the group to describe the assumptions that are behind their estimates. Each person who is different from the group consensus thus gets to affect the group's estimates. After all of the outliers have spoken, the group is asked to again estimate their answers, taking into account what they have just heard. The new estimates are then portrayed on the screen and the process repeated until the group gets suitably close to a consensus. The Zyndor case, which is on the Alloc Web site, shows how a pharmaceutical firm used the Delphi technique and this system to make a $25 million revenue increase.

The two other empirical ways of getting estimates should be used as input to the Delphi group after the group has expressed their first estimates. Statistical analysis of past naturally occurring experiments can sometimes tease out historical changes in revenue in response to changes in effort or resources. If these relationships cannot be teased out, then it can be beneficial to experimentally change allocations and monitor the impact on revenues. See Chapter 6, "Entrepreneurial Advertising That Works— Vaguely Right or Precisely Wrong?," for examples of these analyses for advertising decisions. It is not a good idea to just use these empirical methods without also doing judgmental estimates like the Delphi. The empirical methods can only describe *the past*. All of these resource allocations are based upon alternatives *in the future*. Thus, it is good practice to have codified a group's consensus about the future before being exposed to historical analyses. Then, the historical analyses can be another input into a group's consensus-building activities.

HOW VICTORIA'S SECRET ALLOCATES AND DEPLOYS RESOURCES

This chapter's conceptual methods are being used at a very gross level by Victoria's Secret and the Limited Brands when they make decisions about deploying resources around the globe. Les Wexner, the Limited founder and leader, wants to deploy the firm's resources where they will contribute the best long-term return versus the resource costs for implementing the strategic initiatives. They have been making these judgments somewhat qualitatively, but using the concepts of this chapter. We discuss these initiatives in more detail in Chapter 4, "Distribution/Channel Decisions to Solidify Sustainable Competitive Advantage," but it is worthwhile to review the allocation principals that the Limited applies.

For their Internet site, it has been very cost effective to deploy resources across the globe to service demand because the very small incremental costs are easily justified by the incremental sales generated. They also retain complete control over how the products are portrayed and how the sales process works—thus being able to remain *true to their positioning.* They also experimented with catalogs with some success in some areas of the world, but there was not enough incremental revenue for the incremental costs to justify diverting resources from domestic initiatives that were evaluated as more cost effective.

Similarly, based on their best estimates of longer-term incremental revenue versus longer-term incremental costs, the Limited Brands corporately has decided so far not to expand their stores globally. The perceived *long-term costs* of complex intermediaries necessary in many countries, as well as the loss of total control of how the product offering is delivered, was judged too large versus the potential *incremental revenue* and the opportunities to use those limited Limited resources more profitably domestically. The corporation judged that their domestic initiatives such as "Pink," Henri Bendel, and C. O. Bigelow were better long-term uses for their discretionary resources. Rather than use any arbitrary rules for allocating resources, the Limited Brands is attempting as best they can to allocate their resources to obtain the maximum long-term profit from them. As we put it, they are trying to be "vaguely right versus precisely wrong."

The concepts of evaluating incremental revenue versus incremental costs over all feasible alternatives, using experimentation to improve judgments of incremental revenue and costs, and doing all of this while remaining true to your positioning are reinforced in this chapter.

CONCLUSION

Along with this book, you get access to the Alloc software Web site. There is an extensive help menu to answer your questions as you work with the software. We hope you will use it along with appropriate estimating techniques to improve the marketing resource decisions you make. Most managers use precise methods for these decisions—typically either what we did last year or allocating proportional to either current sales or potential. As we've shown in our example, these methods are precisely wrong. The techniques and models in this chapter have been termed "vaguely right." Our research has shown that these models and procedures have been very helpful in increasing marketing productivity. In practice, firms have been able to increase their productivity from 3–30% using these techniques.

Chapter 11 Appendix: The Conceptual Problem Structure and Its Implementation in the Alloc Software

The problem solved by the Alloc Web-based software first assumes that resources are allocated and need to be reallocated to "buckets." A *bucket* is any entity that can have resources applied to it. In the implementation of the software program, what we call buckets are named "subsections." Examples of buckets might be sales regions or districts, countries, clients, prospects, and so on. Each bucket is assumed to have a certain level of *resources* currently allocated to it. Resources might be salespeople, advertising dollars, promotion dollars, coupons, and so on. For a *planning horizon*, each bucket is assumed to have a level of resources called the *planned level*. For that planned level, there is assumed to be a certain level of revenue over the planning horizon that will be obtained if the planned level of resources is continued. This *planned level of revenue* is the revenue that would be obtained if the planned level of resources is continued during the planning horizon. The job of the Alloc software is to find better levels of resources to apply to each bucket.

The planned level of resources is conveyed to the system in units that are chosen by the user.

Each bucket is assumed to have a relationship between the revenue in the planning horizon and the resources applied to the bucket during the planning horizon. In order to convert the revenue to a measure of profit contribution, the predicted revenue is multiplied by a *profit margin*. The profit margin is defined as the value to the company of each unit of incremental revenue. For most applications of the software, the profit margin should be the percentage of incremental revenue that contributes to profits before fixed costs. If, for example, for each new $100 of incremental revenue, $55 would be incremental costs, then the profit margin to put for that bucket would be 45%. This profit percentage should not include the allocation of fixed costs. By definition, fixed costs will be incurred regardless of the level of revenue. The software has been used to maximize profit contribution to fixed costs in most of its applications to date.

A key part of the problem input is the development for each bucket of a response function that relates the changes in revenue during the planning period to changes in resources applied during the period. For every level of resources, the system needs to know what the impact on revenue will be. It gets this response function by asking the system user for four inputs on this response function and interpolates between them. The inputted four estimates are for the percentage change in revenue during the planning period if 0%, 50% of the planned level, 150% of the planned level, and saturation level of the resource were applied to the bucket instead of the planned level. The *saturation level* is the level above which revenue will no longer increase. The system fits a smooth curve through these four estimates and the revenue anticipated at the planned resource level. Samples of these revenue response relationships are in the following examples.

ALLOCATING SALESPEOPLE TO SOUTHEAST ASIAN AREAS

The following example is a real problem with the data multiplied by a factor to maintain confidentialities. The input data for the problem is summarized by the Alloc system in Figure 11-1.

The V.P. of sales for the region shown in Figure 11-1 is evaluating her allocation of 23 salespeople to 8 areas from Jakarta to Balikpapan. The **Current Effort** row is the number of salespeople she has planned for each area—ranging from a high of 11 in Jakarta to 1 in a number of areas. She wants to evaluate the addition or deletion of salespeople in the territories in units of whole salespeople. Thus, the **Smallest Increment of Effort** row has 1's for all of the areas. The **Minimum Effort** and **Maximum Effort** rows are the minimum and maximum number of salespeople our V.P. wants to consider for each area. Notice all of the minimums are zero—indicating that if an area cannot justify a salesperson by the sales and profit being brought in, it is okay to leave it without a salesperson. **Current Sales** are the sales she expects during the planning period, assuming that the **Current Effort** number of salespeople is used in the area. In this example,

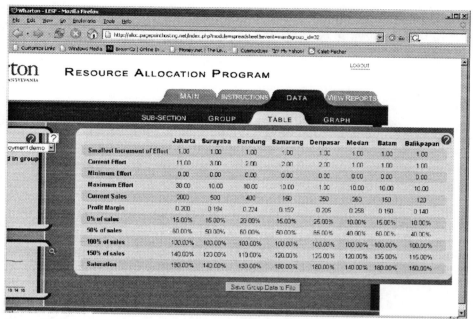

Figure 11-1   Input data for the S.E. Asian example

the planning period is one year, but two years in the future. The V.P. is assuming that whatever allocation she makes in number of salespeople per area will happen over the next two years. She is evaluating options based upon what she forecasts during the third year of any reallocations. She estimates that three years is enough time for any changed sales force allocations (especially drastic reductions) to have completed their impact on the areas' revenue. **Profit Margins** are the percentage of incremental revenue that is contribution to fixed costs. The next five rows are the VP's estimates of what would happen in percentage terms over the planning period if the sales effort were reduced to **0%** and **50%** of the current sales effort if the *current* effort were continued, or increased by **50%**, **100%**, or **150%** of current effort, or if **Saturation** effort were applied over the planning period. The computer program then fits a smooth curve to interpolate between those points to estimate the revenue implications of all feasible salespeople allocations to each area.

Figure 11-2 shows how the computer starts with minimums required in each area and continues to add salespeople to the areas so that each added person is contributing the most to incremental profit over the planning period.

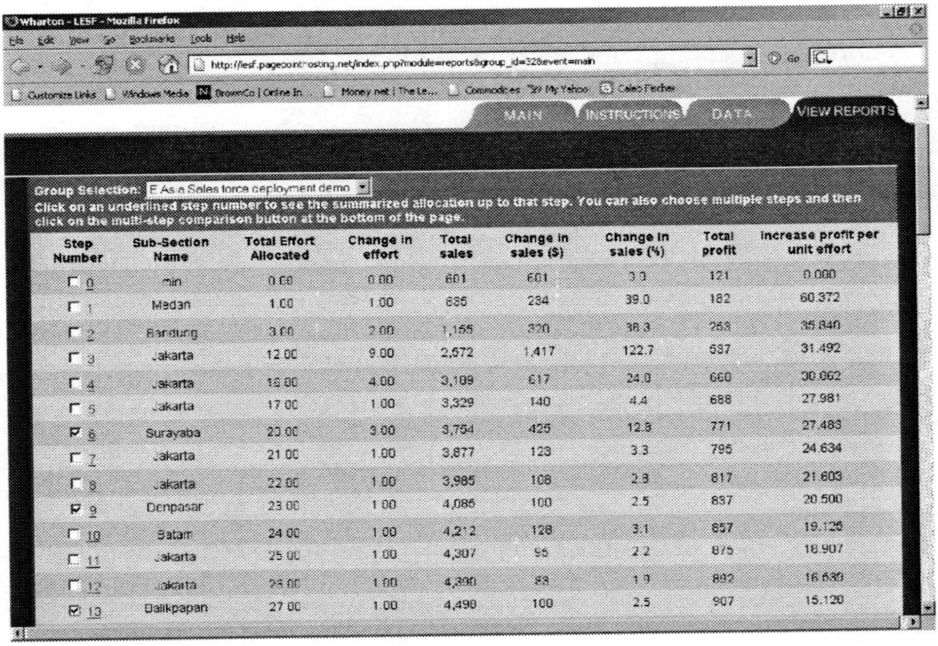

Step Number	Sub-Section Name	Total Effort Allocated	Change in effort	Total sales	Change in sales ($)	Change in sales (%)	Total profit	Increase profit per unit effort
0	min	0.00	0.00	601	601	0.0	121	0.000
1	Medan	1.00	1.00	835	234	39.0	182	60.372
2	Bandung	3.00	2.00	1,155	320	38.3	253	35.840
3	Jakarta	12.00	9.00	2,572	1,417	122.7	537	31.492
4	Jakarta	16.00	4.00	3,189	617	24.0	660	30.062
5	Jakarta	17.00	1.00	3,329	140	4.4	688	27.981
6	Surayaba	20.00	3.00	3,754	425	12.8	771	27.483
7	Jakarta	21.00	1.00	3,877	123	3.3	795	24.634
8	Jakarta	22.00	1.00	3,985	108	2.8	817	21.603
9	Denpasar	23.00	1.00	4,086	100	2.5	837	20.500
10	Batam	24.00	1.00	4,212	128	3.1	857	19.126
11	Jakarta	25.00	1.00	4,307	95	2.2	875	18.907
12	Jakarta	26.00	1.00	4,390	83	1.9	892	16.639
13	Balikpapan	27.00	1.00	4,490	100	2.5	907	15.120

Figure 11-2 The Alloc incremental allocation analysis

In Figure 11-2, Step 0 shows the beginning of the routine where each area gets the minimum salespeople effort—in this case, zero for all areas. The total sales is 601 and the profit is 121. The sales come from the estimates of what would happen in each area if no salespeople were there for the planning period. The next step (1) adds resources to the area in which the incremental profit per incremental person (sales effort) is highest. It is one person allocated to Medan. Sales go up by 234 to 835, and profits go up to 182, an increase of 61 for the first person added. The last column shows the incremental profit contribution per each sales person (unit of effort) for the last incremental addition to the sales force allocation. In Step 2, the system added two salespeople to Bandung as the next most productive place to add effort. It added two salespeople because of economies of scale in the sales response to effort estimates for the area. The sales go up by 320 to 1,155, and profits go up by two times 35.84 to 253. Each step continues to add salespeople (effort) to areas that are incrementally most profitable per each unit of effort (salespeople) added.

The last column shows the incremental profit contribution for each unit of effort added. Notice that this last column is constantly decreasing as less-effective uses for sales effort is applied. Conceptually, it makes sense to continue allocating sales effort until the incremental contribution per person added is just equal to the cost of that person. It is this point in which incremental revenue equals incremental cost. In practice, managers will stop allocating resources before this point is reached, leaving themselves a margin of error. The reason for this conservatism is that the estimates for incremental costs for adding effort (salespeople) are usually pretty good. The estimates for how revenue and profits will change as effort is added are typically much less accurate. In the salespeople example, it also is relatively easy to add salespeople to a force, but much more difficult to subtract people from the force if the force turns out to be too large. Morale implications of firing people are very important.

You can check any steps for which you would like to see an allocation. In the preceding example, Steps 6, 9, and 13 are checked in order to look at optimal allocations of 20, 23, and 27 people. Step 9 with 23 people shows how the system would reallocate the same 23 total salespeople as planned for. This output is shown in Figure 11-3.

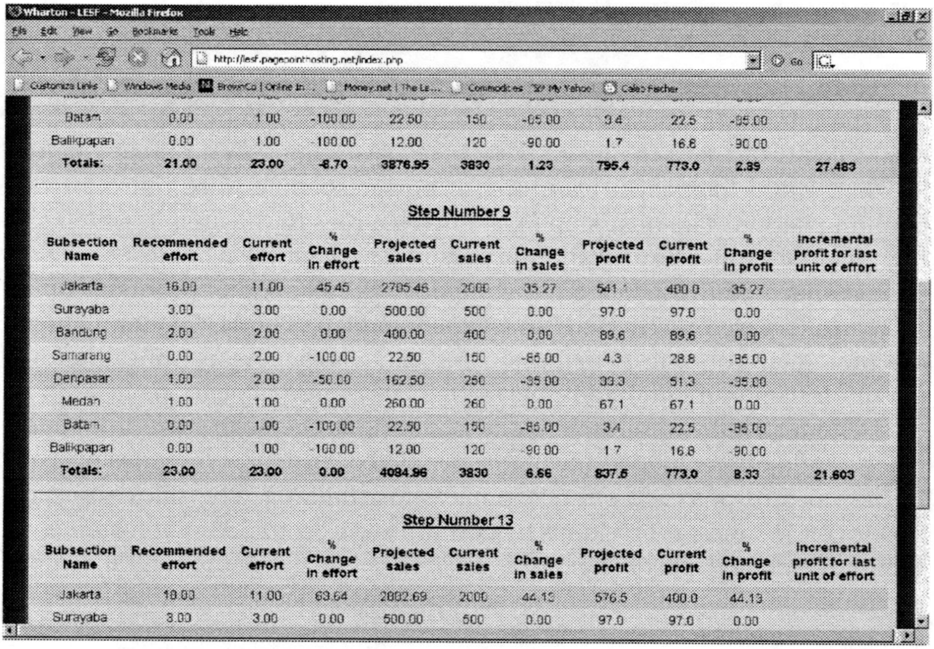

Batam	0.00	1.00	-100.00	22.50	150	-85.00	3.4	22.5	-85.00	
Balikpapan	0.00	1.00	-100.00	12.00	120	-90.00	1.7	16.8	-90.00	
Totals:	**21.00**	**23.00**	**-8.70**	**3876.95**	**3830**	**1.23**	**795.4**	**773.0**	**2.89**	**27.483**

Step Number 9

Subsection Name	Recommended effort	Current effort	% Change in effort	Projected sales	Current sales	% Change in sales	Projected profit	Current profit	% Change in profit	Incremental profit for last unit of effort
Jakarta	16.00	11.00	45.45	2705.46	2000	35.27	541.1	400.0	35.27	
Surayaba	3.00	3.00	0.00	500.00	500	0.00	97.0	97.0	0.00	
Bandung	2.00	2.00	0.00	400.00	400	0.00	89.6	89.6	0.00	
Samarang	0.00	2.00	-100.00	22.50	150	-85.00	4.3	28.8	-85.00	
Denpasar	1.00	2.00	-50.00	162.50	250	-35.00	33.3	51.3	-35.00	
Medan	1.00	1.00	0.00	260.00	260	0.00	67.1	67.1	0.00	
Batam	0.00	1.00	-100.00	22.50	150	-85.00	3.4	22.5	-85.00	
Balikpapan	0.00	1.00	-100.00	12.00	120	-90.00	1.7	16.8	-90.00	
Totals:	**23.00**	**23.00**	**0.00**	**4084.96**	**3830**	**6.66**	**837.6**	**773.0**	**8.33**	**21.603**

Step Number 13

Subsection Name	Recommended effort	Current effort	% Change in effort	Projected sales	Current sales	% Change in sales	Projected profit	Current profit	% Change in profit	Incremental profit for last unit of effort
Jakarta	18.00	11.00	63.64	2882.69	2000	44.13	576.5	400.0	44.13	
Surayaba	3.00	3.00	0.00	500.00	500	0.00	97.0	97.0	0.00	

Figure 11-3 An optimal reallocation of 23 salespeople

The results of the reallocation of the planned 23 people in Step 9 is somewhat typical of many reallocations that we have seen. The system cuts out sales effort to three markets completely and reallocates most of the effort to Jakarta, the biggest market. The last row of totals shows that sales resulting from this reallocation will go up a projected 6.66% to 4084, and profits go up by 8.33% to 837. Keep in mind that the system is maximizing profit contribution, not sales. Based on the V.P.'s input and estimates, he or she could use the same number of salespeople, reallocate their effort geographically, and increase her region's profitability by over 8%.

In Figure 11-4, Step 6, which allocates 20 people instead of 23, shows that reallocating the smaller number of people can still obtain the same profit contribution that the 23 people would have made without reallocating their effort.

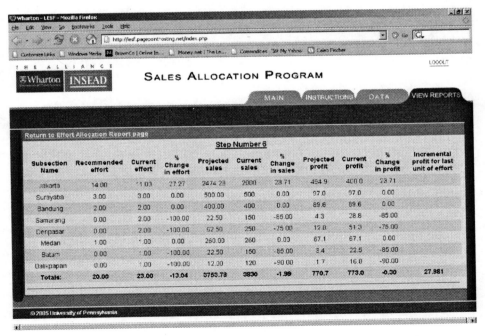

Figure 11-4 Step 6 allocates 20 salespeople

Notice that with only a 13% reduction in salespeople, only half of the areas are given sales force coverage.

Figure 11-5 shows how the system would allocate 27 people, an increase of 17% in sales effort. Based on the last column, if the marginal cost of keeping a salesperson in the field (including expenses and prorated management expenses) is less than 16.52 per year, then an increase to the sales force size of 27 could be justified.

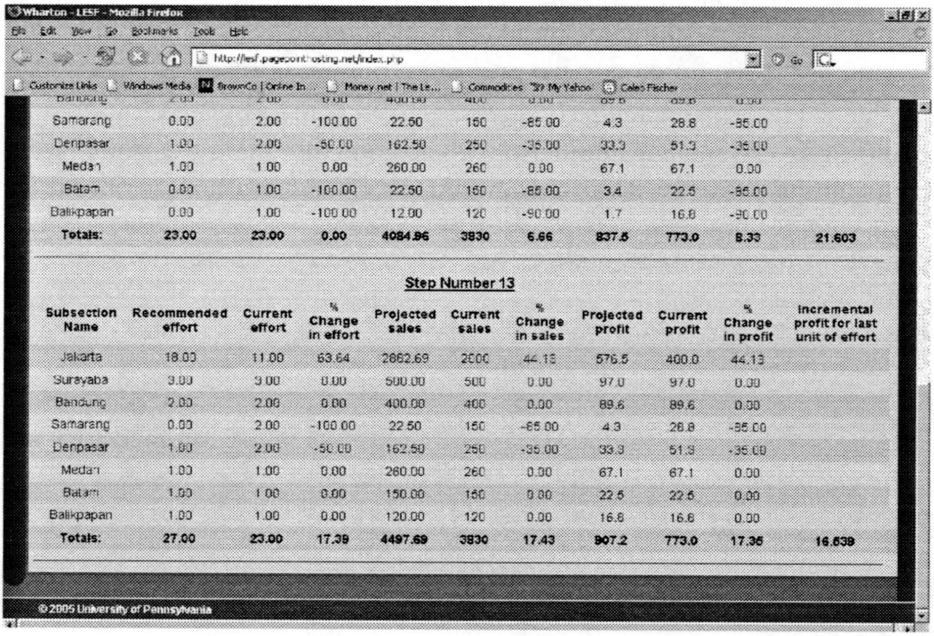

Samarang	0.00	2.00	-100.00	22.50	150	-85.00	4.3	28.8	-85.00	
Denpasar	1.00	2.00	-50.00	162.50	250	-35.00	33.3	51.3	-35.00	
Medan	1.00	1.00	0.00	260.00	260	0.00	67.1	67.1	0.00	
Batam	0.00	1.00	-100.00	22.50	150	-85.00	3.4	22.5	-85.00	
Balikpapan	0.00	1.00	-100.00	12.00	120	-90.00	1.7	16.8	-90.00	
Totals:	**23.00**	**23.00**	**0.00**	**4084.86**	**3830**	**6.66**	**837.6**	**773.0**	**8.33**	**21.603**

Step Number 13

Subsection Name	Recommended effort	Current effort	% Change in effort	Projected sales	Current sales	% Change in sales	Projected profit	Current profit	% Change in profit	Incremental profit for last unit of effort
Jakarta	18.00	11.00	63.64	2882.69	2000	44.13	576.5	400.0	44.13	
Surayaba	3.00	3.00	0.00	500.00	500	0.00	97.0	97.0	0.00	
Bandung	2.00	2.00	0.00	400.00	400	0.00	89.6	89.6	0.00	
Samarang	0.00	2.00	-100.00	22.50	150	-85.00	4.3	28.8	-85.00	
Denpasar	1.00	2.00	-50.00	162.50	250	-35.00	33.3	51.3	-35.00	
Medan	1.00	1.00	0.00	260.00	260	0.00	67.1	67.1	0.00	
Batam	1.00	1.00	0.00	150.00	150	0.00	22.5	22.5	0.00	
Balikpapan	1.00	1.00	0.00	120.00	120	0.00	16.8	16.8	0.00	
Totals:	**27.00**	**23.00**	**17.39**	**4497.69**	**3830**	**17.43**	**907.2**	**773.0**	**17.36**	**16.639**

© 2005 University of Pennsylvania

Figure 11-5 Allocating 27 salespeople, an increase of 17% in sales effort

It is interesting to observe here that even with 17% more resources, it still doesn't pay to keep salespeople in Samarang. The value of two people has more estimated incremental profit contribution in other areas.

12

Entrepreneurial Marketing for Hiring, Growing, and Retaining Employees

	Products/Services	Equity/Shares	Image
Customers			
Users			
Investors			
Supply Chain/ Channel Partners			
Employees			

The three key items that fuel high growth are ideas, people, and money. We have discussed generating ideas in the previous chapters, and will discuss raising capital in the next chapter. All successful companies need a continuing supply of great people to bring the ideas to fruition. Selling to potential recruits is a marketing problem like any other, and many of the same elements need to be considered.

POSITIONING

Great people want to work with winners. One of the key marketing challenges for the human resources (HR) group in a company is to generate the perception that your company is going to be the winner in your product/service space. The same public relations techniques discussed in Chapter 5, "Product Launch to Maximize Product/Service Lifetime Profitability," can be applied to this dimension. Have the influencers meet the founders and describe the company as a sure winner, and recruits will flock to your door.

MetricStream, the enterprise compliance software company mentioned in earlier chapters, proactively uses public relations to assist in recruiting, especially for their Bangalore, India operation. Although MetricStream doesn't currently sell their solutions in India, they aggressively seek out interviews and article placements in Indian media. The sole purpose is to raise the company's awareness in a highly competitive hiring market. The strategy has paid off. In 2005, the company was able to grow their Bangalore division from 25 to over 80 employees in spite of its small size. In addition, their attrition was less than half the market rate.

People usually like to work in compatible environments—that is, they want to work with people who are more like them than not. Google, for example, has created the perception that the world's smartest people work there. To support this idea, they sponsor an annual global competition called Code Jam. Code Jam presents three difficult problems that must be solved correctly in 75 minutes. Google's 2005 Code Jam attracted over 14,500 applicants from around the world, of which 99 were selected to enter the competition. Code Jam serves to both raise Google's awareness as a seeker of highly intelligent engineers and be used as a recruiting tool. As a result, they are able to hire many of the world's smartest folks—not just programmers, but also writers, marketers, salespeople, and so on.

Apple Computer, Inc. has fostered the perception that people who work there "think different" and are not afraid to challenge the status quo. Their consumer advertising campaign and their hiring speeches make the same point. When Steve Jobs was trying to lure John Sculley away from his senior post at Pepsico, he asked, "Do you want to change the world, or just sell soda the rest of your life?" Jobs successfully put forth the message of Apple in its hiring as well as its operations.

For other large companies, there are specific positioning messages—McDonald's is "everyone's first job," and, as they try to hire more senior citizens, may be everyone's last job as well. Goldman Sachs, Disney, and McKinsey & Company are perceived as the best places to learn strategic thinking and to become part of the American corporate elite. Procter & Gamble is the place to learn all about brand marketing.

For the high-growth company, positioning to prospective employees should be simple and straightforward. They are, after all, going to have to work very long hours, usually for low pay, with most of the rewards coming psychologically in the early stages, and through stock option exercise much later. The company's mission and culture must come through in a few sentences or images. Just as important as "the elevator speech" that you should be able to give to a prospective investor is your firm's first encounter with a prospective employee. The prospective employee should know exactly why your company is a different and better place to work. Steve Jobs says: "We hire people who want to make the best things in the world." The focus is not on profit, but on making great things and doing what you love.

SEGMENTATION

Almost every market segments itself along certain dimensions. The hiring market is no exception, and is segmented by functional specifications, by geography, by skill level, and by experience level required. In addition, the risk propensity of applicants causes the more conservative folks to shy away from entrepreneurial startups.

Functional segmentation is the seemingly obvious differentiator. You need to market differently to find accounting personnel rather than manufacturing workers. Yet in the early stages of entrepreneurial companies, each person may have to take on several jobs and functions. The CFO may also run operations, be a purchasing clerk, and work on sales of company equity. It is hard to decide between a candidate with several years of direct experience as a CFO who has come up through the accounting and finance ranks, and someone with a CPA who has also been an operating officer or perhaps run their own business.

Geographical segmentation is an especially difficult hiring hurdle to overcome. There are different lifestyles in Boulder, San Jose, New York City, or Atlanta. People who are attracted to a particular place to live can color the applicant pool for your new venture. It is much easier to find people willing to work all day and night in Silicon Valley than in Atlanta—not that the Georgians are any less productive, just that their culture is built around more family time. Similarly, locating your office where most employees have long commutes (by train or auto) puts bigger limits on total in-office time.

Hiring people who have to change locations in a significant way is fraught with risks for both parties. For the applicants, there is great risk that they simply won't like the new location—or their accompanying family members won't. For the company, such employees are subject to the stresses of a young, fast-growing venture on top of the difficult home situation. Infonautics, Inc. found it difficult to recruit people into the Philadelphia suburban area. Even though applicants saw that the housing and school opportunities were far superior to other cities, they remained reluctant, because there were too few other companies to go to if the venture did not succeed. Now, as more Internet companies have located in the "Philicon Valley," it has become much easier to convince potential employees that, even if the job that moved them here doesn't work out, there will be ample opportunity for them in their specialty.

With the advent of the Internet, companies can now hire some people who break the geographic boundary limits via telecommuting. With one or two visits a month to the corporate facility, the telecommuter can retain enough personal contact and credibility for the rest of his or her work, which is arriving via email. Hiring telecommuters means marketing to them where they live—on the Net. Jobs.com, Monster.com, and the other services provide a way to reach this key group of innovative and hard-working technical and creative people.

Experience also segments the marketing job. Entrepreneurial companies often have the luxury of hiring not on the basis of experience, since they are going into business and product areas in which there may be no relevant experience, but more on the basis of "raw" skill. Young MBAs who can serve as Jacks or Jills of all trades may be more responsive to the hiring message of an Internet startup than someone with 5–8 years of experience and career track at a bigger company. But there really is no substitute for experience. The less training a company needs to provide, the faster they can get their product to market.

Although some recent, relevant experience is critical, many of the jobs that seek 5–10 years of time in related positions are not appropriate for the Internet space. Few people were on the World Wide Web much before the mid 1990s, narrowing the pool of such applicants too severely. What is most important in an entrepreneurial company is the right mix of experienced people, with entry-level talent, who have some idea of how things can be done, and who know no limits to what can be accomplished.

BUILDING A TEAM AND CORPORATE CULTURE

While every hiring decision is critical, and needs to be looked at on an individual basis, the collection of early hiring decisions determines what type of team spirit and corporate culture will be created. In order for a corporation to be successful, it needs to have each of the key personality types as well as each of the critical skills. You need people who enjoy the detail-oriented administrative tasks, as well as entrepreneurs and visionaries who can work at the 50,000 foot level and not be deterred by small uphill battles that occur each day, along with people who will grind out the work, and those who can manage and integrate the people and processes of the organization.

Showing a new recruit that the team works together with common purpose is a key marketing element in successfully hiring the best. Having the applicants come on days when there are pizza parties or other social occasions is a good way for them both to meet many more people than the interviewing schedule permits, and to get a sense for the community that they'll be joining in a less-pressured manner.

REACHING THE PROSPECTS

Traditional want ads and classified job ads are rarely the mainstay of the startup. Most of the candidates are reached via networking, job fairs, headhunters, and online media. Often, if the publicity surrounding the company is strong enough, resumes will flow in unbidden, from those who want to latch onto the hot new company.

Every employee, from the founder down, must be told to keep watch for any good talent, and encourage those who qualify to apply, even when a specific job is not open. Your own employees are great judges of the "chemistry" fit of a candidate, and since one of the keys to successful organizations, and to job satisfaction, is having a best friend at the office, letting people recommend and potentially hire their best friends is a good way to ensure success. Such hires have lower turnover rates, and better prospects. They also cost the company far less than standard headhunter fees.

Job fairs are an efficient way to focus your startup on hiring. Post at local colleges and universities, advertise on the Internet, and hold an open house for 2–3 hours late some afternoon (typically 5–8 p.m.). This allows those who have jobs to get there and talk with people from many different functional areas in the company. In the idealab! incubators, where there are always 5–10 companies, they held job fairs in which each of these incubating companies, and the other 20 companies created that have moved away, set up a table with a few of their people. As a control mechanism, each applicant talks with a limited number of companies—usually 3–5. That way, the number of competing offers is limited, and the amount of duplicate processing is cut down. The applicants sort themselves by degree of risk averseness by the companies they choose to talk to, since those that have been in business for years (such as CitySearch and GoTo.com) get the lower risk takers, and the ones that have started in the past week get the high risk takers.

Networking with local faculty members at a college or university near your company is crucial to seeing the best talent before it is preemptively taken off the market. If the professors know what you're looking for, they can recommend people to you long before they would think of themselves as being in the job market. One good way to get access to this talent pool is the use of students as interns. There are many well-defined tasks—market research, for example—which can be done by a student or student team during a semester course. This allows the student/prospect and the company to evaluate one another with no obligations, and without having to make the hiring decision until after you have really seen both the work and work ethic of the candidate.

PRICING

Compensation packages at entrepreneurial companies are widely varied. Especially in the first few months of the company's existence, offers may be custom tailored to match the applicant's needs for cash, deferred compensation, equity, and other benefits. The perceived value of a package of salary, options, and perks will vary widely with the age, maturity, stage of life, and relocation status of the employee.

The idealab! formula is to try and keep all salaries below $100K per year in the first 6–12 months. To balance this, employees get faster vesting on a portion of their options than is typically industry norm. This is an especially important recruiting tool when dealing with senior people who are leaving highly paid positions, since it ensures that they will have a stake in the company even if their own job doesn't work out. It is much easier for a CEO who is taking a small amount of cash compensation to convince his or her subordinates to stay below the CEO salary level.

CHOOSING THE PROSPECT

There are many people who play a role in the hiring process, and each needs to be trained in the marketing and sales function associated with recruiting. When the Human Resources person (or department, as a company grows) starts out, they should have the mission statement and position description clearly in mind. A key differentiator in entrepreneurial companies, however, is that whatever the position description says, there are likely to be other responsibilities, since there are never enough employees to fill all the roles in a new venture. This message has to be put across to the recruit.

In the army, it is "unit cohesion," the sense of belonging to a small tightly knit group, which makes men and women willing to give their lives to save their fellow unit members. Entrepreneurial companies are also fighting key battles, and unit cohesion is critical. Hence, it is very important to have potential hires interview not only with HR and the specific workgroup manager, but also with most members of the group in which they'll work. Each of these members has to market not only the company's mission and vision, but also the ethos of their own unit, and has to be convinced that the recruit will contribute to the cohesion and success of the unit.

Programmers each have their own style. Development departments—so important to success in the Internet area—create their own sets of rules and conventions. Making sure that a new entrant into an existing group can work within, and perhaps extend, the group's styles can be the difference between the success and failure not only of the recruit, but of the company. In one open source software venture, the head of the group was a maverick who defied most standard programming rules to create a much more efficient e-commerce engine. When hiring for his group, he made sure that he kept a mix of mavericks and traditionalists, so that the creative energy led to productive code, not chaos. This involved meetings and votes among all the existing team members, who ranked each new recruit on several scales, along with an overall "I'd like to work with this person" rating.

CONCLUSION

EPinions, now a Shopping.com division, was a Silicon Valley Internet startup that created a Zagat type guide to almost anything. The company provides convenient places on the Web for people to input their opinions, aggregate them, and make them available to the Web community. Product reviews, movie reviews, and so on are all in the plan. It was started by a small team who had all done successful startups (such as NetScape and Oracle). They faced one interesting hiring challenge in the beginning—they were unwilling to tell potential recruits about the business plan until after they were hired. This meant having the recruits completely believe in the team, and be excited about working with the team on whatever they chose.

They were able to tell the recruits that there was going to be nothing illegal involved—no pornographic or gambling-related stuff—and little else. What helped was that they could say they were funded by Benchmark Ventures, one of the most successful Silicon Valley backers (eBay, etc.). They could also say that they hoped to launch within six months, so there would not be a long delay in finding out if they could be successful.

As the examples in this chapter have shown, hiring and keeping good people needs entrepreneurial marketing to make the process as productive as possible. All the concepts for helping improve the interface between the company and its customers are also important for improving the interface between the company and its current and prospective employees.

13

Marketing for Financing Activities

	Products/Services	Equity/Shares	Image
Customers			
Users			
Investors			
Supply Chain/ Channel Partners			
Employees			

One of the most important jobs of marketing is to help an entrepreneurial venture show its best side when raising money or maintaining stock price. Some of these concepts are applicable to early stage companies, some to later stage, and many to all companies no matter what their stage of growth and financing. It is critical to note that when marketing to potential investors, your product is a share of stock (or debt instruments), not the product or service the company hopes to sell. Although investors may, at times, be customers also, their motivation for being a customer for stock is to maximize a risk-adjusted return. Hence, they are most likely to provide funds, at good valuations, to companies perceived as winners. It is marketing's job to position the company as a (the) winner, leader, most advanced, world-class competitor in its space. Being a leader will most often lead to good financial returns on the products, which in turn will cause the company's valuation, in either public or merger transactions, to rise.

The other function of a good financial marketing plan is to create a sense of urgency, to counteract the oft-given venture response of "I'll put money in if you have a lead." The long drawn out no, which is the response of most venture firms, is painful for a company that needs capital today for expansion, growth of sales forces, or to complete product development. Since there is a natural tendency to not be the first one to jump into the pool, a great marketing plan will provide the incentives to act early. The right pitch aids in finding the lead investor, who will negotiate the specific terms, take a board seat, and help set direction.

The marketing group (or individual in the early stages) must work with the CEO and whoever is taking on the CFO role (often just one person) to create an investor presentation that concentrates on the target market segment (venture capitalists, banks, strategic partner investors). The CFO needs to provide the detailed financial information, while marketing has to boil that down to two slides that help sustain the proper level of excitement. Too much hyperbole, and the pitch may lack credibility or generate legal liability. In a recent pitch, one of the authors heard a group start out with, "Our new Internet business will take over the users of Amazon, eBay, and Google because of our easier-to-use interface." Their financial projections were then based on taking tens of millions of users from these well-established leaders, all in the first year and a half of operation. With such total lack of credibility, none of the people present even heard much of the rest of the pitch.

At later stages, marketing for an IPO and working with investment bankers to create a book for potential acquirers, there is a key role for the proper and legally limited ways to present the financial and product prospects for the company. And crisis management, as discussed in Chapter 7, "How to Leverage Public Relations for Maximum Value," may also be called for if problems arise in the company's operations and affect its share prices.

PRODUCT VERSUS FINANCIAL MARKETING

There are many differences between product marketing and financial marketing, but the similarities are even more numerous. In both, one needs to target the consumer of the goods and services, by working through the chain of influencers and key decision makers, gatekeepers, and naysayers, in order to have maximum impact. In both, getting key benefits understood by all is crucial.

One major difference between product and financial marketing is timing. While the product marketing campaign can often be postponed to coincide with completion of a set of product features, failure to execute financial marketing may mean loss of funds and nowhere to turn—shutting down the business. The key elements of naming, pricing, and positioning still apply, but to the stock, not the product itself.

A FINANCIAL MARKETING PLAN

A typical one-page summary in the New York Angel format is shown in Figure 13-1. The New York Angels is a group of angel investors who invest in venture capital. Because you only have a limited time to get your message across, figuring out how to sell your shares in this format is an important step. It gets at the product, the people, the prospects, and the finance all in one easy page. This template provides a valuable lesson in how to pitch to entice a longer meeting.

THE BUYING CENTER

Just as every product marketer has a set of hurdles to jump through, so too do the CFO and CEO when selling the image of the company. For many venture firms or investors, the first test is the analyst or associate who screens the business plan. They are hired to keep too many plans from cluttering the partners' desks or minds, and get points for saying no early. However, they lose double points if a competitor gets a deal they should have bid on. Thus, telling the analyst at Firm 1 that Firm 2 is preparing a bid can short circuit the turndown.

After the analyst, the venture firms will often bring in outside "experts" to help them in fields in which they are not *au courant*. These consultants have their own agendas, along with the formal assignment from the venture fund. It is quite common for them to offer their services directly to the company after they have made a positive recommendation. They may facilitate the communications between a technically-oriented founder and the financially-oriented venture capitalist. The company should use their

NewCompany	Leonard Lodish, CEO	Walnut Street, Philadelphia, PA, 19103
www.newco.com	lodish@wharton.upenn.edu	215-555-1212

Management:
Leonard Lodish, CEO
Howard Morgan, CTO
Shellye Archambeau, CMO
Industry: Media
Stage of Dev.: Early
Employees: 9 (including contractors)
Founded: 2004
Tech Platform: LAMP
Monthly Net Burn: 40k
Breakeven Date: 2007
Financing Sought: 500k (250k+ already committed)
Pre-Money Valuation: N/A
Use of Funds: Sales & Marketing, Product Development, Administration & Legal
Capital Raised to Date: 200k
Current Investors: Friends and Family, NY Angels:
Law Firm: Dewey Cheatham and Howe
Accounting Firm: Sarbanes & Oxley
Referred By: Jerry Wind

Business Description:
NowPublic is a platform that collects, organizes, and distributes reports from students. The technology powers the Newco.com website and is also available to new organizations as an ASP solution. The website makes money from advertising, licensing fees, and value-added services and the ASP earns recurring monthly fees.

Products/Services:
The Newco website is an Internet destination where people can read and contribute to college news. The Newco ASP solution is a technology platform and syndicated news wire that news organizations can license to manage the disruptive change that vast numbers of mobile recording devices in the hands of students have wrought.

Target Markets:
The Newco website serves the news reading collegian. This is a large market. Students spend more time consuming media than anything else. The ASP model targets media companies – large and small – as well as local portals.

Strategy/Barriers to Entry:
Our competitors will be kept out of the marketplace because of our strong technological leadership as well as demonstrable brand recognition and market share. Our strategic partnerships with handheld manufacturers and new organizations offer additional protection against new arrivals.

Customers: *Wall Street Journal* would be nice.

Competition: Citizen journalism clearinghouses like Scoopt and Spy Media. Local bloggers in key news markets.

Business Model: Advertising and ecommerce supported website. Monthly recurring revenues on ASP business.

Distribution/Sales Model: Direct and reseller channels in ASP business. Blogger supported viral marketing strategy for Newco website.

Technologies/IP: Newco platform includes proprietary formats.

Financials ($mlns):	2004a	2005a	2006e	2007f	2008f	2009f	2010g
Revenue	-	-	1.8	2.2	5.7	9.9	35.6
EBITDA	-	1.2	0.3	0.0	2.1	4.8	18.8
Capital To Be Raised	0.2	1.5	2.5				

Key Problem Solved for Customers: Collegians spend 7 hours a day consuming media. Much of this is news but news organizations are struggling to cope with a new relationship with their readers as they increasingly become contributors as well as consumers. Newco tools help individuals and news organizations manage and profit from these new relationships.

Figure 13-1 Typical one-page summary

review time as an opportunity to gain valuable competitive intelligence, since these experts have a broader view of the competitive space than most founders.

SEGMENTATION OF INVESTORS

The customers for fledgling company stock fall into several categories: angels, venture capital companies, incubators, corporate strategic buyers, or institutional investors. Each has a particular place in the investment food chain, and is matched to certain types of companies. By far the largest share of investment funds for new business comes from angel investors. These are friends, family, and retired executives who have extra cash and are willing to take risks and back someone they know. Over 60% of the money raised is in this category, and that is growing, according to the Ewing Marion Kauffman Foundation, which supports research in entrepreneurship.

ANGELS

While angels used to be approached one at a time, the high-tech world has organized this channel so that it can be more easily reached. Ron Conway, founder of Palo Alto's Band of Angels, manages monthly dinners in which entrepreneurs can present their plan to almost a hundred current and retired high-tech executives. If they like the plan, they can invest from $25,000 to several hundred thousand dollars. The companies also get the network and expertise of senior people at such firms as Hewlett Packard, Apple, Netscape, Sun, and the like. The Band has been so successful that it has spawned a true venture fund, so that the members can participate in more investments with a little less time.

The New York Angels, formed in 2004, has a rigorous screening process for new business plans. In the second week of each month, a subset of the members see quick pitches from about 15 companies. They select three to four to present to the members during the last week of the month. Each of those companies gets some marketing help (presentation training and critique) during the week before the presentation. If some of the members like a company, due diligence sessions are held at the beginning of the next month. Many of the members offer not just money but access to their networks of contacts, which can be of great help in establishing market awareness of a new company.

The Angel Capital Association was formed in late 2004 to help share best practices among the hundreds of angel groups. Almost 100 groups have joined by now. Its Web site, http://www.angelcapitalassociation.org/, has descriptions and contact information for angel groups throughout the world.

MIT Entrepreneur's Forums are held in several cities, Philadelphia has the League of Retired Executives (LORE) and PPIG (Pennsylvania Private Investor Group). Los Angeles has the Tech Coast Angels. In each of these, members agree to invest at least $25,000 in a startup each year. They get to make the choice. Negotiating valuation with angel groups is very idiosyncratic, and often results in higher valuations than the venture capital firms would provide.

To get the opportunity to reach these organized angel groups, a company must find a member to sponsor them. Lawyers, accountants, professors, or other successful entrepreneurs can make the introductions for new startups that don't already have a link to this community.

VENTURE CAPITAL FIRMS

The most visible and helpful investments come from the established venture capital firms. More than 4,000 funds belong to the National Venture Capital Association, and there are undoubtedly hundreds of other funds. The typical venture partnership has $50–$500 million to invest over a three- to four-year period, and assumes that their initial investment will require at least as much in later rounds. Because the scarce asset of these firms is partner time, they need to put $2–$10 million into each deal. (The most recent megafunds are trying to put five or ten times that amount.) Firms such as Benchmark Capital, Kleiner Perkins, or Sequoia want to take an active role in helping the portfolio companies grow, and provide a *keiretsu* (Japanese for a corporate family) to help their companies help one another.

The largest venture firms now see tens of thousands of business plans each year, and fund only a handful (typically fewer than one per month). How can a company work to maximize its chances with these 1,000-to-1 odds? First, almost all of the venture firms only fund plans that have been referred to them by someone they know and trust. This first screen is extremely important, and requires that a company have an advisor (lawyer, accountant, technologist, professor) who is known to the venture firm. That person can make a telephone call or send an email that describes the key business idea or differentiator in a few sentences. If the venture firm has any interest, it will then request either a plan or a meeting. Here the entrepreneur's marketing skills are put to the test. A few slides and a prototype must tell the story, show how the market being attacked is large enough to be worth the venture firm's valuable time, and transmit the passion of the entrepreneur to the partners. Venture firms are looking for markets that can get to between $100 million and $1 billion in a few years, while angel investors can fund companies that may only do $25–$100 million.

INCUBATORS

The incubator is a more recent innovation as a source of help, including capital. idealab!, CMGI, and a large number of universities are all business incubators, which provide space, infrastructure, and funding to help entrepreneurs get a fast start. Pitching to these incubators is similar to the venture capital presentation, but the business team does not have to be as well formed. An incubator often provides accounting services, general office services, and some technical consulting to the various companies, as well as overall business advice. Many are funded through industrial development funds, to try and heighten job creation in a particular region.

CORPORATE STRATEGIC PARTNERS/INVESTORS

Many large corporations have started venture type funds, partly for the financial gains that can be earned, but mainly to keep a strategic eye on new developments in their sphere of interest. Many of the innovations that change industries start in the smallest rather than the largest companies. Intel, Cisco, and even Nokia all have venture funds so that they can benefit from the technologies and business models that new companies have started.

If your entrepreneurial venture has received any visibility at trade shows, in the trade press, and so on, you may be contacted by these groups. They are often brought in as co-investors by the established venture firms.

INSTITUTIONAL INVESTORS

Finally, there are hundreds of investment bankers and finders who will try to help you raise money from qualified institutional buyers. These investors usually want to make large investments ($10 million and up). They are usually willing to pay placement fees. Early stage companies that don't have such large cash requirements may find this market hard to tap.

NAMING

It is easier for people to remember who you are, and what your company does, if it has a well thought-through name. At idealab!, names may be crucial—in more than one instance, the fact that a sufficiently catchy URL was not obtained stopped the investment into the company. The URL for Tickets.com, along with the 1-800-TICKETS phone number, were purchased for a substantial sum in order to get the benefits of quick consumer and investor recognition and remembrance of the company's business area. CarsDirect.com, for example, immediately says that you'll be dealing with a company in the automotive sector.

As with any non-functional name—for example, Google, eBay, Amazon.com—both the product and investor marketing are required to attach the business plan to the name in the minds of customers or investors. In some of these cases, there is high brand value to the name in both consumer and investor contexts.

In many cases, the name used to market to investors is quite different than the name used to market to customers. IAC (Barry Diller's InterActive Corp.) is well known to investors as the place to buy shares in a company that owns Ticketmaster, City Search, Expedia, Hotels.com, and about 40 other businesses. Internet Brands was chosen by CarsDirect.com when they expanded into mortgages, housing, and other businesses—each of which have multiple channels to the consumer. Those consumers are not the ones buying shares, and hence a name that makes more sense to the investment community was chosen.

PRICING—THE VALUE OF YOUR VENTURE

Just as product pricing is an art as well as a science, the pricing of offerings in companies is even more so. Once a company is public, and there is a "free market" for its stock, the price will be set in that marketplace. We will come back to this in the discussion of investor relations. In the private markets, there are two types of prices—those set by the buyer (low), and those set by the seller in the face of excess demand (high). What permits a company to get into the latter category is superior marketing.

The key elements that need to be marketed to investors, in addition to the product, are the people (management team), the financial model, and any strategic relationships that the company may have entered into. Because the investor is buying a fraction of the company, not an instance of the product, it is the expected exit value that is most important. When there is an Internet stock mania, this value may be projected high by some investors, and lower by others. Post crash, there was a period where no value was low enough, and the venture community stopped investing in all but the "sure things" that came their way. Five years later, rationality has returned to the pricing process, and both entrepreneurs and investors have more realistic views of how to price their shares.

As we write in late 2006, an idea from a new, untried entrepreneur and group of qualified engineers, marketers, and so on may be worth 30–65% of the equity of a company for an initial cash investment of $250,000–$1 million. With a seasoned team of entrepreneurs, located in Silicon Valley, raising $5 million for 50% of the equity would not be unusual. The marketing message around a successful team is clear—"They did it before, they'll do it again." Particularly, if the team has either taken a company public or sold at a good price to a major player (e.g., Cisco), their "product" has a seal of approval. In addition, the success of Google and Yahoo! has led to them buying small technology companies, pre-revenue, for about $1 million per engineer. It lets them get hiring done, and prevents folks from getting established and commanding much more money later on.

Many angel investors will invest in the form of a note that will convert to shares that are priced later by more professional investors. For example, the New York Angels often invests $300,000–$500,000 in a convertible note, which converts with a 25–50% discount into the next round. There is also a cap on the price of that next round, so that a giant success still yields what would have been a rational price at the time of the angel's entry. This also protects against the angels offering too high a price, and then being "crammed down" by a later, lower valuation when the company next needs funding.

VENTURE MARKETING

In the pre-public stage, reaching investors can be done by getting mentioned in the key influencer magazines (and online e-zines) such as *Red Herring*, *AlwaysOn*, and *Wired*. The technologic publications are also a source that many venture capitalists use to try and find deals.

In each region of the country, there are also weekly and monthly business magazines that cover startup firms. *Crain's New York Business*, *Philadelphia Business Journal*, and *TechCapital* magazine are examples of publications that can get a young company noticed by potential private (pre-public) investors.

INITIAL PUBLIC OFFERING (IPO)

For many companies in the software and Internet world, much of the reason for going public is marketing related. The mantra for seasoned Internet entrepreneurs is: "The IPO is the premier branding event for an Internet company." In fact, the amount of publicity and brand recognition that can be generated by a successful, high-profile IPO is enormous. Planning for an IPO is an arduous task, and the actual road show and offering are several of the most grueling months that a CEO and CFO will ever face. But each meeting and luncheon presentation is selling the company's products, message, and positioning, as well as its stock.

The first part of getting the message out is accomplished during the underwriter selection phase. At this stage, the various investment bankers are trying to sell the company on choosing their firm to participate in the lucrative fees associated with the IPO. From the company's point of view, however, this is a chance to familiarize many of the Wall Street analysts who might later cover, or be asked to comment on, the company's business and stock prospects.

Too many companies make the mistake of talking to only a small set of bankers. If they want a "first tier" or "bulge bracket" firm, such as Goldman Sachs, Morgan Stanley, or Merrill Lynch, they may feel it isn't worth their time talking with 10–15 smaller players that want to be part of the offering. In fact, just as you wouldn't tell a potential good customer to go away without speaking to them, you shouldn't do the same to the bankers. It is often best to hone the pitch that will be given to the first-tier folks on some of the other firms. Their analysts can constructively criticize the positioning, projects, and passion your company shows in its presentation. This feedback can be very valuable in getting the highest valuation from these firms. It is common to have one or two smaller, boutique firms as part of the offering underwriters. More and more, online Internet firms such as Jeffries/Broadview, eTrade, or DLJ Direct are also participating. These relationships may well be needed in later months, after the IPO, if there is any slip in the company's performance.

Just as you wouldn't run a TV ad that wasn't professionally scripted and produced, the IPO road show pitch itself requires the same care and professionalism. We have observed Power Presentations' Jerry Weissman, whose company helps create road show presentations, and then coaches the speakers in dealing with audiences—large and small—in the most effective way. Jerry says that he can help add a few dollars to the stock price, and we actually believe it.

The buyers for the IPO fall into several groups: institutional investors focused on momentum, long-term institutional holders, retail holders, and flippers. A balanced mix of all of these types are needed to have the company's stock in strong-enough hands, yet trade enough to be interesting to market makers who support the stock.

INVESTOR RELATIONS

Once the IPO has been completed, a company has to communicate with its investors to keep them informed, and to keep the stock price consistent with the company's performance and promise. While there are a number of firms that can help, in the same way that traditional public relations firms help with product positioning, most companies should have an in-house designee to handle investor queries, provide copies of reports, and coordinate the company's release of information on a quarterly basis, as well as its conference calls with analysts.

The conference call gives the company a chance to present itself to 30–100 key influencers each quarter. Many of the analysts on the call will be writing a report or set of comments for their clients—recommending whether or not to buy, sell, or hold the stock. We recommend following four simple rules for these communications, as follows:

- Tell the truth, the whole truth, and nothing but the truth.
- Tell the bad news first.

- Don't over "spin" the good news.
- Don't get on the message boards.

While point one should be obvious, the temptation to omit some of the bad news, or to hold back or spin the positive news, can sometimes feel overwhelming. Don't succumb! There is a large group of plaintiff's lawyers just waiting for any misstatements they can use to successfully sue you. (Note "successfully"—they'll often sue anyway on bad news, whether or not you've been telling the truth.)

Dealing with bad news is never easy. Getting it out of the way of the market, so that its impact on stock price has been felt, and then allowing the price to recover on good news, is far better than wasting some good news immediately before the bad news comes out. It is also important that everyone gets all the bad news at the same time—avoiding the selective disclosure that could give an unfair market advantage to those who hear before others. Most companies schedule their press releases and conference calls outside of market hours. Now that the markets are moving toward 24-hour trading, this is becoming more difficult, but it still makes sense to schedule outside the standard 9:30 to 4:00 Eastern time window when the bulk of the trading takes place.

Finally, one is also tempted to add some "spin" to good news. A small contract may be touted as a harbinger of much bigger ones, or a move from losses to breakeven may be spun as a major turnaround. It is better to let the investors draw their own positive conclusions than to force them on the market.

Over the past few years, there has been a dramatic rise in the availability of information on public companies, which has been good for investors. At the same time, the message board phenomenon has cropped up. On Yahoo!, Raging Bull, Silicon Investor, AOL, Motley Fool, and other places, there are places where "investors" (usually rank amateur speculators) can post any comments they want about your stock. Although there are occasional nuggets, most of it is drivel—uninformed, meant to hype or cut the price when a smarter speculator has gone short or wants to go long. The SEC has been working with the providers to curb the worst of the abuses—outright lies meant to manipulate a stock—but there is still far too much misleading information on the boards.

When your Investor Relations executives read these, they, or other employees or officers, may be tempted to correct the misstatements.

DON'T. Once you start correcting, the public may feel that you have taken on the obligation to always correct them, a task that the company should not, and may not legally, be able to do. False merger rumors, for example, abound on these boards. Companies must say "No Comment" to any questions about unannounced merger activity or, the courts have ruled, they must always respond accurately. This makes it difficult to have secret negotiations, since any leaks would have to be dignified by the company's comments.

You can get help from Yahoo! and the other providers if there is harm being done. In one case, a message poster falsely took on the name of the company's CEO. Since Yahoo! generally allows anyone to get any unused email, they didn't stop this until they were informed of the ruse. At that point, they took away the email address. But the anonymous nature of posting makes it too easy to lie and deceive.

CONCLUSION

Each company has its basic product or service, and the separate product called "shares." Treating the customer base for those shares with the same care and attention as those customers for products and services is crucial to success. In many young companies—including Internet, biotech, wireless communications, and other capital-intensive companies—far more cash comes in during the first five years through financing activities than through product sales.

14

Building Strong Brands and Strong Companies

	Products/Services	Equity/Shares	Image
Customers			
Users			
Investors			
Supply Chain/ Channel Partners			
Employees			

In previous chapters, we have shown how to tackle all elements of the marketing mix for entrepreneurial marketers. All of these marketing mix chapters had very similar formats. Regardless of whether the decision was pricing, public relations, advertising, distribution channels, sales force, or product or service design, the format of the decision-making process was similar. The process began with a given positioning and target market and then asked the role of the marketing mix element in furthering the positioning toward the target market segments. Each marketing mix decision process then described various paradigms for developing mix elements that contributed to the incremental revenue to the company in comparison to the incremental costs of the marketing mix element. Both revenue and costs are estimated over the lifetime of the impact of the marketing mix element. Each chapter emphasizes that the marketing mix elements must be justified based on revenue that they contributed over and above the incremental costs of gaining that revenue.

Given this orientation toward incremental revenue and incremental cost, a reasonable question to ask is: Do these marketing mix procedures contribute to the long-term health of the growing company? Are we performing marketing activities for the short-term that help short-term sales for our products or services, but that will hurt the long-term revenue and profit potential of our company? These are legitimate questions. In order to try to answer them, we will turn to an expert on brand equity and building strong brands, David Aaker. Aaker has written two books and many articles on how to manage brands for the long term. His book, *Building Strong Brands*,[1] has as its goal to guide managers in how to build brands that are strong and will endure and prosper over time. We will examine two major concepts that he uses in the book and see how compatible they are with the entrepreneurial marketing approach we advocate. The two Aaker concepts we will examine are: 1) Why it is hard to build brands; and 2) His ten guidelines for building strong brands. In order to make our examination come alive, we will use two examples of entrepreneurial companies that have been very successful in building a strong brand and strong company—Synygy, Inc., and Victoria's Secret of the Limited Brands.

SYNYGY, INC.: A STRONG, ENDURING, ENTREPRENEURIAL COMPANY

The first successful entrepreneurial company that we will discuss is Synygy, Inc., "the Incentive Compensation Company." Mark Stiffler, an MBA from M.I.T.'s Sloan School, founded Synygy in 1991. The firm began as a service to automate the analysis of sales data for pharmaceutical companies. This experience in automating sales analysis led the firm's customers to ask if Synygy could help in managing their sales force incentive compensation plans. It was a perennial problem for the pharmaceutical firms and their large sales forces. The compensation plans developed by the sales managers were very difficult to implement because of the large amounts of sales data that needed to be processed to tell whether the salesperson had met a quota or what his or her commission or bonus should be. This was the same sales data that Synygy had been analyzing. Most firms were using mostly manual processes that led to late reports, inaccurate compensation calculations, and salespeople who did not trust the veracity of the numbers upon which they were paid. It was a problem that no one had built a business on nor spent much effort against. Many companies were using home-grown systems that were very expensive to build (when all of the real costs were calculated), and very complex to modify if the compensation plan were to change. There was a real need for a more efficient, more valuable approach to the management of compensation plans. Mark and his firm began to develop more and more expertise by becoming the outsourcing vehicle for the administration of plans. They became a group whose expertise grew with each plan they administered. They also developed generalizable computer and information systems to reproduce what their people were doing manually. These systems also were continuously improved. By being very close to their initial customers, they understood how important it was for the plan calculations to be right, but even more importantly, to be understandable. The salespeople needed to be able to relate their own actions and effort to how their compensation would be affected. Over time, the Synygy team developed a series of graphical reports that communicated extremely well to salespeople. Their experience kept building into better and better systems to handle compensation plan administration with a very effective combination of computer systems and expert people. They now do the complete outsourced administration of incentive compensation plans. Since 1991, Synygy has grown fast enough to be on the Inc. 500 list of fastest-growing private companies for five years and is a member of Inc.'s Hall of Fame.

The only real competition to challenge Synygy (aside from in-house home-grown solutions) has been the entry of enterprise software vendors who sell software, but do not provide ongoing plan management services. From its beginnings in the pharmaceutical industry, Synygy has expanded into other industries that employ many salespeople and have incentive compensation as an important part of their plans. As we examine how hard it is to build brands, we will use Synygy, Inc. as one example of a successful strong brand. We will try to understand why Synygy has been able to overcome the obstacles to building an enduring brand and an enduring company.

We will do the same for Victoria's Secret, a division of Limited Brands that we have been discussing throughout this book.

WHY IS IT HARD TO BUILD BRANDS?

Aaker outlines eight reasons that many companies find it difficult to build strong, enduring brands. His orientation is more toward mass-market consumer products, but the concepts are appropriate for any entrepreneur to consider. Figure 14-1 shows these eight reasons.

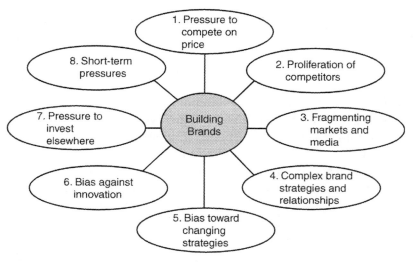

Figure 14-1 Why is it hard to build brands?[2]

We shall reinterpret these reasons from the viewpoint of the person who is beginning a new venture or has been operating a high-growth entity. The *first reason, pressure to compete on price,* can cause an entrepreneurial marketer to make decisions that are counter to building her brand. A lower price, all other things being equal, signals to the marketplace that the value of the product offering is going down also. However, if the perceived value of the offering compared to competition is not going down, then the entrepreneur should not change her price compared to the competition. Many high-tech market categories have price levels that are continuously decreasing as technology lowers costs for all of the players. However, the strong brands within the category will have aspects of their offering that add incremental perceived value versus the competition. This price premium compared to competition based upon perceived incremental value is the essence of what excellent entrepreneurial marketing enables. There is no reason to lower this premium unless something else in your marketing mix is changing the perceived value of your offering by the market participants.

Synygy really does not compete on price with anyone for the total outsourcing solution. They do compete with some enterprise software vendors for the software portion of the implementation. However, in order to capitalize on their distinctive competence in complete plan management, Synygy has partnered with their major software competitors to offer the implementation and ongoing administration of the plans using their competitor's software. Thus, potential customers can buy either a complete solution from Synygy, or they can buy software from someone else and pay Synygy to manage the plan. Synygy bases their pricing on a value-in-use argument. According to a Synygy brochure:

> "Don't buy software. Don't build systems yourself. Outsource to Synygy. Synygy's incentive compensation solution costs less than building, maintaining, and running a home-grown system, or buying, customizing, and operating packaged software.
>
> Many of our customers have saved millions of dollars. That's because outsourcing to Synygy increases the top line, improves margins, cuts costs, and improves cash flow by eliminating the huge upfront investment in software and hardware."[3]

Victoria's Secret has been raising its prices as its positioning has become stronger in its target market. In a recent 10-year period, VS quadrupled its revenue and doubled its average selling price.

The *second reason* for it being hard to build strong brands, *proliferation of competitors*, always makes entrepreneurial life interesting. However, if you are managing the perceived value of your offering versus these competitors, you should fare well. Also, if your initial positioning strategy is soundly based on your distinctive competence that is the source of sustainable competitive advantage, then you should be ready for proliferating competitors.

Synygy was ready to compete when, late in 1998, major enterprise software developers such as Oracle Corp., Siebel Systems, or Trilogy began to offer software to manage incentive plans. Because Synygy's software and operating methods had been continuously improved by their experience and because the operational issues of actually managing the plans on an ongoing basis are so difficult, no competitor has yet challenged Synygy for the complete outsourcing solution. These new competitors are also not finding it easy to finish applications that are referenceable. However, that does not mean that Synygy can sit still.

Recently, Synygy experimented with repositioning their offering more as software and less as a total outsourced solution. They re-priced their offering as a big upfront software purchase, and hired a heavy duty Sales V.P. from Oracle and a number of "software salespeople" to compete with their new competition. After a year and a half of this experiment, Mark Stiffler, the Synygy CEO, dismantled the "software" organization, fired the Sales V.P., and went back to "their roots."

According to Mark, "I hated the culture and lack of teamwork; I hated the prima donna attitudes; I hated the lack of process and discipline. We are now back to our roots: focused on selling hosted and managed service solutions (with emphasis on people who understand client problems and improve their processes . . . the software is secondary . . . I say 'demo our people not our software'); We also went back to pricing as a recurring subscription fee like I did for the first 10 years in business (after having gone down the path of upfront license fees)."[4]

What Mark realized was that the enterprise software orientation was inconsistent with his desired positioning and was seriously hurting his perceived value. There were significant short and medium costs to going back to his roots, but they were worth it. He has recently introduced a one-year contract as his pricing vehicle, just like SAS. His clients can stop any time after a year if they are not satisfied. He has lost no clients, but it makes his service easier to sell if it is perceived as less risky.

In order to keep its competitive edge, Synygy invested money in Web-based software that was essential to deliver the value in a way that was efficient for their clients. In addition to Enterprise Incentive Management (EIM) services, they added three new performance management solutions: referrals management, quotas management, and objectives management. EIM is still the focus, and other solutions are only sold as add-ons to EIM and not by themselves. Mark now realizes that EIM can be their enduring competitive edge, but it needs to always be improved to be perceived as better than the current and potential competition.

Synygy is continually concerned as to how the target markets *perceive* Synygy's offerings as opposed to how much better they actually are. In this situation, word of mouth from satisfied customers is the best weapon

Synygy has. As long as Synygy continues to build its distinctive competence and increases its ability to be perceived as adding the most value to
its target markets, it may be able to stay ahead of its competitors.

Similarly, Victoria's Secret actively manages and measures their market
perception with ongoing consumer research. Because they own their own
retail stores and have much clout with mall operators because of their
association with other Limited Brands' mall stores, VS has not had major
competitive threats in their core business.

We can combine reasons three and four for why it is hard to build brands
for entrepreneurial marketers. These relate to keeping the positioning of
the brand consistent regardless of which media or market is used and considering the brand's relationship to other of the firm's brands. These reasons should typically not be very salient for most entrepreneurial marketers. Most successful ventures are targeting niche markets, not mass
markets, so they should be using very targeted media vehicles and public
relations. Most entrepreneurial ventures also have only one brand, their
first. In many cases, their brand is their company. As they grow, some of
these issues may become more salient.

For Synygy, a key strategic issue they faced was the best way to grow.
They could expand their services to existing clients by performing other
analyses on the same sales data they used for their incentive plan management or offer other plan management services such as the referral,
quota, and objectives management services. They could alternatively
expand their incentive plan management offering to other markets than
pharmaceuticals. Both of the options were somewhat consistent with the
firm's initial positioning and distinctive competence. However, the potential perceived value and distinctiveness of their incentive plan offering was
much higher than the other services. Synygy correctly decided to prioritize the expansion of their core incentive plan management offering to
other target markets. For their current users, they will do further analysis
of the sales data or the other plan management programs as value-added
services. However, Synygy's marketing budget and sales resources are
used primarily toward expansion to new customers and new markets,
leveraging their core distinctive competence. The tag line "The Incentive
Compensation Company" was adopted after Synygy made this strategic
decision to strengthen their company and "brand." Please note that if
Synygy would have known this strategy decision when they named their

firm, it would have been more productive to name the company more consistent with its positioning. However, hindsight is clearer than foresight.

In Chapter 10, "Entrepreneurial Promotion and Viral Marketing to Maximize Sustainable Profitability," we shared the change in advertising copy that Synygy made that increased their short-term advertising productivity by over 15 times. This new advertising copy was still consistent with the basic positioning and segmentation strategies of the firm. The advertising just got the point across much more effectively.

As we have shown throughout this book, VS has done an excellent job of making sure that every marketing activity they do reinforces their positioning. That discipline has paid handsome dividends in their strategic position, financial returns, and market value.

Reasons *five—bias toward changing strategies*—and *six—bias against innovation*—are issues with which entrepreneurs constantly struggle. For many entrepreneurial companies, the issue of developing a scaleable marketing-sales-business model is very difficult. The really successful firms succeed in developing a way of going to market, and getting and serving new customers that becomes routine and scaleable, like a formula. The founding entrepreneur no longer has to go to close each sale. The company's positioning and perceived value become known well enough in the market so that sales come somewhat easier. Growth can accelerate quickly when this happens.

However, the entrepreneur can become bored and lose focus. He or she may want the firm to move into other more interesting products or markets. This changing of strategies can seriously harm the venture; especially if the new products and/or markets are not leveraging the distinctive competence and positioning that have become the heritage of the company. Scarce resources need to be allocated to where they can provide the most long-term value to the firm, not necessarily to the most interesting new idea.

On the other hand, the entrepreneurial marketer cannot stand pat with the formula without continuously seeking to improve the firm's perceived value to its customers and leverage its distinctive competence. He or she must constantly keep ahead of current and potential competition. However, all the innovation should be leveraging the existing positioning and distinctive competence of the firm. If the marketplace needs are changing, then sometimes the positioning and associated product offering needs to adapt to the changing needs. However, adaptation to market changes always should be done to leverage the firm's distinctive competence relative to the competition.

Synygy's market needs and competition are constantly changing. We already discussed the new software competition. The market is also moving toward Web-based systems and applications service providers as new ways to solve information systems problems. The information technology officers at their potential client companies are causing this movement. Synygy is broadening its offering to include different ways of delivering their service. They will provide either a complete outsourced solution, be an application service provider, provide just the enterprise software for purchase, or provide the ongoing management and implementation of someone else's software. However, all of these options are consistent with its core positioning and leverage their distinctive competence. Synygy knows the "nitty-gritty" of implementing incentive plans to improve their customers' productivity better than anyone. All of their new, broadened offerings are consistent with and leverage that core competence.

VS has also continually innovated to reinforce their positioning. The "Pink" new product line supporting breast cancer research and their Web fashion extravaganzas are two good examples.

The *seventh reason* for brands being hard to build, *pressure to invest elsewhere,* may not be as salient for entrepreneurs whose companies, or executives whose divisions, typically have only one brand. The big problem is getting enough resources to invest in the company's main product offering. Many of the new Internet companies of 2000 and 2001 were spending on their core brands, but spending it ineffectively. They did not evaluate the incremental revenue due to the different marketing mix options they could use.

As we discussed earlier, VS (and the Limited Brands) have shied away from big global investments because they were more confident that they could improve their competitive position with investments in their U.S. home market where they could leverage their large retail infrastructure.

The *eighth and last reason* Aaker posits for brands being hard to build is *short-term pressures.* It is sometimes very tempting to sacrifice positioning and the brand's perceived value to do some activity that will help short-term sales and profits. For consumer products, the activities that can cause the most problems are temporary price-oriented price promotions. If these promotions are not reinforcing the product offering's targeted perceived value, they can harm this perceived value. If consumers see a brand as always "on sale," it may cheapen its perceived value. Even if such promotions cause some incremental short-term sales and profits, if they are not consistent with the positioning of the brand, they should not be done.

In Chapter 4, "Distribution/Channel Decisions to Solidify Sustainable Competitive Advantage," we documented what happened to Marantz when they brought in the discount stores to augment their then high-end retail distribution channels. The tactic was very successful short-term, but ruined the company and brand for the long term.

Probably the most common short-term pressure for entrepreneurs in business-to-business markets is from their salespeople to discount their product in order to "close the sale." Here, if the customer does not perceive enough incremental value to justify the normal price, then the salesperson has not done his job, or the customer is not in the target market. Unless the entrepreneur can be confident that the "special" price reduction will not become widely known, then it does not make sense to reduce the price to "close" this one sale. The other potential customers who would have been willing to pay the normal price will no longer be willing, if they learn that someone else has gotten a lower price. Thus, the price received will trend down to match the "special discounts" over time and hurt the long-term profitability of the venture. It is very hard for most entrepreneurs to lose sales, but sometimes it is the right thing to do, especially if the potential customer will not receive as much value as some other customers. As we show in Chapter 3, "Entrepreneurial Pricing—An Often-Misused Way to Garner Extraordinary Profits," a good pricing policy implies that not every potential customer will buy our offering.

Synygy has been able to rapidly grow its business without having to resort to "special" price reductions to get certain clients. They have a given price list to which all companies are subject. Obviously, there are different prices for different numbers of salespeople and for the different levels of service that Synygy can provide. One of the reasons that Mark was unhappy with the "Enterprise Software" strategy was that the software salespeople were accustomed to giving discounts and negotiating special deals. Mark correctly was concerned that this was cheapening the perceived value of his offering and was dangerous.

We discussed earlier how VS consciously limited big price reductions and increased their sales prices, even though in the beginning there was a short-term hit to profits when the constant price promotions were significantly reduced.

CAN ENTREPRENEURIAL MARKETERS OVERCOME THESE EIGHT DIFFICULTIES IN BUILDING BRANDS?

The answer to this question should be obvious. If the entrepreneurial marketer has followed the prescriptions in the previous chapters, she will always be building the long-term health of her company and its brands while she simultaneously contributes to the venture's short-term revenue and profits. Every marketing mix activity—and, in fact, all venture activities—must be consistent with the perceived value the firm wants to deliver to its customers and potential customers. The venture must be dedicated to continuously improving this perceived value versus competition by building and leveraging its distinctive competences and communicating this value to its target markets.

One of the strongest brands built in recent years, Google, has followed these precepts. They have kept the identity, and used the colorful logo, in each of the offerings (gMail, Chat, etc.). They are continuously investing in the brand image, even as their dominance in search grows. And they know that the value for their customers (advertisers in the search marketing) is best perceived through a strong brand.

TEN GUIDELINES FOR BUILDING STRONG BRANDS

Aaker also provides ten guidelines for building strong brands. These are good guidelines for entrepreneurial marketers in general; however, some of them need to be modified to the circumstances in which most entrepreneurs find themselves. The last guideline, in particular, merits significant modification for entrepreneurs. Following are the ten Aaker guidelines for building strong brands.[5]

1. *Brand identity.* Have an identity for each brand. Consider the perspectives of the brand-as-person, brand-as-organization, and brand-as-symbol, as well as the brand-as-product. Identify the core identity. Modify the identity as needed for different market

segments and products. Remember that an image is how you are perceived, and an identity is how you aspire to be perceived.

2. *Value proposition.* Know the value proposition for each brand that has a driver role. Consider emotional and self-expressive benefits as well as functional benefits. Know how endorser brands will provide credibility. Understand the brand-customer relationship.

3. *Brand position.* For each brand, have a brand position that will provide clear guidance to those implementing a communication program. Recall that a position is the part of the identity and value proposition that is to be actively communicated.

4. *Execution.* Execute the communication program so that it not only is on target with the identity and position but achieves brilliance and durability. Generate alternatives and consider options beyond media advertising.

5. *Consistency over time.* Have as a goal a consistent identity, position, and execution over time. Maintain symbols, imagery, and metaphors that work. Understand and resist organizational biases toward changing the identity, position, and execution.

6. *Brand system.* Make sure the brands in the portfolio are consistent and synergistic. Know their roles. Have or develop silver bullets to help support brand identities and positions. Exploit branded features and services. Use sub-brands to clarify and modify. Know the strategic brands.

7. *Brand leverage.* Extend brands and develop co-branding programs only if the brand identity will be both used and reinforced. Identify range brands and, for each, develop an identity and specify how that identity will be different in disparate product contests. If brand is moved up or down, take care to manage the integrity of the resulting brand identities.

8. *Tracking brand equity.* Track brand equity over time, including awareness, perceived quality, brand loyalty, and especially brand associations. Have specific communication objectives. Especially note areas where the brand identity and position are not reflected in the brand image.

9. *Brand responsibility.* Have someone in charge of the brand who will create the identity and position and coordinate the execution over organizational units, media, and markets. Beware

when a brand is being used in a business in which it is not the cornerstone.

10. **Invest in brands.** Continue investing in brands even when the financial goals are not being met.

These guidelines are self-explanatory and should be helpful to entrepreneurs as well as the consumer products corporate types to whom Aaker's book is directed. Guideline six, about the brand system, and seven, brand leverage to new products, may be over-kill for most entrepreneurs who have one brand that keeps their hands full. Guideline eight, tracking brand equity, should be observed more in spirit by many entrepreneurs. They should remain close to their existing and potential customers to assess how their product offering's value is being perceived. They should put cost effective means in place to check whether the perceived value of the offering is changing over time. Usually, this would be in the form of customer satisfaction surveys as well as getting periodic readings from potential customers on how they perceive the value of the offering versus its competition.

The last guideline needs some modification for entrepreneurial marketers. In fact, depending how one interprets it, the guideline may be not consistent with research we discussed in Chapter 6, "Entrepreneurial Advertising That Works—Vaguely Right or Precisely Wrong?" The guideline says to continue to invest in the brand even when the financial goals are not being met. We have discussed research that needs to be considered in this investment decision. That research (on TV advertising) basically said that *if the advertising didn't work short-term, it had no long-term revenue impact.* It also said that *if the advertising worked in the short term, it had a long-term impact that more than doubled the short-term impact on the average.* There is no academic research that says that this conclusion would be any different for other elements of the marketing mix such as public relations or different media. Thus, the key determination that the entrepreneur needs to make is: Does the investment in my brand have an *incremental impact* on the short-term revenue of the product offering? This incremental impact must be determined relative to *what revenue would have been had the investment not been made.* If the brand would be going down if the advertising were not done, and its revenue would *go down less* with an advertising program, then the advertising program has a *positive incremental impact.*

Thus, for entrepreneurial marketers, we would modify the last guideline to read: *Continue to invest in the brand as long as the investment has a positive incremental impact on the brand's revenue.* If your brand-marketing investments are not impacting revenue compared to what the revenue would have been without the investment, then it won't help either the long-term or the short-term sales for the brand. The entrepreneurial marketing challenge is to continually find investments in the brand that will have short-term incremental impact. In Chapter 6, we outlined methods for managing these marketing investments so that they will more likely have the required impact.

CONCLUSION

In this chapter, we have shown how the entrepreneur can simultaneously build short-term revenue and a strong entrepreneurial venture by following the prescriptions in the previous chapters. Entrepreneurs cannot be satisfied to spend money just for "brand building" without having an impact on their revenue. Many advertising and marketing agencies would advocate this unproductive "brand-building" activity. The entrepreneur must resist this advocacy and insist on brand-building programs that have an incremental impact. If not, the entrepreneur is throwing away her money with a very high probability. During the Internet "bubble," many of the new Internet ventures were throwing away lots of money in "brand-building" spending, but had no idea whether it was working or not. Effective entrepreneurs should not let this happen. Chapter 10 shows how to manage this process.

ENDNOTES

1. Aaker, David A., *Building Strong Brands*, New York: The Free Press, 1996.

2. Source: Aaker, op. cit, p. 27.

3. Synygy brochure, 1999. Bala Cynwyd, PA.

4. Personal communication of Leonard Lodish with Mark Stiffler, August 2005.

5. Source: Aaker, op. cit., inside rear cover.

INDEX